SO-EAR-237

Programming MapPoint
in .NET

Chandu Thota

Beijing · Cambridge · Farnham · Köln · Paris · Sebastopol · Taipei · Tokyo

Programming MapPoint in .NET
by Chandu Thota

Copyright © 2006 O'Reilly Media, Inc. All rights reserved.
Printed in the United States of America.

Published by O'Reilly Media, Inc., 1005 Gravenstein Highway North, Sebastopol, CA 95472.

O'Reilly books may be purchased for educational, business, or sales promotional use. Online editions are also available for most titles (*safari.oreilly.com*). For more information, contact our corporate/institutional sales department: (800) 998-9938 or *corporate@oreilly.com*.

Editor:	Simon St.Laurent
Production Editor:	Reba Libby
Cover Designer:	Karen Montgomery
Interior Designer:	David Futato

Printing History:

December 2005:   First Edition.

 This book uses RepKover™, a durable and flexible lay-flat binding.

ISBN: 0-596-00906-2
[M]

To my wife, Taarinya

Table of Contents

Part II.   MapPoint Web Service

Foreword

It's not surprising that discovery has always been rooted in the art and science of mapping. Maps represent many complex relations and hordes of data, yet a child is intuitively able to navigate and comprehend them. Maps have long been the information windows through which explorers and others have peered to find answers. Maps tell the story of the past, record the present, and reveal the future.

Today is no different from the past in that most information—whether business or personal—has a strong relational tie to the place where we reside. The real world provides a commonly understood framework for the endless fields of digital data—whether it lives on the Internet, your corporate network, your desktop, or your mobile device.

The conventional map is changing quickly into a digital representation of the real world. Traditional maps are quickly merging with immersive imagery, local content, 3-D models, and real world sensors. The digital map will have life through its vibrant contributing community of authors and experts that fulfill the dream of global access to local knowledge. Imagine a world where you pivot information in a highly visual place to discover what it's like somewhere else. Layers of information—whether you seek the news, classifieds, weather, stores, restaurants, photos, local businesses, tourist attractions, sporting events, music venues, or recreational activities—are easily discoverable. Your friends and colleagues share favorites and experiences among each other. The community adds pictures and content, corrects data and information, and provides currency and expertise in specialized knowledge until the map takes on a life of its own. If these concepts excite you, you share the passion of the Virtual Earth and MapPoint team.

For many years, unleashing the power of location technology within business or consumer applications was daunting. Geographic Information Systems were limited to companies with inelastic needs and ample resources. Developers were relinquished to niche departmental, non-mainstream applications due to the heavy lifting involved with data management, legacy proprietary GIS development environments, and the lack of an easy way to distribute mapping functionality. Deploying a simple real estate application to a national field sales team would have required a developer to distribute hundreds of megabytes of aging geographic data with desktop code only to have IT revisit this task frequently to update the application with new features or new street data. Web services provided developers with the first means to build broad, scalable, horizontal applications across the network. Web services abstract the developer from the intricacies of GIS and the anchor of large data sets and provide the developer with a means to update features and data quickly and inexpensively.

As a team set to build platforms for location-based application development, we embraced the change years ago with the first commercial SOAP/XML MapPoint Web Service and continue to lead the next charge with Virtual Earth. Virtual Earth, in conjunction with MapPoint Web Service, is both a platform and a user experience that revolutionizes the way users experience location information both online and offline. Given the simplicity of adding location technology to your application, the awesome user appeal of an immersive, well understood real-world user dimension, and the realization of significant business and user benefits, there is no better time to develop location technology and services.

Chandu Thota is an accomplished developer on the Microsoft Virtual Earth and MapPoint team, as well as an influence on much of the early thinking in the next wave of the Internet and mapping technologies. He knows firsthand the best way to develop applications in a quick and effective way using MapPoint technologies. In this book, he narrates a developer story about a platform that has been his work, play, and passion at Microsoft. Whether you are an enterprise developer or hobbyist programmer, *Programming MapPoint in .NET* will set you apart from other developers in the field.

Unleash your application and data with the power of location,

—Stephen Lawler
General Manager, Virtual Earth and MapPoint

Preface

Location is everything! Whether you are trying to find driving directions to the airport or looking for a good restaurant in town, location information has become an essential ingredient of our daily life. Enterprises today consider providing location-based services to their customers an important part of their service offerings. Using MapPoint products and services, you can answer questions such as:

- Where am I?
- How do I get from here to there?
- Where is the nearest coffee shop?

Whether you want to answer these questions using an online application, a web service, or a mobile phone in real-time, or offline, this book is for you. MapPoint provides an integrated set of products, servers, and services that helps enterprises improve their customers' experience by applying mapping and location.

 If you are looking for more programming resources on MapPoint 2004, MP2K Magazine provides excellent online resources and the most up-to-date technical articles on MapPoint 2004 programming. Check it out at *http://www.mp2kmag.com*.

Who Should Read This Book

Programming MapPoint in .NET will be useful to anyone who wants to develop a location-based application using the following MapPoint technologies:

- MapPoint 2004
- MapPoint Web Service
- Microsoft Location Server
- MSN Virtual Earth

This book provides a jump-start for working with these technologies with in-depth discussions about the core concepts and sample code provided in C#.

What's in This Book

This book is organized into 4 major sections with a total of 11 chapters. Each product/technology has a dedicated section in the book:

Chapter 1, *Hello, MapPoint!*
Introduces the MapPoint suite of products and technologies, setting the stage by discussing the basics of each technology and usage scenarios.

Part I, MapPoint 2004

Chapter 2, *Programming with MapPoint 2004*
Covers programming with the MapPoint 2004 ActiveX control and MapPoint 2004 object model for rendering maps, finding places and addresses, and calculating routes.

Chapter 3, *Working with Data in MapPoint 2004*
Covers dealing with business data, rendering data maps, and adding thematic shapes using geographic data.

Chapter 4, *Advanced MapPoint 2004 Programming*
Covers integration with GPS for obtaining real-time location and extending MapPoint capabilities by writing add-ins.

 Future versions of MapPoint (such as MapPoint 2006) are fully backward-compatible with the MapPoint 2004 APIs, so the contents of these chapters are still relevant for MapPoint 2006 and future backward-compatible versions of MapPoint.

Part II, MapPoint Web Service

Chapter 5, *Programming MapPoint Web Service*
Introduces the basics of programming with MapPoint Web Service.

Chapter 6, *MapPoint Web Service Find APIs*
Covers creating applications using the Find APIs of the MapPoint Web Service, including techniques for finding places, addresses, and nearby points of interest.

Chapter 7, *MapPoint Web Service Route APIs*
Covers programming with the Route APIs, such as calculating routes and getting driving directions.

Chapter 8, *MapPoint Web Service Render APIs*
Covers programming with the Render APIs available with MapPoint Web Service, including rendering maps, routes, LineDrive maps, and polygons.

Part III, MapPoint Location Server

Chapter 9, *Programming Microsoft Location Server*
  Covers the basics of programming with Microsoft Location Server and deployment scenarios.

Chapter 10, *Programming with Location Server APIs*
  Covers programming with the Location Server Web Service to get real-time location using mobile phones; also covers the basics of managing the Location Server, contacts, and privacy settings.

Part IV, MSN Virtual Earth

Chapter 11, *Programming with Virtual Earth*
  Covers the basics of programming with the new MSN Virtual Earth (undocumented) APIs.

Appendixes

Appendix A, *Managing Your Data on MapPoint's Customer Services Site*
  Provides programming information for the MapPoint Customer Data Service.

Appendix B, *Working with Polygons*
  Provides basic information on understanding polygons in MapPoint Web Service.

Appendix C, *Implementing Spatial Search Using SQL Server*
  Provides a solution for implementing a proximity search within your enterprise network that doesn't require you to upload your data to MapPoint Web Service.

This book covers the most common application development scenarios with the MapPoint platform. If you feel that something important has been left out that should be included, let me know. I'll work to get it in a future edition. For contact information, see the "We'd Like Your Feedback!" section later in the preface.

Conventions in This Book

The following typographical conventions are used in this book:

Italic
  Introduces new terms, URLs, commands, file extensions, filenames, directory or folder names, and UNC pathnames.

`Constant width`
  Indicates command-line elements, computer output, and code examples.

`Constant width italic`
  Indicates placeholders (for which you substitute an actual name) in examples and in registry keys.

`Constant width bold`
  Indicates user input.

Indicates a tip, suggestion, or general note. For example, we'll tell you when you need to use a particular version or whether an operation requires certain privileges.

 Indicates a warning or caution. For example, we'll tell you when Active Directory does not behave as you'd expect or whether a particular operation has a negative impact on performance.

Method, Property, Field Name Qualification
> When introduced for the first time, the methods are qualified with their class names; for example, when you see the FindAddress method from the FindServiceSoap, you see it as the FindServiceSoap.FindAddress method, while in subsequent sections you see it as only FindAddress.

Code Samples
> All code samples are presented in C#. Many code samples and snippets are not wrapped in try/catch blocks for the sake of simplicity; however, it is good practice to wrap the application logic in try/catch blocks to avoid unexpected errors.

Companion Material

This book comes with companion material that includes sample code for:

MapPoint 2004
> All code samples have references to MapPoint 2004; however, since future releases will be backward-compatible with MapPoint 2004, you should not have issues when running samples on future versions of MapPoint.

MapPoint Web Service
> Samples require credentials. The companion material contains shared credentials for the MapPoint Web Service staging environment. Please note that these credentials are only included for the sake of convenience, and it is recommended to request your own credentials when you start developing with MapPoint Web Service. Abuse of these credentials may result in denied access to the Web Service, causing inconvenience to your fellow readers of this book.

MSN Virtual Earth
> Sample code uses the undocumented Virtual Earth APIs.

Using Code Examples

This book is here to help you get your job done. In general, you may use the code in this book in your programs and documentation. You do not need to contact O'Reilly for permission unless you're reproducing a significant portion of the code. For example, writing a program that uses several chunks of code from this book does not require permission. Selling or distributing a CD-ROM of examples from O'Reilly books does require permission. Answering a question by citing this book and quoting example code does not require permission. Incorporating a significant amount of example code from this book into your product's documentation does require permission.

We appreciate, but do not require, attribution. An attribution usually includes the title, author, publisher, and ISBN. For example: "*Programming MapPoint in .NET* by Chandu Thota. Copyright © 2006 O'Reilly Media, Inc., 0-596-00906-2."

If you feel your use of code examples falls outside fair use or the permission given above, feel free to contact the publisher at *permissions@oreilly.com*.

Other Resources

Writing a technical book is never complete, especially when four different products and technologies are covered in one book. For more information, you can always go to the MSDN online developer center for all your documentation needs. You can read about all of the MapPoint products at *http://www.msdn.com/mappoint*.

You can also check my MSDN weblog at *http://blogs.msdn.com/cthota*.

Safari® Enabled

 When you see a Safari® Enabled icon on the cover of your favorite technology book, it means the book is available online through the O'Reilly Network Safari Bookshelf.

Safari offers a solution that's better than e-books. It's a virtual library that lets you easily search thousands of top technology books, cut and paste code samples, download chapters, and find quick answers when you need the most accurate, current information. Try it for free at *http://safari.oreilly.com*.

We'd Like Your Feedback!

The information in this book has been tested and verified to the best of our ability, but mistakes and oversights do occur. Please let us know about errors you may find, as well as your suggestions for future editions, by writing to:

O'Reilly Media, Inc.
1005 Gravenstein Highway North
Sebastopol, CA 95472
800-998-9938 (in the United States or Canada)
707-829-0515 (international or local)
707-829-0104 (fax)

You also can send us messages using email. To be put on our mailing list or to request a catalog, send email to:

info@oreilly.com

To ask technical questions or comment on the book, send email to:

bookquestions@oreilly.com

For corrections and amplifications to this book, check out O'Reilly Media's online catalog at:

http://www.oreilly.com/catalog/mappoint/

Acknowledgments

Thanks to O'Reilly for signing this book. I'd also like to thank my editor, Simon St. Laurent, for being patient with me and providing words of encouragement throughout the process.

Thanks to the MapPoint team for creating a fantastic set of products to write about!

Thanks to Wayne S. Freeze, Michael Schmalz, and Dylan Vance for serving as the technical reviewers for this book. All of them caught numerous oversights and mistakes and made the book much better as a result. I'd like especially to thank Dylan's thoughtful and thorough feedback.

I would like to thank Stephen Lawler for writing the foreword and laying out the vision for the future of MapPoint Development Platform for this book. I also would like to extend my special thanks to Anurag Sharma and Jay Nanduri for their encouragement and cooperation throughout this effort.

Writing a book is a collective effort and it was simply not possible to finish this project without help from the following people: Amit Dekate, Andrew Hwangbo, Brian Jepson, Caleb Thompson, Chris Pendleton, David Buerer, Eric Frost, Norm Bryar, Rachel Falzone, Richard Waymire, Stuart Macrae, and Steve Lombardi.

Finally, I would like to thank to my wife, Taarinya, for putting up with me when I essentially ignored the world writing this book through many weeks, long weekends, and late nights.

CHAPTER 1

Hello, MapPoint!

So, you want to develop location-based applications using .NET! Microsoft Map-Point technologies offer a wide variety of applications, services, and tools to enable you to develop powerful location-based applications using .NET technologies.

In this introductory chapter, I will go through different location-based application categories and architectures and explain which MapPoint product or technology is appropriate to use in certain scenarios; specifically, I will discuss the fundamental differences between the following three products and technologies from MapPoint:

- MapPoint 2004
- MapPoint Web Service
- MapPoint Location Server

Location-Based Application Categories

Fundamentally, location-based applications are applications that either know how to process location-based information or make use of their location for other processing. To that end, location-based applications can be categorized into two major categories: location-enabled applications and location-aware (or real-time) applications.

Location-Enabled Applications

Location-enabled applications understand location and know how to process it. For example, a conventional store locator is a location-enabled application—simply specify a location and provide a distance within which you want to find stores. Another example is a simple maps-and-directions application that can calculate driving directions using starting and ending addresses and display them on a map. These applications know how to interpret and process the location information.

Location-Aware Applications

Location-aware applications are similar to location-enabled applications except that they are aware of their own location, so they can use it for processing information. For example, a simple maps-and-directions application connected to a GPS device can provide you with up-to-date driving directions based on your current location, or it can even recalculate the driving directions if you leave your planned route! Another example is a store-locator application that knows where you are and automatically recommends nearby stores based on your current location. Location-aware applications are usually known as *real-time location applications*.

The intelligence of location awareness comes from the real-time location information obtained either by using an external hardware device, such as GPS, or by other means, such as mobile phone operator networks.

Location Application Architectures

Beyond the application categories, you need to be aware of application architectures when building location-based applications. Location-based applications can be built using two different architectures:

- Disconnected location-based applications
- Connected location-based applications

Let's look at each of these categories in detail.

Disconnected Location-Based Applications

Disconnected location-based applications contain location information and related processing framework locally on the hosted computer hard disk, which means that network connectivity is not required for the application's functionality. A typical disconnected location-based application architecture is shown in Figure 1-1.

The main advantage of this architecture is that the location data resides locally, so the applications can provide a faster and richer user experience; however, having data locally may also be viewed as a limitation for other reasons, such as the size of the application (since location data can easily grow to a few Gigabytes) and the data becoming out-of-date due to lack of frequent updates. The advantages include:

- Continuous availability of the application and data with no dependency on network connectivity
- Rich user interface
- Ideal architechture for thick client scenarios, where computing power and memory are available to handle complex processing on the client device

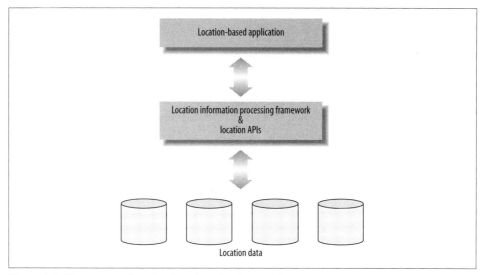

Figure 1-1. Disconnected location-based application architecture

However, there are also disadvantages:

- Larger application footprint
- Local location data that becomes out-of-date over time
- Different applications for different platforms (Windows versus Mobile)
- Not ideal architecture for thin client (such as web) scenarios

The decision to develop a disconnected location-based application should be based entirely on factors such as connectivity and functional richness of the application, which we will discuss in more detail later in this chapter.

Connected Location-Based Applications

Connected location-based applications contain location information and related processing framework on remotely located servers instead of the local hard disk, which means that a network connection is essential for the application to run. Typical connected-location based application architecture is shown in Figure 1-2.

The main advantage of this architecture is that the location data and the related processing framework reside remotely, so the applications can be lightweight. Since the applications are loosely coupled to the location data, it is easy to update the data frequently to keep it up-to-date. The advantages of this architecture include:

- Smaller application footprint
- Ideal architecture for thin client scenarios

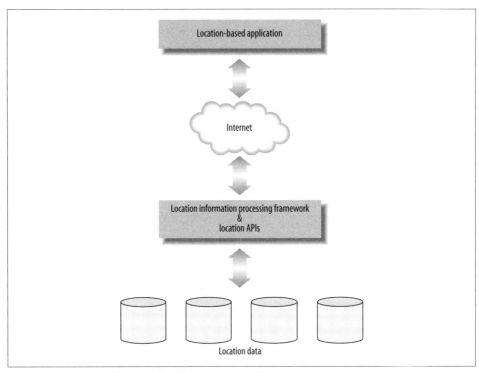

Figure 1-2. Connected location-based application architecture

- Easy architecture in which to keep data up-to-date
- Easy architecture in which to develop applications for different platforms (Windows and Mobile)

However, there are still disadvantages:

- Architecture that requires continuous network connectivity
- Architecture in which you may be charged for each transaction in a commercial Web service scenario

Now that you have been introduced to location application categories and different architectures, let's see how Microsoft MapPoint technologies enable you to build both connected and disconnected location-based applications.

Developing Location-Enabled Applications

Location-enabled applications know how to interpret and process location information. The kinds of applications that fall into this category include:

Generic maps and directions

Provide basic planning-related functionalities, such as displaying a desired location on a map and calculating driving directions from one point to another point. For example, both MapPoint 2004 and Streets & Trips 2004 provide this functionality right out of the box.

Location-based data visualization (or thematic mapping)

Helps you to visualize the data using geographic extent. For example, using MapPoint 2004, you can view information such as population statistics in any given city in the United States, or color-code the map based on population density.

Store Finders, ATM Finders, and similar applications

Find points of interest around a desired location. For example, you can find a nearby coffee shop when you are traveling in a new town or find local bloggers in the area in which you live.

To build this category of applications using MapPoint technologies, you have two choices: disconnected applications using MapPoint 2004, and connected applications using MapPoint Web Service.

Disconnected Applications Using MapPoint 2004

MapPoint 2004 is a powerful desktop mapping application that provides a rich set of APIs for both managed and unmanaged application development. MapPoint 2004 is well-suited for disconnected location-enabled application architecture, which means that the location-enabled application and required location data reside locally on the host computer's hard disk, and no network connectivity is required for the application's functionality.

Along with normal location-based APIs, such as Find, Route, and Render, MapPoint 2004 also offers a rich set of functions (also APIs) for thematic mapping, territory management, and spatial data import from a variety of source formats such as Excel, Access, Txt, and so on.

The APIs provided by MapPoint 2004 are COM- (Component Object Model) based APIs; however, thanks to .NET Framework runtime callable wrappers, you can program with the COM APIs using .NET's managed code. MapPoint 2004 also provides an ActiveX control that enables MapPoint 2004 application integration into your applications so that you can reuse most of the MapPoint 2004's application user interface.

Figure 1-3 shows how your applications stack on MapPoint 2004 architectural layers.

When you redistribute applications that you have developed using MapPoint 2004, make sure that the target machines have MapPoint 2004 installed as well. It is also possible to include MapPoint 2004 runtime and data along with your application if

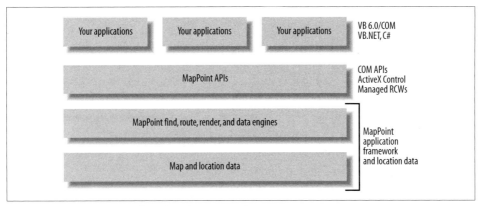

Figure 1-3. MapPoint 2004-based application stack

you become a MapPoint 2004 application reseller. Also, note that the MapPoint 2004 licensing model prevents you from developing web-based applications using the ActiveX control.

 For further details on application redistribution using MapPoint 2004 information, go to *http://msdn.microsoft.com/library/?url=/library/en-us/mappoint2004/BIZAPIAboutDistributingMapPointControl. asp?frame=true.*

With this introduction, let's look at a simple Windows application that uses Map-Point 2004 ActiveX control to display a map.

Hello, MapPoint 2004!

Using Visual Studio .NET, you can program with MapPoint ActiveX Control just like any other .NET Windows Forms Control.

 If you do not have MapPoint ActiveX Control added to your Visual Studio .NET Toolbox, see Chapter 2 to learn about how to prepare your development environment to use MapPoint ActiveX control.

When you drag-and-drop the MapPoint ActiveX Control onto a Windows Form, Visual Studio .NET automatically adds a reference to your project and defines a private instance of the ActiveX control:

```
private AxMapPoint.AxMappointControl axMappointControl1;
```

Using this ActiveX control instance, you can open up a map and place a pushpin at its center:

```
//Create a new map
axMappointControl1.NewMap(MapPoint.GeoMapRegion.geoMapNorthAmerica);
//Get map center location
MapPoint.Location location = axMappointControl1.ActiveMap.Location;
```

```
//Add a pushpin at this location
MapPoint.Pushpin pushpin
      = axMappointControl1.ActiveMap.AddPushpin(location, "Center");
//Assign a symbol
pushpin.Symbol = 64;
//Select and highlight the location
pushpin.Select();
pushpin.Highlight = true;
//Write annotation
pushpin.Note = "This is the centroid of America!";
//Show tooltip (Balloon State)
pushpin.BalloonState = MapPoint.GeoBalloonState.geoDisplayBalloon;
```

When you place the above code in the Form.Load event handler and run the application, the Windows Form displays the map as shown in Figure 1-4.

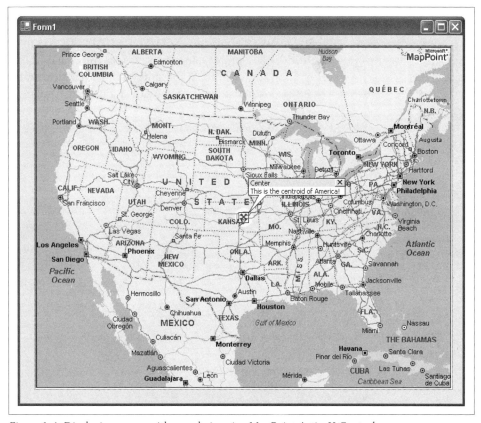

Figure 1-4. Displaying a map with a pushpin using MapPoint ActiveX Control

Finally, MapPoint 2004 provides required location data locally; however, the data available with MapPoint 2004 contains only map data for the United States, Canada, and Mexico. To access map and location data for Europe, use MapPoint 2004 Europe Edition. At the time of this writing, MapPoint 2004 supports only North America, Western Europe, and some parts of Eastern Europe.

Connected Applications Using MapPoint Web Service

MapPoint Web Service is a Microsoft-hosted XML Web Service that is fully compliant with SOAP and WSDL standards. MapPoint Web Service makes it very easy for you to develop connected location-enabled applications. One of the advantages of using MapPoint Web Service is that the location data and the necessary processing framework are hosted by Microsoft on MapPoint servers, so your applications remain very thin and always have up-to-date location data. In addition, since MapPoint Web Service is a SOAP XML Web Service, it is possible to develop location-based applications that are both platform agnostic and programming language agnostic.

Along with normal location-based APIs, such as Find, Route, and Render, MapPoint Web Service also offers a full set of APIs for custom points of interest data upload and download to enable automated data management.

The APIs provided by MapPoint Web Service are SOAP-based APIs that can be accessed using any XML-enabled programming languages. Using the .NET framework makes it easy to develop applications with MapPoint Web Service; for example, using the following code, you can render a map with a pushpin similar to Figure 1-4:

```
//Create an instance of the render service object
RenderServiceSoap renderService = new RenderServiceSoap();
renderService.Credentials =
        new System.Net.NetworkCredential("myid", "mypassword");

//Create an instance of MapSpecification
MapSpecification mapSpec = new MapSpecification();
//Assign data source name
mapSpec.DataSourceName = "MapPoint.NA";

//Add pushpin
//Create and add a pushpin
Pushpin pin = new Pushpin();
//Assign data source
pin.IconDataSource = "MapPoint.Icons";
//Assign icon name
pin.IconName = "1";
//Assign label
pin.Label = "This is the centroid of America!";
//Assign location
pin.LatLong = new LatLong();
pin.LatLong.Latitude = 38.79;
pin.LatLong.Longitude = -98.79;
//Add pushpin to map specificiation
mapSpec.Pushpins = new Pushpin[] {pin};

//Create options
mapSpec.Options = new MapOptions();
```

```
//Assign options
mapSpec.Options.Format = new ImageFormat( );
mapSpec.Options.Format.Height = this.mapImage.Height;
mapSpec.Options.Format.Width = this.mapImage.Width;

//Assign view by height and width if it is the view
ViewByHeightWidth vbh = new ViewByHeightWidth( );
vbh.Height = 400;
vbh.Width = 600;
vbh.CenterPoint = pin.LatLong;

//Zoom out to see the entire country
mapSpec.Options.Zoom = 10;

//Assign view
mapSpec.Views = new MapView[] {vbh};

//Get map
MapImage[] mapImages = renderService.GetMap(mapSpec);

this.mapImage.Image = new Bitmap(new System.IO.MemoryStream(mapImages[0].MimeData.
Bits));
```

If you don't understand anything about these steps, don't worry—we will look at Map Rendering in detail in Chapter 8. When the code is run, the map is displayed as shown in Figure 1-5.

It looks like a lot more code than MapPoint ActiveX Control, but it is very simple once you understand the MapPoint Web Service object model. Also, it is important to note that the above code returns the binary form of the map image, which displays the map in a .NET Windows Forms Picture Box control; when you use a Web Form application using ASP.NET, you can request the map in a URL format, which can be used in an HTML IMG tag.

Figure 1-6 shows how your applications build on top of MapPoint Web Service architectural layers.

Location data in MapPoint Web Service is hosted on Microsoft MapPoint servers, and all of the map and location data is available for developers via the programmable APIs. This provides greater flexibility in building global location-based applications that work for multiple countries and regions.

Location data in the MapPoint Web Service environment is represented in terms of *data sources*; each dataset represents data for a particular country or region; for example, North American region map and location data is contained in the MapPoint.NA data source. So, if you develop a store finder application using MapPoint Web Service using the MapPoint.NA data source, and you want to reuse the application code for Europe, change the data source name from MapPoint.NA to

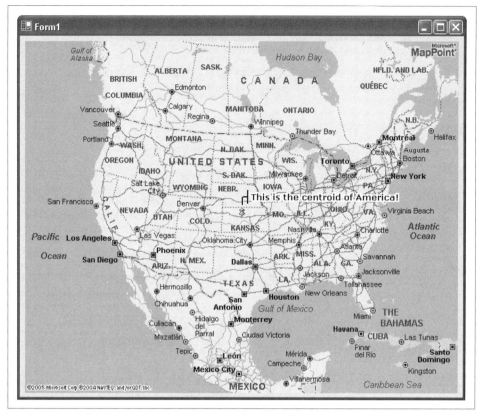

Figure 1-5. Displaying a map using MapPoint Web Service

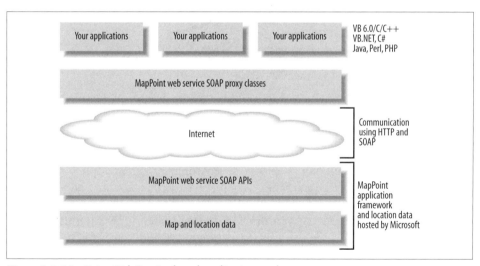

Figure 1-6. MapPoint Web Service-based application stack

`MapPoint.EU` (compare the procedure used here to one using MapPoint 2004). Location-based applications can be configured to use just about any map data, since MapPoint Web Service provides the loose coupling between your application layer and the data layer.

MapPoint Web Service currently supports map and location data for countries and regions in North America, Europe, and Pacific Asia.

Developing Location-Aware Applications

Location-aware applications (or real-time location applications) apply your current location when processing information to provide smart choices. The kinds of applications that fall into this category are:

- Real-time navigation software
- Fleet tracking applications
- Friend and family finder applications

To build this category of applications using MapPoint technologies, you have two choices (yes, again!): disconnected and connected applications.

Disconnected Applications Using MapPoint 2004 and GPS

MapPoint 2004 provides necessary APIs and location data to build location-enabled applications; however, you can also build disconnected location-aware applications using MapPoint 2004 by interfacing a location-aware hardware such as Global Positioning Satellite (or simply GPS) devices. Even though MapPoint 2004 does not provide ready-to-use APIs for GPS interfacing, it is relatively easy to use real-time information from a GPS device in the MapPoint application environment.

Figure 1-7 shows how your location-aware applications build on MapPoint 2004 and a GPS device.

This architectural layer is not very different from Figure 1-3, except that this application uses a GPS device for real-time information.

 For further details on how to interface MapPoint 2004 with a GPS device, see Chapter 4.

The most common scenarios for this architecture include real-time navigation applications, real-time location based information logging applications.

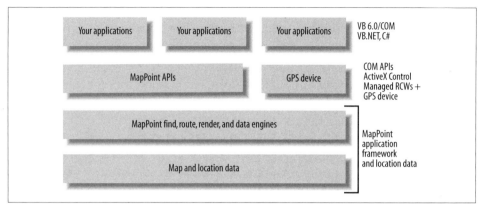

Figure 1-7. Location-aware application using MapPoint 2004 with a GPS device

Connected Applications Using MapPoint Location Server

MapPoint Location Server is an enterprise-hosted server that enables real-time location scenarios using a locatable device, such as a mobile phone or a pager. MapPoint Location Server does not require any location-related hardware, such as GPS devices; instead, it locates a provisioned (registered) user's mobile device by communicating with a mobile operator. In a typical scenario, a user requests his position using a mobile device equipped with a client that communicates with MapPoint Location Server. When MapPoint Location Server receives the request from the client, it identifies the mobile operator for the user and sends a location request to the mobile operator, which responds by sending back the real-time location of the user, expressed as latitude and longitude coordinates. MapPoint Location Server then requests a map or other location information from MapPoint Web Service to process the user's real-time location.

All communications specific to a mobile operator are hidden from end users and developers. Thus, MapPoint Location Server works as an aggregator for mobile operators by abstracting implementation details that are specific to the mobile operator to obtain a real-time location. Once the location is obtained, it can be used for many purposes, such as finding nearby ATMs, calculating driving directions based on current location, and so on.

Figure 1-8 shows the overall architecture for a location-aware application using MapPoint Location Server.

MapPoint Location Server exposes a SOAP XML-based web service that provides methods to obtain real-time location using a mobile phone number or a pager number. This functionality was intentionally exposed as a web service, since it can be

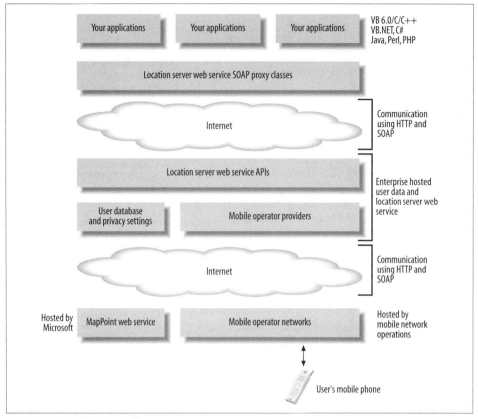

Figure 1-8. Application architecture using MapPoint Location Server

consumed by any client on any platform with minimal effort; it is very easy to develop connected location-aware applications for Windows or mobile platforms. Also, while MapPoint Location Server obtains real-time location using mobile devices and mobile operator networks, it uses MapPoint Web Service to obtain other location-based information.

How It All Fits Together

By now, you might be confused about which product to use for each type of application. To clarify your choices, Figure 1-9 summarizes your options.

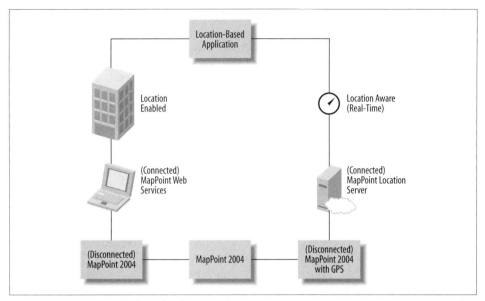

Figure 1-9. MapPoint Platform development choices

Where Are We?

Microsoft MapPoint technologies provide a wide variety of applications, services, and tools to develop location-enabled applications and location-aware applications for both connected and disconnected scenarios. To recap:

- To develop disconnected location-enabled applications, use MapPoint 2004.
- To develop connected location-enabled applications, use MapPoint Web Service.
- To develop disconnected location-aware applications, use MapPoint 2004 with GPS.
- To develop connected location-aware applications, use MapPoint Location Server.

If you are wondering how to digest so much information about all these products in one introductory chapter, don't worry; I will discuss MapPoint 2004, MapPoint Web Service, and MapPoint Location Server in detail in the upcoming chapters.

Let's get started!

PART I

MapPoint 2004

CHAPTER 2

Programming with MapPoint 2004

MapPoint 2004 provides a rich set of APIs and an ActiveX Control that lets you build powerful location-based business applications. Originally, the MapPoint APIs and ActiveX Control were designed for use with COM technologies, but thanks to .NET interoperability with COM, you can use those COM APIs to build applications using .NET programming languages such as C# and VB.NET.

 Keep in mind that it is sometimes tricky to make the COM interfaces work with your .NET code, but I will discuss the tips, tricks, and workarounds in detail.

This chapter explores using the MapPoint 2004 APIs and MapPoint 2004 ActiveX Control to accomplish basic location-oriented tasks, such as finding places, addresses, and points of interest, routing between places, and other lightweight business-oriented tasks, such as optimizing a route. To follow the examples in this chapter, you'll need Microsoft MapPoint 2004 North America/Europe Edition installed on the development computer, and the Microsoft .NET Framework, Version 1.1 or later.

The MapPoint 2004 Object Model

The MapPoint 2004 APIs and MapPoint 2004 ActiveX Control are designed for building disconnected Windows applications. Since all map data is installed locally on your hard drive, you can build Windows applications that don't need any network connectivity. However, if you need to build a connected web-based mapping application to keep your application footprint to a minimum size, consider instead the MapPoint Web Service, which is discussed later in this book in detail. Building a web-based application using the MapPoint 2004 APIs (or ActiveX Control) not only results in a poorly-performing web application but also violates the MapPoint license model! So, MapPoint 2004 can be used only for building Windows applications.

For a more detailed discussion on which platform to choose for your application development, refer to Chapter 1.

You can develop three kinds of applications using MapPoint 2004:

Location data-processing applications
Use MapPoint 2004 automation internally but don't create maps.

Location visual applications (with map display)
Display location and thematic maps embedded into applications using MapPoint2004.

MapPoint 2004 Add-Ins
Extend the capabilities of MapPoint 2004.

Location data-processing applications are typically used in the business intelligence part of an enterprise application. For example, a goods-delivery company must optimize the stops in a delivery route to save on fuel costs and drivers' time. These applications are developed using the MapPoint 2004 APIs.

The visual application category applies when you want to display a map to represent business data thematically. For example, a map displaying sales across the country based on zip code gives an immediate understanding of whether location plays a crucial role in sales. For applications that embed maps, it is ideal to use the MapPoint 2004 ActiveX Control; however, you can also use MapPoint APIs to display maps without using the ActiveX Control, as discussed in Chapter 3.

MapPoint 2004 Add-Ins extend MapPoint functionality to include your specific business needs. For example, you might want to use MapPoint 2004 application as a mapping tool in your enterprise but need an additional feature to display sales data that is available as an internal web service. In this case, MapPoint 2004 Add-Ins are ideal for adding features to the MapPoint 2004 application. There are also some specific scenarios where you need to implement your application logic as an Add-In for performance reasons, which we will discuss in Chapter 4.

Whether you are developing with the APIs or with the ActiveX Control, the core concepts behind MapPoint 2004 programming are still the same. The only difference is that the `ApplicationClass` is the root class if you are programming using the APIs, and the `AxMapPointControl` class is the root class if you are programming using the ActiveX Control. However, both these classes expose the `MapClass` (via the `ActiveMap` property), which is the centerpiece of the MapPoint 2004 programming. `MapClass` offers an extensive set of functions, properties, and collections, including a reference to the parent `ApplicationClass` via the `Application` property, which can be used in developing a wide variety of location-based applications.

Figure 2-1 shows the relation of these classes, while Table 2-1 gives you a selective list of the methods exposed on the MapClass object.

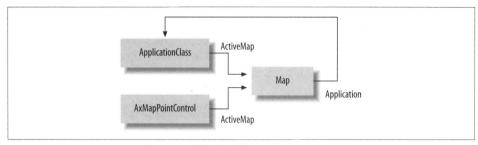

Figure 2-1. MapPoint 2004 Object Model—key objects

Table 2-1. Important methods available on the Map Class

Method name	Description
FindAddressResults	Finds addresses and returns FindResults collection
FindPlaceResults	Finds places (by name) and returns FindResults collection
FindResults	Combines the functionality of FindAddressResults and FindPlaceResults into one method; takes an input string, tries both address and place finding, and returns the successful results as FindResults collection
ObjectsFromPoint	Takes the x and y coordinates on the map and returns a collection of Locations and/or Pushpins that are located at that point
LocationToX and LocationToY	Converts any given location into x and y coordinates on the screen
XYToLocation	Converts any given x and y coordinates on the screen to a MapPoint Location object
AddPushpin	Adds a pushpin at a specified location

The Map class exposes a set of methods that does basic methods to find, mark (by adding pushpins), and convert screen coordinates to loctation objects and vice versa.

Apart from the Map object, the other two important and most frequently used objects are the FindResults and Location objects. The FindResults object represents a collection of Location and/or Pushpin objects. You can access the individual collection items using the FindResults.get_Item method (discussed in more detail later in this chapter). The Location object, on the other hand, represents a real location in MapPoint 2004. The Location object exposes methods such as FindNearby to find nearby points of interest and DistanceTo to find the distance between two points (locations).

Programming with MapPoint 2004 API

The MapPoint 2004 APIs were originally designed for use with the COM programming model. In order to build applications using the Microsoft .NET Framework, you need the interoperable assemblies for the MapPoint COM library. Let's look at how to add the MapPoint 2004 APIs as references for use in your project.

Adding MapPoint 2004 References Using Visual Studio .NET

If you are using Visual Studio .NET Version 2003 or later, it is easy to add a reference to the MapPoint 2004 APIs using the Add Reference option from the project context menu, as shown in Figure 2-2.

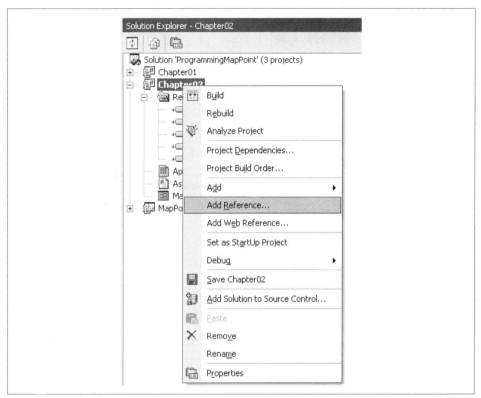

Figure 2-2. Project Add Reference menu

 If you are using MapPoint ActiveX Control, you don't need to add this reference manually, since Visual Studio .NET adds it automatically when you drag-and-drop the control on your Windows Form.

When you see the Add Reference dialog window, select the COM tab and select the Microsoft MapPoint 11.0 Object Library (North America) to add the MapPoint 2004 type library as a reference to your project, as shown in Figure 2-3.

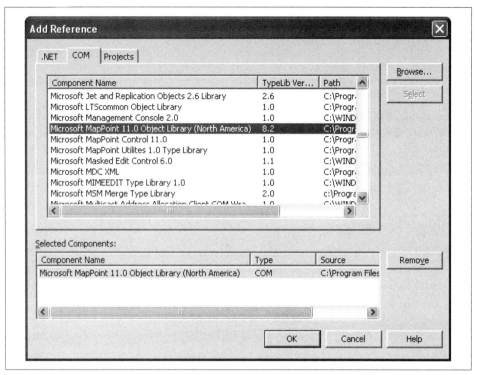

Figure 2-3. *Adding the MapPoint 2004 library as a reference*

If you are using the MapPoint 2004 European Edition, select the Microsoft MapPoint 11.0 Object Library (Europe) to add the reference. Also, note that if you have both MapPoint North America and MapPoint Europe installed on the same computer, you can develop an interop assembly for either product for use with both applications.

In this process, Visual Studio .NET automatically creates an interoperable assembly and adds it as a reference to your project. By default, the namespace of the newly created assembly is set to MapPoint.

Adding MapPoint 2004 References Using TlbImp.EXE

If you do not have Visual Studio .NET, or if you chose to do the hard work of creating the interoperable assembly yourself, you can use the *TlbImp.EXE* tool (located in the *Microsoft Visual Studio .NET 2003\SDK\v1.1\Bin* directory) that ships with the

.NET framework. For example, to generate the interoperable assembly for MapPoint 2004 type library with the namespace Interop.MapPoint, use the following command-line command:

```
C:\>tlbimp.exe "C:\Program Files\Microsoft MapPoint
\MPNA82.tlb" /out:"C:\Interop.MapPoint.dll" /namespace:Interop.MapPoint /sysarray /
transform:dispret
```

This command generates the interoperable assembly *Interop.MapPoint.dll* in the *C:* directory; add it to your project as a reference as you would do with any other .NET assembly.

Now that you have added the MapPoint 2004 object library to your project as a reference, let's get started with a simple application.

Finding a Place

When you think of mapping in general, the first thing that comes to mind is finding a location—whether it is a place or an address. A *place* is a general location referred by its commonly known name; an *address* is a more detailed specification of a location. For example, one of the best-known places in Seattle is the Space Needle, but the actual address of the Space Needle is 498 Broad St, Seattle, WA 98109. Using MapPoint 2004, you can find both places and addresses, as well as other elements that I discuss later.

Let's start off by building a simple Windows application that finds a place and returns the address for that place. This application contains a text box to input a place name and a button that can be used to fire an event to find the input place. When the input place is found, the address of the place is displayed in the text box labeled Address. The Windows form layout, which you can lay out in Visual Studio, is shown in Figure 2-4.

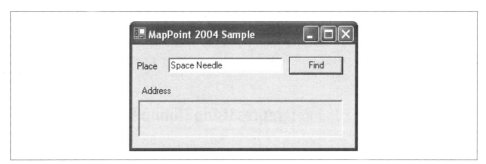

Figure 2-4. Find Place sample application

Because the user interface code is highly repetitive and generated by Visual Studio, I won't list it here. It is included in the sample files in the download.

Now, let's write the code that is invoked when the Find button is clicked. The root of MapPoint 2004 API programming is the ApplicationClass, so let's start by creating an instance of ApplicationClass:

```
//Create an instance of ApplicationClass
//Important Note: You need to clean up after you are done with the
//application class. For more informantion, see the section
//"Cleaning Up After You're Done"
MapPoint.ApplicationClass app = new MapPoint.ApplicationClass();
```

After creating the ApplicationClass, access the Map instance via the ActiveMap property:

```
//Get a reference to the Map instance via the ActiveMap property
MapPoint.Map map = app.ActiveMap;
```

The MapClass exposes a method, FindPlaceResults, that returns all places matching the input query. This method takes the place name string as input and returns FindResults, which is a collection of locations found. The following code shows the FindPlaceResults method call:

```
//Call FindPlaceResults on the MapClass instance
MapPoint.FindResults findResults = map.FindPlaceResults(this.textBox1.Text);
```

When the method call is complete, the FindResults instance will contain all the locations that matched the input query. The number of matches is represented by the Count property of the FindResults instance. In our example, the search for "Space Needle" resulted in 25 matches. Next, we need to go through the list to figure out which instance represents the Space Needle in Seattle. So, let's add a modal dialog to show a ListBox control with all found locations so that we can disambiguate the results manually.

Each location that matched the input place is represented as an instance of MapPoint. Location class in the FindResults object. Even though the FindResults class is essentially a collection of Location objects, its behavior is quite different from any .NET collection—you cannot directly access the Location items in the FindResults collection using the index number:

```
FindResults.Items[index]
```

In fact, the Items indexer is not exposed in the FindResults class in the interoperable assembly; however, there are still two ways to get the Location objects from the FindResults collection, using either the get accessor method or an enumerator.

Using the get accessor method

Collections are implemented using two special accessor methods called get_Item and set_Item. For read-only properties, only the get_Item method is implemented. These special methods are generated by the .NET compiler for every publicly exposed property. In case of FindResults instance, even though the read-only Items property is not exposed in the interoperable assembly, the get_Item method is still implemented internally. The only differences from the conventional .NET get_Item method are that this method takes the index value as an object passed by reference (for COM marshalling purposes) and the index starts from 1 instead of 0.

The following code shows how to use the get_Item accessor method to iterate through the list of Location objects in the FindResults collection:

```
//Create an object to hold index value
object index = null;
//Start with index 1 instead of 0
for(int i=1; i<=findResults.Count; i++)
{
    //Box the integer value as an object
    index = i;
    //Pass the index as a reference to the get_Item accessor method
    MapPoint.Location loc = findResults.get_Item(ref index) as MapPoint.Location;
    if(loc != null)
        this.listBox1.Items.Add(loc.Name);
}
```

Using an enumerator

You can also access the list of Locations from FindResults instance using the enumeration. The FindResults instance exposes a method, GetEnumerator, to get an enumerated list of locations. Using this enumerator instance, you can loop through the list of locations as follows:

```
//Get an enumerator using the GetEnumerator method
IEnumerator locationEnumerator = findResults.GetEnumerator();
//Loop through the location instances to get the names
while(locationEnumerator.MoveNext())
{
    MapPoint.Location loc = locationEnumerator.Current as MapPoint.Location;
    if(loc != null)
        this.listBox1.Items.Add(loc.Name);
}
```

The net effect is same for both methods, but the code in the enumerator approach looks cleaner than the get_Item accessor approach. However, the get_Item accessor approach performs better than the enumerator approach, especially when a large number of locations is found. The get_Item accessor method also provides a way to access the desired item directly instead of looping through the entire list.

We can use either method to populate the list of locations in the ListBox of the modal dialog, as shown in Figure 2-5.

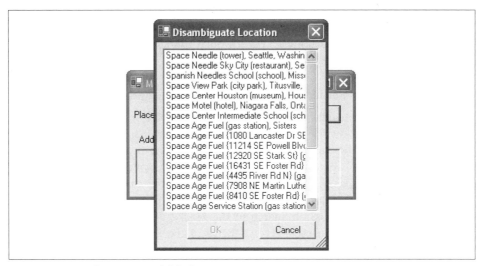

Figure 2-5. Disambiguation modal dialog

Look at the list to get the address. From the list of 25 found locations' names from our query, the first name reads "Space Needle [tower], Seattle, WA," which is what we are looking for. Since this is the very first instance in the list, you can use the index to obtain the Location object and the StreetAddress property to get the actual address:

```
object currentLocationIndex = findResModalDlg.SelectedIndex + 1;
MapPoint.Location loc = this.findResults.get_Item(ref index) as MapPoint.Location;
//Access the StreetAddress property for address
if(loc != null)
{
    if(loc.StreetAddress != null)
        this.textBox2.Text = loc.StreetAddress.Value;
    else
        this.textBox2.Text = loc.Name;
}
```

There are a couple of things of note in this code:

- We are adding 1 to the selected index because the items in the ListBox are zero-index based, but the locations in FindResults collection start with index 1, so to offset this difference, you need to add 1 to the selected index manually.

- Not all locations have addresses. Although it sounds strange, what address would be returned if you searched for "Seattle" and the returned location was "Seattle, WA"? In cases like this, it is sufficient to return the name of the location.

After obtaining the desired Location object from the FindResults collection, you can access the street address from the Location.StreetAddress property. We now have the address for the Space Needle, which is "498 Broad St, Seattle, WA 98109."

You may be wondering why MapPoint 2004 can't tell you whether there is a best location match instead of making you go through the list to disambiguate the locations each and every time. Actually, it does tell you.

Programmatically disambiguating the results

The locations in FindResults collection are always ordered in the best match order, so the first location is always the best possible match according to MapPoint 2004. However, the results depend on the input received by the program; for example, if you misspell the name "Space Needle" as "Spac Neele," MapPoint 2004 won't necessarily display the best possible match first; it is up to you to disambiguate the results using the given list of locations. How do you know as a programmer that MapPoint 2004 has made the best possible match in the FindResults collection? It's actually very simple. Using the ResultsQuality property of the FindResults collection, you can tell whether MapPoint 2004 succeeded in finding the exact match to the input location or whether it is offering a list of possible matches and expecting you to disambiguate. The ResultsQuality property is of GeoFindResultsQuality type, which is an enumeration with the values shown in Table 2-2.

Table 2-2. Values for the GeoFindResultsQuality enumeration

ResultsQuality value	Meaning	Need to disambiguate?
geoAllResultsValid	All location matches are exact matches to the input query.	Not applicable. This value is not returned for finding places or addresses; instead, it is returned for finding points of interests (discussed later in the chapter).
geoFirstResultGood	The first location is an exact match for the input query.	No. You can safely return the first location from the FindResults instance.
geoAmbiguousResults	At least the first two locations are good matches.	Yes. You can safely return the first location from the FindResults instance.
		However, since at least the first two results are best possible matches, sometimes you may have to disambiguate between the two.
geoNoGoodResult	There are some location results, but none of them is really a good match according to MapPoint 2004.	Yes. In this case, you don't know what the input query intended to find, so you have to disambiguate the location results.
geoNoResults	No locations found at all.	Not applicable.

Now, with this background, let's extend our sample application to disambiguate the location results programmatically:

```
//See if the FindResults.ResultsQuality is either
//geoFirstResultGood or geoAmbiguousResults
```

```
if(findResults.ResultsQuality ==
        MapPoint.GeoFindResultsQuality.geoFirstResultGood
   || findResults.ResultsQuality ==
        MapPoint.GeoFindResultsQuality.geoAmbiguousResults)
{
    //No need to disambiguate, just return the street address
    //of the first location
    currentLocationIndex = 1;
    //Get the Location object
    MapPoint.Location loc
        = this.findResults.get_Item(ref currentLocationIndex) as MapPoint.Location;
    //Access the StreetAddress property for address
    if(loc != null)
    {
        if(loc.StreetAddress != null)
            this.textBox2.Text = loc.StreetAddress.Value;
        else
            this.textBox2.Text = loc.Name;
    }

}
else
{
    //Add disambiguation process and show modal dialog
    FindResultListDlg findResModalDlg = new FindResultListDlg(ref findResults);
    if(findResModalDlg.ShowDialog() == DialogResult.OK)
    {
        //Process the selected location from the find results list
        . . .
    }
}
```

Adding this code gets the street address of the input query "Space Needle" without requiring any manual disambiguation.

Now, does this application work if you enter an address as input? A quick test with the address "498 Broad St, Seattle, WA, 98109" shows that this application does not work with addresses because the FindPlaceResults method that we are using treats every input location as a place, so to find addresses you need to use the FindAddressResults method.

Finding an Address

MapPoint 2004 API provides a way to find addresses. The Map class has a method, FindAddressResults, which you can use to find addresses. Unlike the FindPlaceResults method, this method takes a full or partial address to find the intended location. So, in order to use the FindAddressResults method, you have to provide at least one of the following parts of an address:

- Street address
- City

- Other city (used for UK addresses)
- Region (or state/province)
- Postal code (or Zip Code)
- Country

The Country parameter is expressed as a GeoCountry enumeration, while the rest of the parameters are strings. For example, if you want to find the address "498 Broad St, Seattle, WA 98109" in the United States, you have to use the GeoCountry.geoCountryUnitedStates value for Country. The following code shows how to invoke the FindAddressResults method on a Map class:

```
//Create an instance of the MapPoint application class
MapPoint.ApplicationClass app = new MapPoint.ApplicationClass();

//Get the Map object from the application object
MapPoint.Map map = app.ActiveMap;

//Call the FindAddressResults method
MapPoint.FindResults findResults = map.FindAddressResults(
                            "498 Broad St",
                            "Seattle",
                            string.Empty,
                            "WA",
                            "98109",
                MapPoint.GeoCountry.geoCountryUnitedStates);
```

Note that when a Country parameter is supplied, the address provided must match that country's address format, or the FindAddressResults method throws an exception. For example, if you pass the above address for GeoCountry.geoCountryUnitedKingdom (UK), the FindAddressResults method throws an exception (since some UK addresses expect the Other City parameter).

 For a full list of the GeoCountry enumeration values, see *http://msdn.microsoft.com/library/default.asp?url=/library/en-us/mappoint2004/BIZOMMFindAddressResults.asp*.

The quality of the locations returned by the method can be determined by the ResultsQuality property of the FindResults object. The rules that we have discussed in the previous section to disambiguate the locations results are applicable to this method as well.

Do you always need to have the address in the previously described format? Our application collects the input location into a simple textbox as a string, so is it possible to have an address entered as a single string so that you can programmatically parse the address before calling the FindAddressResults method? Absolutely; MapPoint 2004 has a method to do this.

Parsing a string into valid street address

The `Map` class has a method, `ParseStreetAddress`, that parses a string into a valid street address represented as the `StreetAddress` class. The `StreetAddress` class has the `Street`, `City`, `OtherCity`, `PostalCode`, `Region`, and `Country` properties that represent various parts of an address. The `Value` property of the `StreetAddress` class gives the full address as one string. The following code shows how to parse a string into a valid address:

```
//Create an instance of the MapPoint application class
MapPoint.ApplicationClass app = new MapPoint.ApplicationClass();
//Get the Map object from the application object
MapPoint.Map map = app.ActiveMap;
//Parse the address
MapPoint.StreetAddress address =
    map.ParseStreetAddress("498 Broad St, Seattle, WA, 98109");

//Now get the values from the
//StreetAddress properties
string streetName = address.Street;
string city = address.City;
```

 If you are using this method with MapPoint 2004 European Edition, it is a good idea to include the country information in the address string to ensure accurate results.

So, which method is right for your application? Is it `FindPlaceResults` or `FindAddressResults` (along with `ParseStreetAddress` method)? The answer depends on the requirements of your application. If you expect users to type a well-formatted address all the time, then it is safe to use the `FindAddressResults` method. On the other hand, if you have an application that expects only place names as input locations, then you should use the `FindPlaceResults` method. However, if you have an application that can accept both place names and well-formatted addresses, which method do you use, `FindPlaceResults` or `FindAddressResults`? Neither—use the `FindResults` method instead.

Finding Both Places and Addresses

The `Map` class has a method, `FindResults`, that can find both places and addresses. This method takes the input location as a string and tries to parse the string into a valid address. If the input string is successfully parsed into an address, then a `FindAddressResults` method is called to find the input location; when the input string cannot be parsed into a valid address, the `FindPlaceResults` method is called. The following code snippet shows how to use the `FindPlaceResults` method:

```
//Create an instance of the MapPoint application class
MapPoint.ApplicationClass app = new MapPoint.ApplicationClass();
//Get the Map object from the application object
MapPoint.Map map = app.ActiveMap;
```

```
//Works with finding addresses
MapPoint.FindResults findAddressResults
    = map.FindResults("498 Broad St, Seattle, WA, 98109");
//Works with finding places
MapPoint.FindResults findPlaceResults
    = map.FindResults("Space Needle");
```

Let's replace the FindPlaceResults method in our application with the FindResults method call to support both place names and addresses:

```
//Call FindResults on the MapClass instance to support both places and
//addresses
MapPoint.FindResults findResults = map.FindResults(textBox1.Text);
```

You know that our application works for both places and addresses and also handles location disambiguation well, but you may be wondering whether you need to create a user interface (UI) to support each method, since each find method's input formats are so different. You actually don't need to—for applications like ours, there is a method exposed by the Map class that uses the pre-built MapPoint UI.

One UI Finds All

The Map class exposes the ShowFindDialog method to show the built-in find dialog, a modal dialog that implements the FindResults and GetLocation methods along with a nice disambiguation process with a great UI. This method returns either a Location or a Pushpin class instance. Don't worry about the details of the Pushpin class yet; I will discuss this class in detail in the next chapter. For now, consider the Pushpin class to be a graphical mark or shape that represents a location. You can access the Location represented by a Pushpin using the Pushpin.Location property.

The ShowFindDialog method takes the input location as a string. The other parameters include:

FindState

This parameter is of GeoFindState type, which is an enumeration. Use GeoFindState.geoFindDefault if you don't know what type of find (place or address versus latitude and longitude) you may be performing. If you know a specific find that you want to show as the default, set the enumeration value to be geoFindAddress or geoFindPlace.

HWndParent

This is an integer that represents the parent window handle of the find modal dialog. Set this parameter's value to 0 if there is an active, visible MapPoint 2004 application window; if not, pass the current window's handle as an argument.

AutoConfirmExactMatch

This is a boolean that tells the find dialog to hide when an exact match to the input location is found. The default value is false.

The following code shows the implementation of this method for our application:

```
//Get a reference to the Map instance via the ActiveMap property
MapPoint.Map map = app.ActiveMap;

//Call the ShowFindDialog to show the find (modal) dialog
object result = map.ShowFindDialog(
                        this.textBox1.Text,
                        MapPoint.GeoFindState.geoFindDefault,
                        (int) this.Handle,
                        false);

//See whether the result is null
if(result != null)
{
    //If the result is a Location type get the
    //Location directly
    if(result is MapPoint.Location)
    {
        currentLocation = result as MapPoint.Location;
    }
    else if(result is MapPoint.Pushpin)
    {
        //If this is a Pushpin type, first get the Pushpin
        MapPoint.Pushpin pushpin = result as MapPoint.Pushpin;
        //Then get the location
        currentLocation = pushpin.Location;
    }
}
else
{
    MessageBox.Show("No locations found. Please verify the input.");
}
```

You need to check for the return type after the ShowFindDialog method returns a value. If it is a Pushpin type, access the corresponding Location object via the Pushpin.Location property.

Figure 2-6 shows the MapPoint find dialog shown for the "Space Needle" search.

We know our application works for place names and well-formatted addresses. Since we also know exactly where the Space Needle is, let's extend our application to do a bit more and find points of interest around the Space Needle.

Finding Points of Interest Around a Location

Points of Interest (POI) are places that may be of some interest; for example, to a tourist in Seattle, the POI could be the Space Needle, among other interesting things to see; for a coffee connoisseur in Seattle, the POI could be a list of coffee shops. If we take the interest out of context, the POI are simply locations. Each location has

Figure 2-6. MapPoint 2004 Find UI dialog

an interest attributed to it and is identified by the category of the place. These categories are defined as broad groups to fit several types of places into one category; examples of such categories are airports, restaurants, coffee shops, and museums.

Using MapPoint 2004, you can find the POI around a location (or around a route) within a specific radius or distance. The location class from the MapPoint 2004 object model exposes the FindNearby method to find the POI around a location.

Let's extend our sample application to find the POI around a location using the FindNearby method. Add a tree view control to add points of interest, a combo box to select distance, and a button to find the POI around a selected location. The new layout is shown in Figure 2-7.

Clicking the Find POI button finds the points of interest around a given location by calling the Location.FindNearby method.

The only parameter that the FindNearby method takes is distance, as type System. Double. The distance must be greater than 0 and less than or equal to 50 miles. The default unit of measurement for distance is miles, but you can change it by setting the appropriate value to the Units property of the ApplicationClass. The Units property is of GeoUnits type, an enumeration containing the values of geoKm and geoMiles. If you want to treat the distances as kilometers, set the Units property to the geoKm value as shown in the following example:

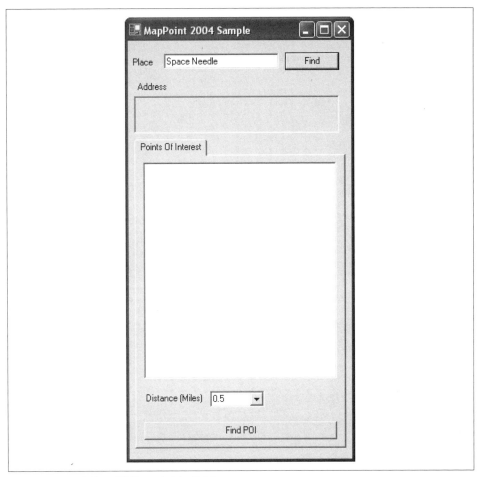

Figure 2-7. Find Place UI Extended for POI

```
MapPoint.ApplicationClass app =
        new  MapPoint.ApplicationClass( );
app.Units = MapPoint.GeoUnits.geoKm;
```

The following code shows the actual FindNearby call from the location found during the FindPlaceResults search:

```
//Call the find nearby on the current location
MapPoint.FindResults poiResults = location.FindNearby(distance);
```

The POI search within a one-mile radius around the Space Needle results in 683 POI; the same search with distance unit set to kilometers results in 288 POI. Figure 2-8 shows the POI found within a one-mile radius around the Space Needle.

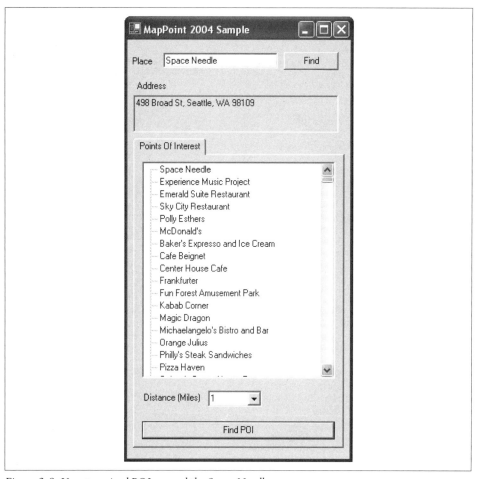

Figure 2-8. Uncategorized POI around the Space Needle

Going through a list of 683 (or even 288) POI would be annoying, as well as intimidating, so we need a better way of handing the POI to give a better view of the POI search results. This is when the PlaceCategory class comes to our rescue. The place categories are names that can be used to group locations together.

Categorizing points of interest using the PlaceCategory class

The PlaceCategory class encapsulates a category name and is exposed as the PlaceCategory property from the Location class. The Parent property of the PlaceCategory gives access to all categories available in MapPoint 2004; there are 48 predefined categories, such as Pharmacies, Restaurants, Theaters, and so on, available in MapPoint 2004. In order to make the POI list more readable by grouping them into meaningful categories, we need to use the PlaceCategory.Name property, which gives the name of the category that a location belongs to. The following code shows how to group locations into categories:

```
//Create an object to hold index value
object findResultIndex = null;
//Create a string instance to hold category name
TreeNode node = null;
int nodeCount = 0;

//Create a hashtable to hold category names
Hashtable categoryNames = new Hashtable();

//Start with index 1 instead of 0
for(int i=1;i<=findResults.Count;i++)
{
    //Box the integer value as an object
    findResultIndex = i;
    //Pass the index as a reference to the get_Item accessor method
    MapPoint.Location loc = findResults.get_Item(ref findResultIndex) as MapPoint.
Location;
    if(loc.PlaceCategory != null)
    {
        object nodeIndex = categoryNames[loc.PlaceCategory.Name];
        if(nodeIndex == null)
        {
            //Create a new category node
            node = new TreeNode(loc.PlaceCategory.Name);
            //Add the current location under this node
            node.Nodes.Add(new TreeNode(loc.Name));
            //Add this node to the tree
            tree.Nodes.Add(node);
            //Store the value in hashtable along with the index number
            categoryNames.Add(loc.PlaceCategory.Name, nodeCount);
            //Increment the node index
            nodeCount ++;
        }
        else
        {
            //Add the current location under this node
            tree.Nodes[Convert.ToInt32(nodeIndex)].Nodes.Add(new TreeNode(loc.Name));
        }
    }
}
```

The category name is checked for each POI location; if the category name already exists in the tree view, the current location is added under that category; if that category does not exist in the tree view, a new category node is added before adding the current location. The final application layout is shown in Figure 2-9.

This POI list is easier to navigate than its predecessor in Figure 2-8, but we still have too many unrelated categories. In this case, we can programmatically hide the unwanted place categories.

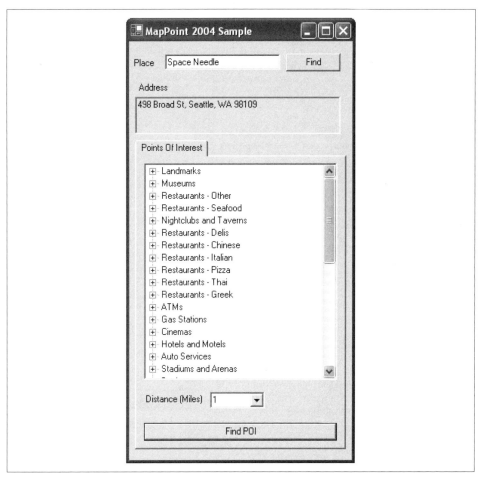

Figure 2-9. Categorized POI around the Space Needle

Controlling place category visibility

The visibility of the point of interest categories can be controlled using the Map-Point 2004 APIs. This PlaceCategories class, which represents the 48 predefined place categories in MapPoint, is exposed as a `PlaceCategories` property from the `Map` class. The `PlaceCategories` class holds the collection of `PlaceCategory` classes that represent individual categories defined in the MapPoint 2004 points of interest. Set the visibility behavior of an individual place category using the `PlaceCategory.Visible` property. The following code shows how to block the "Restaurants—Other" category from the POI list:

```
//Create an instance of ApplicationClass
app = new MapPoint.ApplicationClass();
```

```
//Define the category that needs to be blocked
string blockCategory = "Restaurants - Other";

for(int i = 1; i<app.ActiveMap.PlaceCategories.Count+1; i++)
{
    object index = i;
    //if the name of the category matches the block list
    //set the visible property to false
    MapPoint.PlaceCategory placeCategory =
    app.ActiveMap.PlaceCategories.get_Item(ref index) as MapPoint.PlaceCategory;
    if(placeCategory.Name == blockCategory)
    {
        placeCategory.Visible = false;
    }
    else
    {
        placeCategory.Visible = true;
    }
}
```

Along similar lines, you can also block multiple categories (presented as an array of strings):

```
//Create an instance of ApplicationClass
app = new MapPoint.ApplicationClass();

//Define the category that needs to be blocked
String[] blockCategoryArray = new string[]
            { "Restaurants - Other", "Museums"};

for(int i = 1; i<app.ActiveMap.PlaceCategories.Count+1; i++)
{
    object index = i;
    //if the name of the category matches the block list
    //set the visible property to false
    MapPoint.PlaceCategory placeCategory =
    app.ActiveMap.PlaceCategories.get_Item(ref index) as MapPoint.PlaceCategory;
    if(Array.IndexOf(blockCategoryArray , placeCategory.Name) >= 0)
    {
        placeCategory.Visible = false;
    }
    else
    {
        placeCategory.Visible = true;
    }
}
```

When changing the visibility of a PlaceCategory, keep in mind that the visibility settings of a category persist between application sessions. If you set a category's visibility to false in one session, you must set it to true to see the category again.

But wouldn't it be more useful to show the distance to each point of interest from the input location? In our example, that would mean showing the distance from the Space Needle to each point of interest in the list.

Calculating Distance Between Two Locations

The Location class has a DistanceTo method that calculates the distance to a given location. Keep in mind that the distance calculated using this method is not the same as the driving distance; this method only gives you the straight line ("as the crow flies") distance between the two locations. The DistanceTo method takes another location as an argument; the following code shows how to calculate the distance between two locations:

```
//Get the from location
MapPoint.Location fromLocation
        = this.findResults.get_Item(ref fromIndex) as MapPoint.Location;
//Get the to location
MapPoint.Location toLocation
        = poiResults.get_Item(ref poiIndex) as MapPoint.Location;
//Calculate the distance between the from location and
//to location using the DistanceTo method
double distance = fromLocation.DistanceTo(toLocation);
```

Figure 2-10 shows the POI list when it's updated to show the distances from the input location.

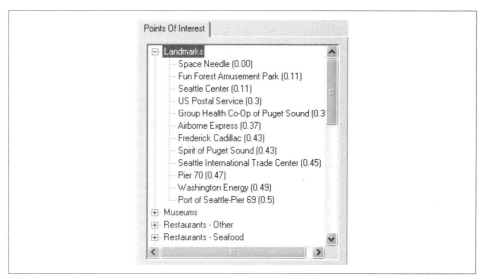

Figure 2-10. POI shown with distances

Another way of calculating the distance between two locations is to call the Distance method on an active Map object:

```
double distance = app.ActiveMap.Distance(startLocation, endLocation);
```

Both startLocation and endLocation are MapPoint.Location type objects.

Keep in mind that both these methods calculate the distance based on the units specified at the ApplicationClass level. To change the units of measurement for the distances (between miles and kilometers), use the Units property on the ApplicationClass object.

After displaying the distances in the POI list, it looks much better with all the information needed to decide which points of interest to visit when you are around the Space Needle clearly shown. However, wouldn't it be helpful if you could actually show the POI on a map? After all, what kind of application would MapPoint 2004 be if it didn't actually display a map? For this next step, we need the MapPoint 2004 ActiveX control.

Programming the MapPoint ActiveX Control

The programming models of the MapPoint 2004 APIs and MapPoint 2004 ActiveX Control are exactly the same, except that you use the AxMappointControl class instead of creating an ApplicationClass object to access the active map instance.

Adding MapPoint 2004 ActiveX Control

The first step towards developing with MapPoint 2004 ActiveX control starts with configuring your development environment. You need to add the ActiveX Control to your Visual Studio .NET toolbox to enable the "Drag-and-Drop" development tool. Create a new tab by selecting the Add Tab option from the toolbox context menu as shown in Figure 2-11.

Figure 2-11. Add Tab context menu

Name the newly created tab MapPoint ActiveX Control and click on it to add the MapPoint 2004 ActiveX Control reference by selecting Add/Remove Items from the context menu, as shown in Figure 2-12.

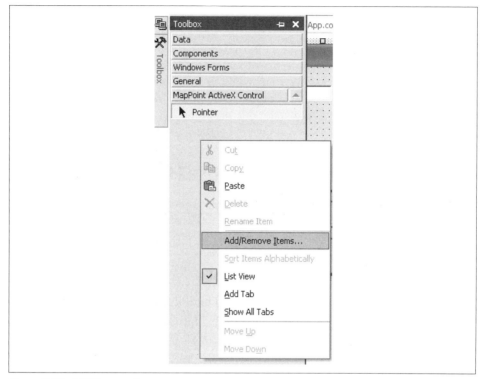

Figure 2-12. Add/Remove Items context menu

When the Customize Toolbox dialog is displayed, select the COM Components tab and Microsoft MapPoint Control 11.0 as shown in Figure 2-13.

Note that if you have MapPoint 2004 APIs already added to your project, you need to remove that reference before you add ActiveX Control; adding ActiveX Control automatically adds the MapPoint 2004 API reference to your project.

That's it! Now you are ready to develop applications using the MapPoint 2004 object model.

Initializing the MapPoint 2004 ActiveX Control

When you drag-and-drop the MapPoint control onto your Windows form, the reference to the MapPoint interoperable assembly is automatically added to your project, along with the control. The drag-and-drop operation also creates and adds an instance of MapPoint control to your code file:

```
private AxMapPoint.AxMappointControl axMappointControl1;
```

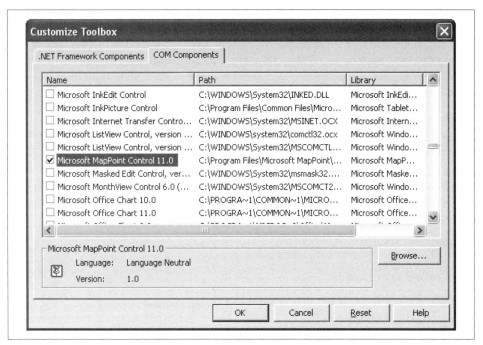

Figure 2-13. The Customize Toolbox dialog

Before you use AxMappointControl, you need to initialize the control by creating new map coverage by calling the NewMap method on the AxMappointControl class. This method takes the map region of type GeoMapRegion enumeration as an argument. There are two valid region values for the map region in MapPoint 2004: GeoMapRegion.geoMapNorthAmerica for North American maps and GeoMapRegion. geoMapEurope for European maps. The following code shows how to initialize the control to show the North American map:

```
axMappointControl1.NewMap(MapPoint.GeoMapRegion.geoMapNorthAmerica);
```

If you are programming with MapPoint 2004 European Edition, you have to initialize the control with GeoMapRegion.geoMapEurope.

You can also open an existing map file using the OpenMap method to initialize the control. The OpenMap method takes an existing map file path as an argument:

```
axMappointControl1.OpenMap("C:\MyMap.ptm");
```

After initializing the map control, you can access the map object via the ActiveMap property:

```
MapPoint.Map map = axMappointControl1.ActiveMap;
```

Using this map object, you can perform all the location-based operations, such as finding places, addresses, and nearby places, as we did earlier in this chapter.

Controlling Toolbars and Panes

The MapPoint 2004 ActiveX map control provides the same set of toolbars as the MapPoint 2004 application. These toolbars are not visible by default, but you can make them appear or disappear programmatically using the MapPoint 2004 ActiveX control's Toolbars property, which is a collection of four toolbars:

Standard toolbar
> Contains common operations, such as opening a new map and printing a map along with main MapPoint features, such as finding nearby places, routing, etc.

Navigation toolbar
> Contains a find textbox to find input places and other menu items, such as zoom in, zoom out, and map style.

Drawing toolbar
> Contains standard drawing tools to draw shapes, such as lines, rectangles, and circles.

Location and Scale toolbar
> Shows the current maps's location and scale.

These toolbars are shown in Figure 2-14.

To access a particular toolbar, use either the index or the name of the toolbar; for example, the following code shows how to show make the Location and Scale toolbar visible using the index:

```
 //Define toolbar indexes
object TOOLBAR_STANDARD = 1;
object TOOLBAR_NAVIGATION = 2;
object TOOLBAR_DRAWING = 3;
object TOOLBAR_LOCATIONSCALE = 4;

//using index
axMappointControl1.Toolbars.get_Item(ref TOOLBAR_DRAWING).Visible
                                              = true;
axMappointControl1.Toolbars.get_Item(ref TOOLBAR_LOCATIONSCALE).Visible
                                              = true;
axMappointControl1.Toolbars.get_Item(ref TOOLBAR_NAVIGATION).Visible
                                              = true;
axMappointControl1.Toolbars.get_Item(ref TOOLBAR_STANDARD).Visible
                                              = true;
```

You get the same effect using the following code, which uses the toolbar's name:

```
object name = "Location and Scale";
axMappointControl1.Toolbars.get_Item(ref name).Visible = true;
```

The Standard toolbar allows users to toggle different panes, such as route pane, find nearby pane, and so forth. However, if you want to control these panes in your application, don't make the entire Standard Toolbar visible in your application—you can

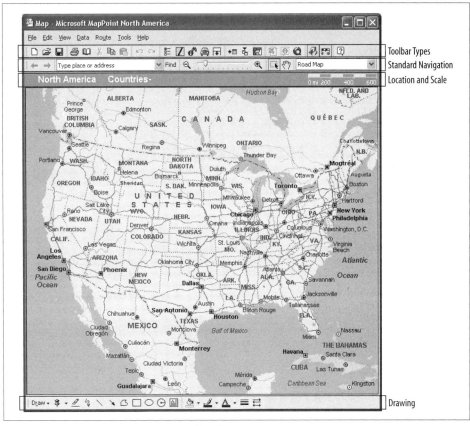

Figure 2-14. MapPoint 2004 MapControl toolbars

control the pane visibility programmatically using the PaneState property of the ActiveX control. The PaneState property is of MapPoint.GeoPaneState type, which is an enumeration. The GeoPaneState enumeration has five values that show no panes, the Legend pane, the Find Nearby Places pane, the Route Planner pane, and the Territory Manager pane, as shown in Table 2-3.

Table 2-3. GeoPaneState enumeration values

GeoPaneState value	Description
geoPaneLegend	Legend pane is displayed.
geoPaneNearbyPlaces	Find Nearby Places pane is displayed.
geoPaneNone	No panes are displayed with the map.
geoPaneRoutePlanner	Route Planner pane is displayed.
geoPaneTerritory	Territory Manager pane is displayed.

For example, to let users find nearby places in your application, you can give them access to that functionality:

```
//Make the route planning pane visible
axMappointControl1.PaneState = MapPoint.GeoPaneState.geoPaneRoutePlanner;
```

Finally, if you want to control the Route Planner pane that displays the detailed driving directions visibility, use the `ItineraryVisible` property of the ActiveX Control:

```
//Hide itinerary pane
axMappointControl1.ItineraryVisible = false;
```

This property is also available from the `ApplicationClass` instance.

Now that we have a map control ready to use, let's start off with some basic actions, such as displaying a location on a map and zooming in and out of maps.

Displaying a Location on a Map

In our sample earlier this chapter, we have implemented the find methods to find places, addresses, and nearby locations. In all these cases, a `MapPoint.Location` instance represents the locations found. To display a location on the map, call the `Location` object's `GoTo` method:

```
//Define a location instance
MapPoint.Location currentLocation = null;

//Get the current location from FindResults method
MapPoint.FindResults findResults =
                map.FindResults("your place input");

currentLocation = findResults.get_Item(ref index);

//Go to the current location on the map
currentLocation.GoTo( );
```

Calling this method zooms in to the location with the best possible view on the map and centers the map on that location. To highlight the location on a map, use the `Location.Select` method:

```
//Highlight the location on the map
currentLocation.Select( );
```

After this implementation, our application looks similar to Figure 2-15.

If there is only one location, you can center the map on it using the `Location.GoTo` method, but you have to use the `Map.Union` method to center the map to display multiple locations on it. This method takes an array of locations and returns the center of the map as a `Location` object for all given locations:

```
//Define an ArrayList to hold location objects
ArrayList locList = new ArrayList();
//Add locations to the array list
for(int i=0;i<findResult.Count;i++)
{
```

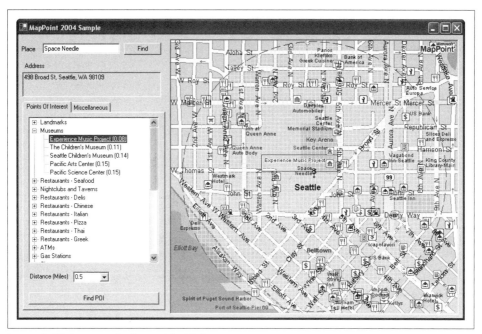

Figure 2-15. Location display and highlight

```
Object index = i+1;
MapPoint.Location location =
        findResult.get_Item(ref index)
        as MapPoint.Location;

locList.Add(location)
}
//Center the map to show all locations
MapPoint.Location center = axMappointControl1.ActiveMap.Union(locList.ToArray( ));
//Now zoom map to the center
center.GoTo( );
```

How do you pinpoint the selected location? Is it possible to annotate that location, or better, to highlight it? Pushpins make this process easy.

Working with Pushpins

Pushpins are visual marks on a map that contain either an annotation or data. Each pushpin on a map is associated with a location. A pushpin in MapPoint 2004 is represented by the Pushpin class. The Name property of a Pushpin object can be used to annotate the pushpin. You can also add notes to the pushpin using the Pushpin. Notes property.

A pushpin is represented pictorially by a symbol. MapPoint 2004 provides a number of symbols to be used with pushpins. These symbols are indexed, and their number should be used to indicate the symbol of a given pushpin; for example, the default symbol is the black pushpin, represented by 0. The valid range for the standard symbols is 0–255. You can also add customized pushpins, but the identity must be in the range of 256–32,766.

 For a full list of available symbols, see the online documentation at *http://msdn.microsoft.com/library/default.asp?url=/library/en-us/ mappoint2004/BIZOMPSymbol.asp.*

The location represented by a pushpin can be accessed via the Pushpin.Location property. Let's look at some code to implement this; to add a pushpin to a predetermined location, call Map.AddPushpin method:

```
//Get map center location
MapPoint.Location location = axMappointControl1.ActiveMap.Location;
//Add a pushpin at this location
MapPoint.Pushpin pushpin = axMappointControl1.ActiveMap.AddPushpin(
                                              location, "Center");
//Assign a symbol
pushpin.Symbol = 64;
//Select and highlight the location
pushpin.Select();
pushpin.Highlight = true;
//Write annotation
pushpin.Note = "This is my favorite place!";
```

This code adds a pushpin to the center of the map. However, the pushpin on the map does not display any information. To display the information associated with the pushpin, such as name, notes, etc., use the Pushpin.BalloonState property. Setting this property displays the pushpin tool tip information. The Pushpin. BalloonState property is of MapPoint.GeoBalloonState type, which is an enumeration. The valid values for this property are:

GeoBalloonState.geoDisplayNone

Does not display any information.

GeoBalloonState.geoDisplayName

Displays only the name of the pushpin.

GeoBalloonState.geoDisplayBalloon

Displays all information including name, notes, etc.

The following code shows how to display the full details of a given pushpin:

```
//Show tooltip (Balloon State)
pushpin.BalloonState = MapPoint.GeoBalloonState.geoDisplayBalloon;
```

You can remove a given pushpin by calling the Pushpin.Delete method. The Pushpin class exposes some other methods, such as Copy and Cut, to copy the pushpin to the clipboard.

Now that we know how to display a location on map, select a location, and add a pushpin to it, let's look at how to interact with the MapPoint 2004 ActiveX Control maps.

Interacting with Maps

The MapPoint 2004 ActiveX Control provides you with a fully interactive map on which to perform actions such as panning, zooming, and tracking mouse clicks. All of this functionality is accessible to both the programmer and the user.

Panning maps

To pan a map, use the `Map.Pan` method. This method takes two arguments:

PanDirection

> Indicates the direction of the pan operation; this property is of `MapPoint.GeoPanCmd` type, which is an enumeration. This enumeration contains values that represent directional values such as east, west, north, south, and northeast.

PanFactor

> Indicates the amount of pan. Even though there are no limits to the pan factor, keep in mind that this value is dependent on the altitude of your map. To give you an idea of what this means, at 1 mile (lower altitudes), a pan factor of 1 pans the map by 0.2 miles, but the same pan factor at 50 miles (a higher altitude) pans the map by 10 miles.

The following code shows how to call the `Pan` method:

```
axMappointControl1.ActiveMap.Pan(MapPoint.GeoPanCmd.geoWest, 1);
```

Given this information, you could write a smart `Pan` method that pans by a certain distance at all altitudes. You would need the altitude to pan the distance ratio to calculate the correct pan value at a given altitude and distance. This ratio is approximately 4.88568304395 for altitudes up to 6,000 miles, above which the factor becomes non-linear. If you want your application to pan the map only by 1 mile irrespective of map's current altitude, you can calculate the pan factor as follows:

```
//Specify desired pan distance
//For example, set to 1 mile in this case
double desiredDist = 1;
//Standard Altitude/Distance ratio
const double ALT2DISTRATIO = 4.88568304395;
//Calcuate the pan factor
double panFactor = desiredDist * ALT2DISTRATIO /
                          axMappointControl1.ActiveMap.Altitude;
//Now pan the map to west
axMappointControl1.ActiveMap.Pan(MapPoint.GeoPanCmd.geoWest, panFactor);
```

This code always pans the map the specified distance. This is very useful if you want to pan your map by a certain distance to show specific locations on the map. Finally, keep in mind that when panning at very low altitudes (say, one or two miles) where street level data is not possible, the MapPoint 2004 ActiveX Control shows a dialog asking to zoom out to higher altitudes before panning.

Zooming Maps

MapPoint 2004 ActiveX Control provides two methods to perform zoom operations on maps:

ZoomIn
> Zooms the map view closer by reducing the map altitude.

ZoomOut
> Zooms the map view farther by increasing the map altitude.

These two methods zoom in or out in steps. There are many levels of zoom effect that you can achieve using them. The levels are defined based on the map altitude. Each time you call zoom methods, the map's altitude is modified accordingly and rerendered to show the map at that altitude. The following code shows how to call a ZoomIn method:

```
axMappointControl1.ActiveMap.ZoomIn( );
```

What if you want to zoom in to a particular level from your current view? For example, if you want to zoom to street level directly without calling the ZoomIn method multiple times, you can do that by modifying the map altitude yourself:

```
//Zoom directly into Street Level by setting 3 mile altitude
axMappointControl1.ActiveMap.Altitude = 3;
```

 When the MapPoint 2004 ActiveX control loads a new map, by default it will be set at a 5,592-mile altitude. Streets start showing up at a 10-mile altitude. For detailed street maps, a 3-mile altitude is ideal.

Tracking mouse clicks

Along with all of its MapPoint-related functionality, the MapPoint 2004 ActiveX Control also provides events and methods to capture your interaction with maps using a mouse. Mouse interaction, in the context of maps, usually includes selecting a point on a map, selecting a pushpin location on a map, and so forth. If you want to process a user's interaction with maps in MapPoint 2004 ActiveX Control, you need to know when and where a mouse is clicked to obtain the location corresponding to a mouse click. Let's look at some of these methods in detail.

Point to location

This map object exposes the XYToLocation method to obtain a location at a given point on the map view on the screen. This method returns the location corresponding to the selected x and y coordinates. In order to use this method, you need to trap the mouse click and capture the x and y coordinates, which can be done using the Map object's BeforeClick event. This event occurs when a user clicks on the map before MapPoint 2004 ActiveX Control actually processes the mouse click. You would have to wire up this event in the InitializeComponent method of your application:

```
axMappointControl1.BeforeClick +=
   newAxMapPoint._IMappointCtrlEvents_BeforeClickEventHandler(
                                    axMappointControl1_BeforeClick);
```

Once you have wired up the event, the axMapPointControl1_BeforeClick method should be implemented so that you capture the mouse click coordinates:

```
private void axMappointControl1_BeforeClick(object sender,
                           AxMapPoint._IMappointCtrlEvents_BeforeClickEvent e)
{
    int XCoord = e.x;
    int YCoord = e.y;
    MapPoint.Location location =
               axMappointControl1.ActiveMap.XYToLocation(XCoord, YCoord);
    if(location != null)
    {
        //Do some processing with location
        . . .
    }
}
```

This event captures only single clicks from the mouse. To capture double-clicks from your mouse, you have to wire up the BeforeDblClick event, which occurs when a user double-clicks on the map but before the MapPoint 2004 ActiveX Control actually processes the double click.

Location to point

The Map object also provides a way to convert a location on the map to a point on the screen. Using Map object's LocationToX and LocationToY methods, you can obtain x and y coordinates for any given location by making separate calls for each coordinate:

```
//Get the center of the map
MapPoint.Location location = axMappointControl1.ActiveMap.Location;
//Get x and y coordinates
int x = axMappointControl1.ActiveMap.LocationToX(location);
int y = axMappointControl1.ActiveMap.LocationToY(location);
//Display the center coordinates
MessageBox.Show(String.Format("Map is centered at ({0}, {1})",
                               x.ToString(), y.ToString()));
```

The LocationToX and LocationToY methods assume that a particular location is on the current map screen limits; if the location is not present in the ActiveX Control map screen limits, these methods fail by returning invalid values (such as a maximum value of int32). To avoid errors in a case like this, it's always a good idea to use the Location.GoTo( ) method before getting the coordinates.

Processing location selections

Sometimes you have to follow the locations or pushpins that users are selecting on a given map; for example, you have displayed 10 pushpins on a map, and when a user selects a pushpin, you want to show the information by using the BalloonState property. In this case, you need the Map object's SelectionChange event. Wiring up this event is no different from any other event that we have seen previously; you have to add the following code in the initialization method:

```
this.axMappointControl1.SelectionChange +=
        new AxMapPoint._IMappointCtrlEvents_SelectionChangeEventHandler(
                                    axMappointControl1_SelectionChange);
```

The SelectionChangeEvent exposes two objects: one for a current or new selection and one for an old or previous selection. So, in the event handler method, you have to capture these two objects to do the processing, as follows:

```
private void axMappointControl1_SelectionChange(object sender,
                    AxMapPoint._IMappointCtrlEvents_SelectionChangeEvent e)
{
    //Get the previous selection
    MapPoint.Pushpin pPrev = e.pOldSelection as MapPoint.Pushpin;
    //Get the current selection
    MapPoint.Pushpin pCurr = e.pNewSelection as MapPoint.Pushpin;
    if(pPrev != null)
    {
        //Turn off the tool tip
        pPrev.BalloonState = MapPoint.GeoBalloonState.geoDisplayNone;
        //Turn off the highlight
        pPrev.Highlight = false;
    }
    if(pCurr != null)
    {
        //Display the information
        pCurr.BalloonState = MapPoint.GeoBalloonState.geoDisplayBalloon;
        //Highlight the pushpin
        pCurr.Highlight = true;
    }
}
```

Since the SelectionChangeEvent captures both previous and new selections as objects, it is possible that these selections are locations if you select a location instead of a pushpin. This event is also applicable for other objects such as shapes, directions, and waypoints. In that case, you need to typecast the object as a Location:

```
//Get the previous selection
MapPoint.Location lPrev = e.pOldSelection as MapPoint.Location;
//Get the current selection
MapPoint.Location lCurr = e.pNewSelection as MapPoint. Location;
```

Disabling map interaction

Now, let's look at how to disable the map for user interaction; this may sound strange, after all the user interaction-related discussions. In some application scenarios, you have to make the map read-only so that users cannot change the information on the map. There is no straightforward way to do this other than disabling all events by overriding them.

You must take the following steps:

1. Turn-off the edge panning by setting AllowEdgePan to false:

```
axMappointControl1.ActiveMap.AllowEdgePan = false;
```

2. Capture any mouse down event and display a message saying that this is a read-only map.

```
//Wire up the mouse down event
private void axMappointControl1_MouseDownEvent(object sender,
                AxMapPoint._IMappointCtrlEvents_MouseDownEvent e)
. . .
//Implement the event handler method by displaying a message
private void axMappointControl1_MouseDownEvent(object sender,
                AxMapPoint._IMappointCtrlEvents_MouseDownEvent e)
{
    return;
}
```

3. Support pan and zoom via mouse wheel and arrow keys by overriding the AfterViewChange event by restoring the original center of the map and altitude.

```
//Obtain the original center location
originalCenterLocation = axMappointControl1.ActiveMap.Location;
//Obtain the original altitude
originalAltitude = axMappointControl1.ActiveMap.Altitude;
. . .
//Wire up the AfterViewChange event
this.axMappointControl1.AfterViewChange +=
        new System.EventHandler(this.axMappointControl1_AfterViewChange);
. . .
//Implement AfterViewChange event handler method
private void axMappointControl1_AfterViewChange(object sender, EventArgs e)
{
        if(originalCenterLocation != null)
    {
        //Re-assign the center point
        axMappointControl1.ActiveMap.Location = originalCenterLocation;
    }
    //Re-assign the altitude
    axMappointControl1.ActiveMap.Altitude = originalAltitude;
}
```

As you can see, the AfterViewChange event handler restores both map center and altitude; this method takes care of both pan clicks and zoom (via the mouse wheel scroll), but keep in mind that performance may be affected by the mouse wheel scroll events. Finally, if you want to disable mouse clicks, set the cancel property of the BeforeClick and BeforeDblClick events to true.

Saving a Map

There are several ways to save a map from your application. You can save the map as a standard .ptm map that can only be opened using MapPoint 2004 application, or you can save it as a web page (.htm) map that can be opened by any browser.

Saving the map as a *.ptm* is very straightforward; you can use the `SaveMapAs` method on the MapPoint 2004 ActiveX Control:

```
axMappointControl1.SaveMapAs(@"C:\test.ptm");
```

To save the map as a web page, use the `SavedWebPages` property of the `Map` object. This property is a collection of web pages, and you call the `Add` method as follows to save a new map as a web page:

```
string path = @"C:\test.htm";
            axMappointControl1.ActiveMap.SavedWebPages.Add(
                    path, axMappointControl1.ActiveMap.Location, "My Map",
                    true, true, true, axMappointControl1.ActiveMap.Width,
                    axMappointControl1.ActiveMap.Height, true, true, true, true);
```

Using the `SavedWebPages` collection also enables you to manage the saved pages from the MapPoint 2004 application UI using the File → Manage Saved Web Pages menu option.

Cleaning Up After You're Done

The MapPoint 2004 object model was originally designed and implemented using COM technologies, so even if you use the COM Interoperable assemblies to write your code, the MapPoint 2004 Application instance will not be collected by the .NET runtime garbage collector. Before quitting your application, you must manually quit the MapPoint 2004 Application by calling the `Quit` method on the `MapPoint.Application` object:

```
//Define MapPoint Application instance
MapPoint.Application app = null;
//Obtain app references either via MapPoint.ApplicationClass or
//MapPoint.AxMapPointControl.ActiveMap.Application
. . .

//Clean up the MapPoint Application before you exit
if(app != null)
{
    app.Quit();
    app = null;
}
```

The `Quit` method discards the current map and unloads all other items, such as add-ins, before exiting the application. However, calling this method asks the user whether she wants to save the map before discarding it. If you don't want users to have this choice, you can set the `Saved` property to `True` on the application's active `Map` object:

```
app.ActiveMap.Saved = true;
```

Setting this value means that the user will not be prompted to make a decision whether to save or discard the current map.

If you fail to implement the cleanup, your application may have memory leaks.

So far, we have covered major APIs offered by MapPoint 2004 for finding places, addresses, and nearby interests, along with some basic map operations, such as placing pushpins, zooming, and panning. A discussion of MapPoint 2004 programming is not complete if we don't mention latitude and longitude, so before we move on to routing and driving directions, let's look at finding addresses for latitude and longitude in MapPoint 2004.

Definition of Latitude and Longitude

Latitude measures how far north or south of the Equator a place is located. The Equator is situated at 0°, the North Pole at 90° north (or simply 90°, since a positive latitude number implies north), and the South Pole at 90° south (or –90°). Latitude measurements range from 0 to (±)90.

Longitude measures how far east or west of the Prime Meridian a place is located. The Prime Meridian runs through Greenwich, England. Longitude is measured in terms of east, implied by a positive number, or west, implied by a negative number. Longitude measurements range from 0 to (±)180.

Dealing with Latitude and Longitude

You know how to find a location using a place name or an address, but do you know how to find a location using latitude and longitude? Using the Map class's GetLocation method, you can easily find a location that corresponds to a given latitude and longitude measurement. This is also called *geocoding* in cartography terminology. This method takes latitude and longitude as System.Double values and returns a Location instance that represents the input latitude and longitude. This method also takes the altitude as an argument, but it is mainly used at the time when the location is displayed on a map, so you can freely pass one mile for the time being. The following code shows how to find a location using latitude and longitude:

```
//Get the reference to the active map instance
MapPoint.Map map = app.ActiveMap;
//Call the GetLocation method to find location
//using the latitude and longitude
MapPoint.Location location =
        m.GetLocation(41.33896, -122.43433, 1);
```

At this point, don't bother to get the street address for the location returned by the GetLocation method because this method doesn't return the address all the time. Don't be disappointed, as there is still a way to find the nearest address using the current location. The idea is to basically do a hit-detection around the found location to see if there are any addresses available. Before we get into the details of how to find out a location's address, let's look at the hit-detection in MapPoint 2004 in detail.

Hit-Detection in MapPoint 2004

What is hit-detection in MapPoint 2004, and how do you programmatically implement it? The Map object in MapPoint has the method, ObjectsFromPoint, which allows you to perform a hit-detection around any given point (x and y coordinates) on the screen. You can already get a point from any given location, so what does this method return? As the method name suggests, it returns an array of objects wrapped in a FindResults instance. The type of objects returned by this method depends on the current map altitude. For example, if you call this method at lower altitudes, it returns locations with street addresses; if you go to higher altitudes and call this method, it returns larger geographic areas, such as Zip Code, county, and time zone of the point. The following snippet shows how to call the ObjectsFromPoint method for any given Location:

```
//Get Location from latitude and longitude
MapPoint.Location location =
        app.ActiveMap.GetLocation(mylatitude, mylongitude, altitude);

/Now use the Map.ObjectsFromPoint method to get points from the
//above location
MapPoint.FindResults findresults =
    app.ActiveMap.ObjectsFromPoint(
            app.ActiveMap.LocationToX(location),
            app.ActiveMap.LocationToY(location));
```

The ObjectsFromPoint method is very versatile and can be used for many purposes, such as querying for address of a given location, determining time zone, querying a territory, and so on. In the following sections, I will show you how to use the ObjectsFromPoint method in a few of these scenarios.

Determining Time Zone for a Given Location

Determining the time zone of any location can be done using the ObjectsFromPoint method. When this method is called at lower altitudes (usually around two to three miles), it returns the time zone as one of the FindResults objects. Using this technique, you can check whether FindResults contains a time zone by looking for the string "GMT" in the name of the each found result:

```
string place = "Redmond, WA";
//Find the location first
MapPoint.FindResults findResults
    = axMappointControl1.ActiveMap.FindResults(place);
if(findResults != null && findResults.Count > 0)
 {
```

```
          object index = 1;
          MapPoint.Location location =
          findResults.get_Item(ref index) as MapPoint.Location;
          //Zoom into it
          location.GoTo();
          //Set low altitudes
          axMappointControl1.ActiveMap.Altitude = 2;
        //Now get points from the location
        MapPoint.FindResults points
            = axMappointControl1.ActiveMap.ObjectsFromPoint(
                axMappointControl1.ActiveMap.LocationToX(location),
                axMappointControl1.ActiveMap.LocationToY(location));
      if(points != null && points.Count > 0)
      {
        for(int i=1;i<=points.Count;i++)
        {
         object index2 = i;
         //Get location
         MapPoint.Location loc
           = points.get_Item(ref index2) as MapPoint.Location;
         //Look for GMT in the name of the location
         if(loc.Name.IndexOf("GMT") > 0)
         {
           MessageBox.Show(loc.Name);
           break;
         }
        }
      }
    }
```

As an example, when this code is executed, the time zone of the New York area is displayed as "Eastern (GMT-5)."

 Note that if you are using a non–North American version of Map-Point, the localized string to match may be different from GMT.

Next, let's see how we can extend the ObjectsFromPoint method to determine the street address of a location.

Determining the Street Address of a Given Location

One of the limitations of the GetLocation method is that you cannot always get the address for a given set of latitude and longitude. The workaround for this limitation is to use the hit-detection technique around the given latitude and longitude.

There are a few ways to do the hit-detection:

- Panning around at the same altitude to see whether we find street addresses
- Zooming in and out trying to find locations with street addresses
- Routing to a place with a known street address (such as the Space Needle) so that the found location automatically snaps to the nearest street

Due to its efficiency and accuracy, I choose to implement the first option, panning around to see whether there is a nearby street. The basic approach to panning around the chosen found location is to move in a general spiral. In this case, the center of the spiral goes to the original location found using the GetLocation method, and I continue increasing the radius until I find a street address. The implementation of this approach is as follows:

```
public static MapPoint.Location GetLocationEx(double latitude,
                              double longitude, ref MapPoint.Application app)
{
    if(app == null)
        return null;

    //Define the altitude
    double altitude = 3;
    //Flag to indicate that a street address is found
    bool found = false;
    //Original latitude and longitude
    double mylatitude = latitude;
    double mylongitude = longitude;
    //Angle to create a spiral
    double theta = 0;
    //Radius of the spiral
    double radius = 0.00003;
    //flag to indicate the original location
    bool first = true;
    //Define a location to hold end-result
    MapPoint.Location foundLocation = null;

    //Approximately corrects for latitude changing the value of longitude
    double latitudeInRadians = latitude * Math.PI / 180;
    double longMultiplier = 1 / Math.Cos(latitudeInRadians);

    //Get the location using the Map.GetLocation method with the given
    //latitude and longitude
    //The altitude plays an important role in getting the better accurate
    //addresses for given lat longs
    while(!found)
    {
        MapPoint.Location location =
                app.ActiveMap.GetLocation(mylatitude, mylongitude, altitude);

        if(location == null)
            return null;

        if(first)
        {
            //Zoom map to the original location
            location.GoTo();
            first = false;
        }
```

```
//Now use the Map.ObjectsFromPoint method to get points from the
//current map center
MapPoint.FindResults findresults =
    app.ActiveMap.ObjectsFromPoint(
              app.ActiveMap.LocationToX(location),
              app.ActiveMap.LocationToY(location));

//Select a point that has street address and return that location
object index = null;
//Now loop through the results
for(int i = 0; i<findresults.Count; i++)
{
    index = i+1;
    MapPoint.Location loc =
            findresults.get_Item(ref index) as MapPoint.Location;
    //Check for the street names
    if(loc != null && loc.StreetAddress != null)
    {
        //Found the steet name
        foundLocation = loc;
        found = true;
    }
}

//Radius increment value; if you want your
//Street address find to be more accurate, keep this
//value at either 0.00001 or 0.00002, but keep
//in mind that lower values may take more time to resolve
Double accuracy = 0.00004;
//Increment the radius
radius = radius + accuracy;
//Increment the angle
theta = theta + Math.PI/16;
//Pan to next latitude, longitude
mylongitude = longitude + (longMultiplier * (Math.Cos(theta) * radius));
mylatitude = latitude + Math.Sin(theta) * radius;
}

return foundLocation;

}
```

An example of how the above algorithm works is shown in Figure 2-16 on a map with blue and red pushpins. The center of the spiral is the original location found for a given latitude and longitude; the pushpin to its right shows the nearest street address found using the spiral method.

You could enhance this algorithm by completing the circle (with no increments to radius) and seeing whether there is more than one intersection between the circle and a street; if there is, the midpoint of that arc would be a closer point to the original location.

Figure 2-16. Finding the nearest street address from a Lat/Long algorithm

The location found using the previously described method can be used to find the nearest street address for a given latitude and longitude. You can find this method in the *ProgrammingMapPointUtilities* project in the *Chapter 02* file included in the companion material.

Finally, if you are using the `ShowFindDialog` method for finding latitude and longitude, use the `GeoFindState.geoFindLatLong` as `FindState` parameter; in this scenario, the method looks for a comma as a delimiter to parse the values correctly. Anything that lies to the left of the delimiter is considered latitude, and the value that lies to the right of the delimiter is considered longitude.

Routing in MapPoint 2004

MapPoint 2004 provides a simple but powerful API to calculate routes between locations. A route in MapPoint 2004 is represented as a `MapPoint.Route` object. You can access a `Route` object via the `ActiveRoute` property of a `Map` object (the `Map` object can be obtained either via the MapPoint.ApplicationClass object or MapPoint.axMapPointControl object using the ActiveMap property):

```
MapPoint.Route route = axMappointControl1.ActiveMap.ActiveRoute;
```

After obtaining a valid route object, you can perform actions such as calculating, optimizing, and personalizing routes; let's see each one of these features in detail.

Specifying a Route

In MapPoint 2004 terms, a *route* is essentially a collection of locations connected in some way—via street, ferry, or highway. These locations in a route are known as *waypoints* and are represented using the MapPoint.Waypoint class. A valid route always contains two or more waypoints. Waypoints in a route are represented in the Route.Waypoints collection, so you use the Waypoints collection to add new waypoints:

```
//Get ahold of route object
MapPoint.Route route = axMappointControl1.ActiveMap.ActiveRoute;
//Add the location to the ActiveRoute
route.Waypoints.Add(loc, loc.Name);
```

You can access the waypoints using the same collection and the corresponding index value:

```
//Obtain a waypoint from a given route
object index = 1;
MapPoint.Waypoint waypoint = route.Waypoints.get_Item(ref index);
```

You can use the MapPoint.Waypoint object in many ways to specify a new route or modify an existing route. To change the location represented by a Waypoint object, use the Waypoint.Anchor property. This property is of type object because it can be either a Location or a Pushpin. If you are assigning a new location to a waypoint, you can do it like this:

```
//Obtain a waypoint from a given route
object index = 1;
MapPoint.Waypoint waypoint = route.Waypoints.get_Item(ref index);
//Assign a new location
waypoint.Anchor = newlocation;
```

You may have noticed that a Waypoint object also exposes the Location property, which returns the Location object that it corresponds to; however, keep in mind that this property is a read-only property, and you cannot change the location using it.

Using the Waypoint object's SegmentPreferences property, you can set the segment preference indicating whether you prefer a shorter route, a quicker route, and so on. This is useful if you have preferences for a segment in a route. This property is of MapPoint.GeoSegmentPreferences type, an enumeration which has the following values:

geoSegmentQuickest

Calculates a route based on the quickest route available between two locations.

geoSegmentShortest

Calculates a route based on shortest distance between two locations.

geoSegmentPreferred

Calculates a route based on the route preferences set using the DriverProfile object at the Route object level (which I will discuss shortly).

The default value is always geoSegmentQuickest, and you can set a different value:

```
object index = 2;
MapPoint.Waypoint waypoint = route.Waypoints.get_Item(ref index);
waypoint.SegmentPreferences = MapPoint.GeoSegmentPreferences.geoSegmentShortest;
```

There is one last concept that you need to understand about waypoints and SegementPreferences; a waypoint represents only one location, but a route segment represents two locations. So, what happens if you set two different segment preferences for each location in a single segment? The answer is that the waypoint (location) at the beginning of the segment always decides the segment's route preference.

Waypoints are categorized into three types:

- Start point
- End point
- Intermediate stop

You can access this information for a given Waypoint object using the Type property. This property is of MapPoint.GeoWayPointType enumeration. This property is useful in determining the type of waypoint when analyzing a route or processing driving directions. You can set a Waypoint's preferred arrival and departure times using the PreferredArrival and PreferredDeparture properties, respectively; MapPoint 2004 uses this information to adjust the itinerary when calculating driving directions. Finally, you can specify a stop time using the StopTime property, which is of Double type and expresses amount of hours as a fraction of a day (24 hours); for example, if you want to stop for 2 hours, you would assign the StopTime:

```
waypoint.StopTime = 2/24;
```

Now that we know how to specify and set waypoints for a route, let's look at how to optimize a route.

Optimizing a Route

You can optimize a route if it has more than one waypoint as an intermediate stop. This is useful if you want to order waypoints (of Intermediate type stops) so that the total distance driven in a route is minimized. To optimize a route, call the Optimize method on the Waypoints collection:

```
//Optimize the route
route.Waypoints.Optimize();
```

Note that the Optimize method does not alter the start and end points; it reorders only the intermediate stops. If you do not have more than three waypoints, calling this method does not effect on the waypoint order.

You can find out whether a Waypoints collection is optimized by using the WayPoints.IsOptimized property. When the Optimize method is called and a route is successfully optimized, the RouteAfterOptimize event is fired; the following code shows how to wire up this event:

```
this.axMappointControl1.RouteAfterOptimize
    +=new AxMapPoint._IMappointCtrlEvents_RouteAfterOptimizeEventHandler(
                        axMappointControl1_RouteAfterOptimize);
```

The following code shows how a simple implementation of this event handler:

```
private void axMappointControl1_RouteAfterOptimize(object sender,
    AxMapPoint._IMappointCtrlEvents_RouteAfterOptimizeEvent e)
{
    //Now display the waypoints in correct order
    MyMethodToDisplayCorrectRouteOrder(e.pRoute);
}
```

You can use this event to record or display the new order of the waypoints.

Remember that calling the Optimize method does not calculate driving directions; it only reorders the intermediate stop waypoints. So, in order to get driving directions, you need to calculate the route as a separate step.

Calculating a Route

You can calculate a route for a given set of waypoints using the Route object's Calculate method:

```
//Calculate the route
route.Calculate();
```

As you can see, this method does not take any parameters. However, when you call it, you need to make sure that you have at least two waypoints added to the Route object; otherwise an exception is thrown. Additionally, it is important to note that this method also throws an exception when two waypoints are not connected by any routable means. When this method is successfully completed, the RouteAfterCalculate event is fired; this event has several functions, including displaying driving directions, storing route cost into a database, and so on. The following code shows how to wire up the RouteAfterCalculate event:

```
this.axMappointControl1.RouteAfterCalculate+=
        new AxMapPoint._IMappointCtrlEvents_RouteAfterCalculateEventHandler(
                            axMappointControl1_RouteAfterCalculate);
```

This code snippet shows a sample implementation of the event handler method:

```
private void axMappointControl1_RouteAfterCalculate(object sender,
        AxMapPoint._IMappointCtrlEvents_RouteAfterCalculateEvent e)
    {
```

```
    //Display diriving directions
    DisplayDrivingDirections(e.pRoute);
}
```

After calculating driving directions, you can get the detailed instructions from the directions using the Route object's Directions property:

```
foreach(MapPoint.Direction direction in route.Directions)
{
    . . .
}
```

The Directions property is a collection of Direction objects. The Direction class has several properties, including driving instructions, starting time, distance, and so forth. Table 2-4 shows some key properties that are exposed on the Direction class.

Table 2-4. Key Properties of the Direction class

Property name	Description
Waypoint	Represents the starting point for the route segment
Distance	Returns the total distance of the current segment
Location	Returns the location that represents the best map view for the current segment
Instruction	Returns the directions text for the current segment
StartTime	Returns the calculated start time for the current segment

Along with these properties, the Direction object also provides the FindNearby method to locate nearby points of interest; since a Direction object connects two locations, FindNearby works as a "find along route" method instead of a finding locations around a specific point. This method is useful in route-planning tasks, such as figuring out where to stop for gas and food along a route.

Personalizing Route Calculations

Personalizing a route is possible with the MapPoint 2004 API using the Route object's DriverProfile property. This property is an instance of the DriverProfile class and can be used to set a preferred start time, end time, speed, road type, and so on. Table 2-5 shows some key properties of the DriverProfile class.

Table 2-5. Key properties for the DriverProfile class

Property name	Description
StartTime	Gets or sets the time to start driving each day
EndTime	Gets or sets the time to end driving each day
Speed	Gets or sets the speed at which the user prefers to drive on different road types

To set preferred roads for your route, use the `set_PreferredRoads` method to indicate the road type and preference setting on a scale of zero to one (least preferred to most preferred) as follows:

```
//Really hate arterial roads
route.DriverProfile.set_PreferredRoads(
                    MapPoint.GeoRoadType.geoRoadArterial, 0);
//Prefer Interstates
route.DriverProfile.set_PreferredRoads(
                    MapPoint.GeoRoadType.geoRoadInterstate, 1);
```

Finally, keep in mind that you need to set the driver profile settings before calculating the route.

Where Are We?

In this chapter, we have discussed how to use MapPoint 2004 APIs to develop applications with basic functionalities, such as finding places, addresses, and latitude/longitude; displaying locations on a map; zooming into a location; and panning maps. When you develop your applications using MapPoint 2004 ActiveX Control, try to reuse the UI that comes with it—toolbars, panes, dialogs, etc. We have also discussed using the MapPoint 2004 routing API to optimize, calculate, and personalize routes. It is important to keep in mind that you are working with a set of COM objects with a managed wrapper around them, so be sure to call the `Quit` method on the `MapPoint.Application` object when you are done with your tasks.

While it seems to be a lot of information, these concepts are really the core of MapPoint 2004 programming, and we will be using them more in the next chapter when we discuss dealing with business data and MapPoint 2004 data APIs.

CHAPTER 3

Working with Data in MapPoint 2004

MapPoint 2004 can process, analyze, and display business data based on location, and it can then create demographic maps, thematic maps, territories, time zone maps, and shapes on maps. MapPoint 2004 ships with extensive built-in demographic data and a set of APIs to import, analyze, and display your business data from variety of sources.

This chapter has three major sections that correspond to the common tasks of working with:

- MapPoint demographic data
- Your own data
- Shapes on maps

I will assume that you are familiar with the basic MapPoint 2004 programming model (if not, refer to Chapter 2 of this book). The sample data and code used in this chapter is available in the book's companion material in the *Chapter03* directory.

Understanding the MapPoint 2004 Data API

In MapPoint 2004, both business data and demographic data are represented using the DataSet class. An active Map object exposes the DataSets collection, which you use to access a valid DataSet object. How does a DataSets collection get its data wrapped as a DataSet object? The DataSets collection is different from traditional .NET collections—it not only exposes a collection of DataSet objects, but it also offers methods to import external data and to access MapPoint 2004 demographic data.

A DataSet object is similar to a data table with rows and columns and regular querying capabilities. However, a DataSet object allows you to query the records or data rows based on location information. Each query results in a Recordset object containing the records that satisfy the location-based query. The DataSet object can also be used to display data on maps. In essence, if you are using any data features (such as data maps, territories, etc.) in MapPoint 2004 APIs, the DataSet class is the root for all these tasks; Figure 3-1 shows the relationships between an active `Map` object, a `DataSets` collection, a `DataSet` object, and a `Recordset` object.

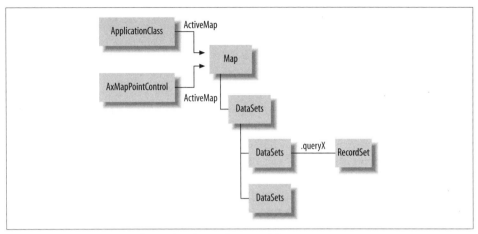

Figure 3-1. MapPoint 2004 data-related API object model

 It is important to note that the `DataSet` and `RecordSet` objects shown in the MapPoint object model are different from the `Dataset` and `RecordSet` classes defined in the `System.Data` namespace in the .NET Framework.

Tables 3-1 and 3-2 show some of the key methods exposed on the `DataSet` and `RecordSet` objects.

Table 3-1. Key Methods in the DataSet object

Method Name	Description
DisplayDataMap	Displays a set of data on a map
QueryAllRecords	Returns all records in a `DataSet` as a `RecordSet` object
QueryShape	Returns records that fall within a specified shape on the map as a `RecordSet` object
ZoomTo	Zooms to the best map view of the specified `DataSet` object

Table 3-2. Key methods in the RecordSet object

Method Name	Description
MoveFirst	Sets the current record of the `RecordSet` to the first record
MoveNext	Sets the current record of the `RecordSet` to the next record

With this introduction, let's look at specifics of dealing with visualization of data using MapPoint 2004.

Understanding Data Maps

Imagine this: if you had a table of data that contained population count and area in square miles per state, and a map of the United States with states color-coded with corresponding population densities, on which one would it be easier to spot the state with the highest population density? Visualizing statistical data on maps makes grasping the key statistics more intuitive, especially if they are based on location.

MapPoint 2004 supports data visualization on maps through its data APIs. You can display data maps using either native MapPoint demographic data or an external data source such as a text file, Excel spreadsheet, or even a SQL Server database. In MapPoint 2004, a data map is represented with a `DataMap` class. A `DataMap` object can only be created using a `DataSet` object by calling the `DisplayDataMap` method. The resulting map displays data on the current active map of the MapPoint ActiveX Control or the `ApplicationClass` object and returns a `DataMap` instance. The `DataMap` object exposes a set of read-only properties that define the data map's behavior. The only property for which you can set a value is the `LegendTitle` property, used in the legend pane.

Before we get into coding details of data maps, there are a couple of details that you need to know: what data map styles (also known as data map types) are, and how to use the `DataSet.DisplayDataMap` method.

Understanding Data Map Styles

MapPoint 2004 supports three broad categories of data map styles:

- Location data map
- Single item data map
- Multiple items data map

Each category is appropriate for a different set of uses.

Location data map

This data map style should be used when you want to display only locations and have no data associated with them. For example, if you want to display your company's retail store locations in the United States, use a location data map. In this data map style, there are two display options to represent locations on maps:

Pushpin maps
Use standard MapPoint 2004 pushpins or custom pushpins to represent each location. For example, locations such as a coffee shop, your office, and your home will be shown using one pushpin type.

Multiple symbol maps

> Use different symbols to represent each location. For example, locations such as a coffee shop, your office, and your home are marked with different pushpins for easy identification.

Single-item data map

This data map style should be used when you have a single data item associated with each location that you want displayed on a map (or when you have multiple data items but want to display only one on the map). For example, to display the annual sales for each retail store in the United States, use a single-item data map. In a single item data map, each location has an associated data item. In this category, you have four display options:

Shaded area maps

> In this map style, shown in Figure 3-2, varying map shades and colors represent the data associated with each location. This map style is useful for displaying data for larger areas, such as states, countries, and Zip Codes. In this map style, a lighter shade represents a lower value, and a darker shade represents a higher value. For example, if you use the shaded area map style to represent annual sales amounts per state for retail stores, all states that have a lighter shade represent poorly-performing stores, and all states that have a darker shade represent the stores that are performing well in sales.

Figure 3-2. Shaded area map (Color Plate 1)

Shaded circle maps

In this map style, similar to the shaded area map style, varying map shades represent the data associated with each location. Since each location is represented as a circle, this map style is suited only for point locations such as cities or addresses. In this map style, shown in Figure 3-3, all circles are the same size, and the shade of the circle represents the data value; lighter shades mean lower values, while darker shades mean higher values. This map style is suitable if you want to display annual sales per store.

Figure 3-3. Shaded circle map

Sized circle maps

In this map style, shown in Figure 3-4, varying circle size represents the data associated with each location. This map style is useful when displaying data for medium to large locations, such as a city, county, state, or Zip Code. In this map style, the circle's size represents the data associated with that location. For example, if you use the sized circle map style to represent annual sales amounts per state for your retail stores, states with smaller circles represent poorly-performing stores, and states with bigger circles represent the stores that are performing well in sales.

Multiple symbol maps

In this map style, shown in Figure 3-5, multiple symbols represent locations, and different colors represent ranges of value associated with each location. For example, you could use the multiple symbol map style to display annual sales of

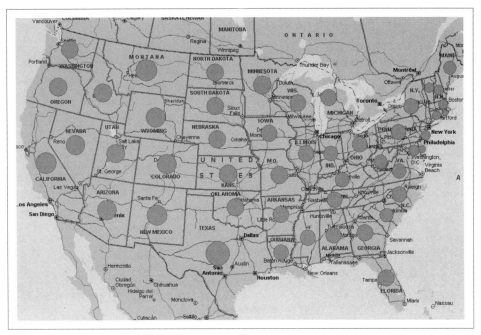

Figure 3-4. Sized circle map

your retail stores by using green to represent top sales range (say, >$10 million), orange to represent medium sales range (say, from $5 million to $10million), and red to represent poor sales range (say, from $1 million to $5 million).

In all these map styles, there is only one dimension being analyzed based on location (for example, retail store sales). But what map styles would you use to display both your sales and your competitor's sales based on location? This situation is when you need multiple item data maps.

Multiple item data map

In multiple item data maps, you display two or more items based on location. For example, you could display your sales and your competitor's sales per state to understand how you are performing against your competitor, or you could display your sales and average spending per state to verify whether you are targeting the right market segments. So, in a multiple item data map, there are two or more pieces of information associated with each location. Again, in this category, there are different map styles that come to our rescue to represent multiple values for each location:

Pie chart map

The pie chart map style, shown in Figure 3-6, is good for displaying multiple data items for each location. The maximum number of data items that can be displayed for each location is 16. Each data item's value is represented by the size of the pie for each location. Use this map style to display sales by product line for your retail stores.

Figure 3-5. Multiple symbol map (Color Plate 2)

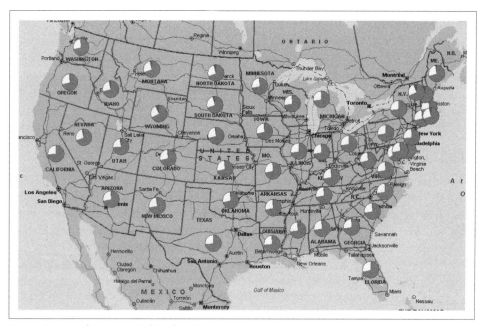

Figure 3-6. Pie chart map (Color Plate 3)

Sized pie chart map

The sized pie chart map style, shown in Figure 3-7, is similar to the pie chart map style except that the size of the pie chart represents the overall value of the data items associated with that location. For example, to see how your sales are doing against your competitor's sales per state as a pie chart, and also to get a sense of overall sales (yours and your competitor's combined) for each state, use this map style. In this figure, a bigger pie chart represents higher overall sales, while a smaller pie chart represents poorer overall sales.

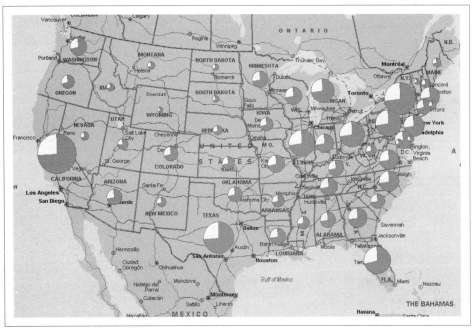

Figure 3-7. Sized pie chart map (Color Plate 4)

Column chart map

In this map style, shown in Figure 3-8, each data item associated with a location is represented by a column. The size of the column represents the value, so the taller the column, the higher the value. You can also assign different colors to each column. For example, to display your sales against your competitor's sales, use a column chart map style. The maximum number of data items that can be associated with a location is 16.

Series column chart map

This map style, shown in Figure 3-9, is identical to column chart map style but all columns are of the same color. This map style is more suitable for representing a series of data. For example, presenting your store sales per month per state is more suited for series column chart map style. This map style also supports associating up to 16 data items per location.

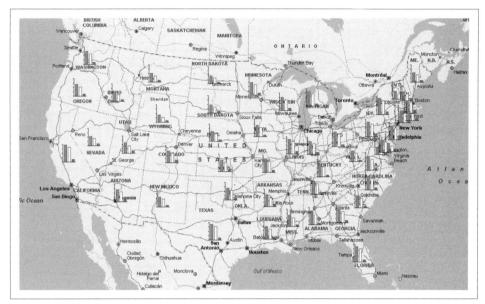

Figure 3-8. Column chart map (Color Plate 5)

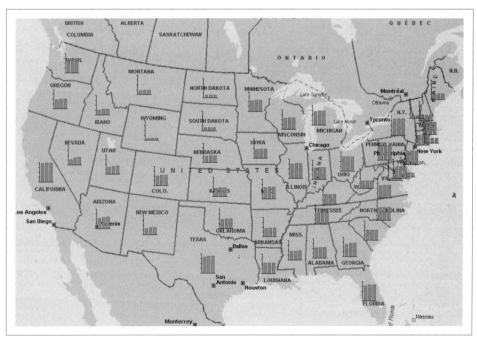

Figure 3-9. Series column chart map

Now that we know what data map styles are and what they are well-suited for, let's look at the DataSet.DisplayDataMap method used to display a data map.

Understanding the DataSet.DisplayDataMap Method

The DisplayDataMap method is called on a valid DataSet object to display a map using the data in the dataset. This method provides a lot of flexibility and control to choose from a wide variety of parameters for data maps, but this flexibility comes with a penalty—complexity.

It is not an exaggeration to say that the DataSet object's DisplayDataMap method is one of the most complex methods available with the MapPoint 2004 APIs because of both the complex inner workings of the method and the sheer number of arguments that it accepts. See the following code snippet of the DisplayDataMap method:

```
//Invoke DisplayDatamap method
MapPoint.DataMap datamap =
    dataset.DisplayDataMap(MapPoint.GeoDataMapType.geoDataMapTypeCategoricalColumn,
                           datafields,
                           MapPoint.GeoShowDataBy.geoShowByRegion1,
                           MapPoint.GeoCombineDataBy.geoCombineByNone,
                           MapPoint.GeoDataRangeType.geoRangeTypeDefault,
                           MapPoint.GeoDataRangeOrder.geoRangeOrderDefault,
                           6,
                           5,
                           arrayOfCustomValues,
                           arrayOfcustomNames,
                           missing,
                           arrayOfcustomLabels,
                           missing );
```

The DisplayDataMap method takes 13 arguments to display a data map; look at the original definition of the DisplayDataMap method signature to understand what each parameter represents in the previous method call:

```
DataSet.DisplayDataMap([DataMapType],
                       [DataField],
                       [ShowDataBy],
                       [CombineDataBy],
                       [DataRangeType],
                       [DataRangeOrder],
                       [ColorScheme],
                       [DataRangeCount],
                       [ArrayOfCustomValues],
                       [ArrayOfCustomNames],
                       [DivideByField],
                       [ArrayOfDataFieldLabels],
                       [ArrayOfPushpinSymbols])
```

Table 3-3 shows how each parameter is used during this method call.

Table 3-3. DataSet.DisplayDataMap method parameters

Parameter Name	Description
DataMapType	The type of data map to display. Default is geoDataMapTypeDefault.
DataField	A Field object or an array of Field objects of the data set to be mapped. String fields are invalid for unsized pie chart, sized pie chart, column chart, and series column chart maps. Default is the first valid field in the data set.
ShowDataBy	The geographical entity by which the data is to be shown on the map. See GeoShowDataBy values for a list of values and descriptions. Default is geoShowByDefault.
CombineDataBy	Used only if data aggregation is required. Data aggregation is required when the geographical entity designated by GeoShowDataBy is larger than the set of data to be mapped. Is ignored (geoCombineByNone) if not needed or if the DataSet object has a HowCreated property of geoDataSetDemographic. Default is geoCombineByDefault.
DataRangeType	Determines the appearance of data on the map by range type. Default is geoRangeTypeDefault.
DataRangeOrder	Determines the order in which data is displayed. Ignored for unsized pie chart, column chart, and series column chart maps. Default is geoRangeOrderDefault.
ColorScheme	An integer that determines the color scheme used for mapped data. See the ColorScheme property topic for color schemes and integer values associated with different data map types. Default is geoColorSchemeDefault (-1).
DataRangeCount	An integer between one and eight that indicates the number of data ranges. Ignored for continuous data ranges and unsized pie chart, column chart, and series column chart maps.
ArrayOfCustomValues	An array of the custom value for each data range. If used, this parameter sets the IsCustomized property of a DataRanges collection, which will be cleared if the user changes the range type. Ignored for unsized pie chart maps.
ArrayOfCustomNames	An array that contains labels for the map legend. Ignored for unsized pie chart maps.
DivideByField	The field or column to which the DataFields property of the DataMap object is compared. If this parameter is not provided, then the current DivideByField is used.
ArrayOfDataFieldLabels	An array that contains color labels for the legend.
ArrayOfPushpinSymbols	An array that establishes the pushpin symbols used with multiple symbol maps.

If you are worried about how to remember all this, thankfully, it is possible to categorize these arguments into one argument and two major categories, as follows:

```
dataset.DisplayDataMap(Data map style,
                       [Data Specification],
     [Range Specification]);
```

Let's discuss this method in detail by starting off with a hypothetical scenario: say your requirement is to display your average annual sales for each product line compared to your competitor's. A hypothetical display data map command (like in SQL) would look like this:

> Display a *pie chart* data map per *state* for *our annual sales* (per *product line*) compared to *our competitor's annual sales* per *product line*.

Also, let's assume that you have data in a table with the schema shown in Table 3-4.

Table 3-4. Hypothetical business data for data maps

County	Our annual sales	Competitor's annual sales	Total product lines lold	....
Pierce	34,561,775	11,701,483	20	....
King	22,456,333	16,995,443	18	....
....	....	....	....	....

Note that your data is categorized based on county and not on state, but the requirement is to display a data map based on states. Next, let's look at the `DisplayDataMap` method to display the data map specified in this hypothetical command.

Defining data map style

This is the first step in displaying a data map. Choose the map style for the data map using the `DataMapType` argument. This argument is `GeoDataMapType` enumeration, and you can choose among the nine available map styles. Setting it to `geoDataMapTypeDefault` allows MapPoint 2004 to decide what map is best suited for the input data and other factors. In our example, we wanted a pie chart map, so set this to `geoDataMapTypeUnsizedPie` enumeration value.

The portion of the hypothetical display data map command completed so far:

> Display a *pie chart* data map...

Next, let's look at the data specification arguments category, which you use to actually specify which data will be be displayed on the map and how to manipulate or process it on the fly before displaying it.

Specifying Data Detail

In this category, the following arguments are used to specify the data and how to process the data before displaying it on a data map. Let's look each of these arguments in detail:

`DataField`

> Indicates field name or names to be displayed as a data map. The field values can be numeric or non-numeric, but they should be linked to a location dimension. This argument is of object type, so you can pass either a string or an array of strings depending on the requirement. In our example, we want to display your company's sales and your competitor's annual sales, so that would be two named columns, *Our Annual Sales* and *Competitor Annual Sales* from Table 3-1.

The portion of the hypothetical display data map command completed so far:

> Display a pie chart data map per state for *our annual sales* compared to *our competitor's annual sales*...

ShowDataBy

Specifies which location dimension you are applying to your data to display a data map. In other words, indicates whether you want to display your data map based on a city, state, country, and so on. This argument is of type GeoShowDataBy, which is an enumeration, and geoShowByDefault is the default value. In our example, we want to display data map of average annual sales per *state*, so you need to pass the GeoShowDataBy.geoShowByRegion1.

 For a full list of values available with the GeoShowDataBy enumeration and their meanings, see MapPoint 2004 help: *mk:@MSITStore:C:\Program%20Files\Microsoft%20MapPoint\MapPoint.chm::/BIZOMVGeoShowDataBy.htm*.

The portion of the hypothetical display data map command completed so far:

Display a pie chart data map per *state* for our annual sales compared to our competitor's annual sales...

However, there is an issue with this command. The sales data we have is at the county level, but we want to display data at state level. How can we do it? Now we need theCombineDataBy argument.

CombineDataBy

An optional argument needed only when data aggregation is used. Aggregation is required when you want to show data at a larger location dimension than the one in the data table. This argument is of GeoCombineDataBy type, which is an enumeration. Since you don't have state level sales data readily available, you have to aggregate (add) the county data to produce a data map at the state level; so, in our example, you have to pass the value geoCombineAdd. Other combine options include average, count, default, and none.

The portion of the hypothetical display data map command completed so far:

Display a pie chart data map per *state* for our annual sales compared to our competitor's annual sales...

DivideByField

Indicates whether there is any divide-by operation to be performed on the data (DataField argument) being displayed. This argument takes a column name from the table. When you pass a valid column for this field, the data used to display on the map will be:

Data displayed on the map = DataField(s)/DivideByField

So, in our example, since we want to display annual sales per product line, we need to divide the annual sales number by the product line count. So, we need to pass the *Total Product Lines Sold* field for this argument.

The hypothetical display data map command is now complete:

Display a pie chart data map per statefor our annual sales *per product line* compared to our competitor's annual sales *per product line*.

We have now finished the display data map task as we specified it at the beginning. Now it's time to address the range specification.

Specifying data range

The range specification argument group consists of the arguments that specify the data ranges and related color scheme to be used with the data map. What is a data range in the data map context? Data range is where you define the limits (lowest and highest) for your data to be displayed on the data map. Some ranges will be narrow, while others will be wide—this depends purely on the input data. Usually MapPoint 2004 does a good job of deciding which range types and orders to use depending on the input data. For most applications, leaving the default values would suffice. Still, let's look at each argument in detail.

The range specification argument group consists of the following arguments:

DataRangeType

> This argument indicates which kind of data range you prefer to use to display a data map. This argument is of type GeoDataRangeType enumeration, which has values to indicate different data range types such as continuous, logarithmic, discrete, equal data, and so on. When in doubt, just use geoRangeTypeDefault, and MapPoint will choose the suitable range for your data. If you are planning to use a specific range type for your data maps, there are some compatibility issues that you need to be aware of (for example, a logarithmic data range type cannot be used with unsized pie chart data maps). For a full list of range types and compatibilities, refer to the DisplayDataMap method in the help documentation.

DataRangeOrder

> This argument indicates whether the data map should display range from low to high or high to low. This argument is of type GeoDataRangeOrder enumeration. The default value is geoRangeOrderDefault, and MapPoint decides which order to use based on the input data.

DataRangeCount

> This argument indicates preferred data range count for the data map. The allowed range is from one to eight. This argument is of type integer. This argument is ignored for maps with a continuous data range (since the range here is continuous, rather than a specific ranges in steps) and for unsized pie chart, column chart, and series column chart map styles.

ColorScheme

> This argument indicates the color scheme to use for your data map. There are 16 different types of color schemes (0–15) available in MapPoint. You have to pass the integer value that represents the suitable color scheme for your data map. You can also pass -1 to let MapPoint pick the appropriate color scheme for you.

For more details on how the color scheme values map to actual colors, refer to the "ColorScheme Property" topic (*http://msdn.microsoft. com/library/en-us/mappoint2004/BIZOMPColorScheme.asp*) in the online help documentation on MSDN.

So far, we have discussed the arguments you need to understand to work with data maps. If you are not anticipating using custom data range specifications, you can safely skip the following section on specifying custom ranges without losing any continuity or context.

Specifying custom ranges

The following sets of arguments are used only to specify a custom data range. Why do you need a custom data range? Say, for example, that you have sales data ranging from $10 to $10,000. If you want to consider a specific range of sales amount in your data map, say from $500 to $5,000, ignoring all other data, you need to use a custom data range specification that sets the range limits as $500 and $5,000. Remember, though, that there is a direct relationship between the DataRangeCount argument and the custom data range values, which is shown in Table 3-5.

Table 3-5. DataRangeCount and custom data range relationship

Data range type	DataRangeCount	Custom data range values	Notes
Continuous / Continuous Logarithmic	Ignored	3	Set only first and third custom range values.
Unique Values	1 to 8	1 to 8	If your data has more than 8 unique values, only first 8 will be displayed.
Discrete Equal Values/ Discrete Logarithmic/ Equal Data Points	1 to 8	Data Range Count + 1	

Similar to the previous range count, range type, and custom range value relationships, there is one more relationship between map style and custom range values. For column chart and series column chart maps, the number of custom values is always set to five, and you need to set only the first and fifth custom range values.

With this introduction, let's take a look at the custom range specification arguments in detail:

ArrayOfCustomValues
Indicates the custom range values used for displaying the data map. Use this argument to pass the custom data ranges.

ArrayOfCustomNames

Lists the names of the custom data range values. The rules applicable to the custom data range values and data range count are also applicable to the custom data range names, which are displayed in the legend pane.

ArrayOfDataFieldLabels

Contains the labels for the colors in the legend pane. This argument size must match the number of colors displayed on the map, which is equal to the number of data fields, except for the series column chart map style, in which case the column charts are always displayed in one uniform color, so only one label is required.

ArrayOfPushpinSymbols

Used only with the multiple symbol map style. For other styles, the size of this array is equal to that of the data range count. The valid values are 0–255.

We have now finished a grand tour of the DisplayDataMap method argument list. If your head is spinning by now, don't worry—I will discuss all of these concepts with some examples later in this chapter. For now, there is one last important issue that you need to understand in order to use this method in .NET: dealing with optional values.

 One of the easiest ways to figure out how data maps work is to experiment with the Data Mapping Wizard of the MapPoint application.

Dealing with optional values

The DisplayDataMap method (along with many other methods in the MapPoint 2004's API) has optional arguments that can be safely omitted by passing nothing in COM/VB era. It's not that simple when you call this method from .NET. Whether it's C#, VB.NET, or any other .NET language, there is no notion of optional values that can be skipped in a method call. However, the .NET framework provides a type, System.Reflection.Missing.Value, which represents a COM optional value. So, when you are working with a method that has optional values, and you do not have any specific value to pass, you need to send the missing value instance:

```
//Define missing argument for optional argument
object missing = System.Reflection.Missing.Value;
....

//Now display datamap
MapPoint.DataMap datamap =
    dataset.DisplayDataMap(
    GeoDataMapType.geoDataMapTypeCategoricalColumn,
    datafields, GeoShowDataBy.geoShowByRegion1,
    GeoCombineDataBy.geoCombineByNone,
    GeoDataRangeType.geoRangeTypeDefault,
    GeoDataRangeOrder.geoRangeOrderDefault,
    6, 3, missing, missing, missing, missing, missing);
```

Now that you have a good understanding of data map styles and the `DisplayDataMap` method, it's time write some code to display data maps. As a first step, let's look at how to use the native demographic data that ships with MapPoint 2004 to display data maps. Next, we'll look at some techniques to display external data (for your business) and to integrate the demographic data and your data.

Working with MapPoint Demographic Data

MapPoint 2004 ships with a lot of *demographic data* (also known as *statistical data*) that includes 136 categories for the United States and Canada and 43 categories for other countries worldwide. This demographic data includes statistics, such as population by location, average age by location, average household income by location, and so on. It is very useful when integrated with your own business data. For example, you may want to see total sales by state in the United Sates and then compare them with total population by state; this gives you an idea of your sales relative to population in each state.

Accessing the Demographic Data Categories Programmatically

Our first task is to see which kind of demographic data is available on a per country basis programmatically. An active `Map` object exposes a `DataSets` collection. You can access the demographic data by calling the `GetDemographics` method on the `DataSets` collection:

```
//Get the demographics dataset by calling the
//GetDemographics method
MapPoint.DataSet dataset
  = map.DataSets.GetDemographics(MapPoint.GeoCountry.geoCountryUnitedStates);
```

The `GetDemographics` method takes the country as an input argument and returns a `DataSet` object containing demographic data for the specified country.

 You can obtain a demographic `DataSet` for other countries using `MapPoint.GeoCountry` enumeration. For example, to get demographics for the United Kingdom, call `GetDemographics` with the `MapPoint.GeoCountry.geoCountryUnitedKingdom` value.

To get all demographic data categories supported by this `DataSet`, loop through its field collection:

```
//Get dataset details
if(dataset != null)
 {
   //Get all field names
   for(int i=1;i<=dataset.Fields.Count;i++)
    {
```

```
        object index = i;
        //Add the field name in a listbox
        listBox1.Items.Add(dataset.Fields.get_Item(ref index).Name);
    }
}
```

This code generates a listbox, shown in Figure 3-10, filled with all demographic categories that are available in MapPoint 2004 North American edition.

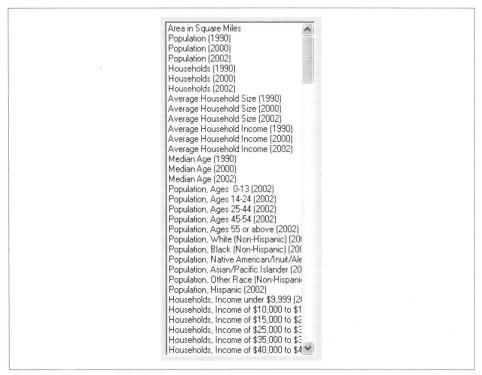

Figure 3-10. MapPoint 2004 demographic categories in a ListBox

In case you are wondering how to interpret the list displayed in Figure 3-10, don't worry—it's really simple: think of a table with rows and columns where the items from the list are the columns in that table. Now add one more column with some form of location information to the left of the existing columns in the table, and that's how the demographic data is organized. So an example demographic table can be interpreted somewhat like Table 3-6.

Table 3-6. Interpreting demographic data

Location	Population (2002)	Households (2002)	Average household size (2002)	....
California	34,561,775	11,701,483	2.88	....
....	....	....	....	....

In the previous example, I have taken State as my location dimension; MapPoint 2004 demographic data supports the following location dimensions:

State
> Demographic data by state/region/province.

Metropolitan area
> Demographic data by metropolitan area.

County
> Demographic data by county/province.

Zip Code
> Demographic data by Zip Code.

Census tract
> Demographic data by census tract/subdivision.

Geography for every zoom level
> The location dimension varies based on scale. For example, for maps at lower altitudes, Zip Code or census tract location dimension can be used; for maps at higher altitudes, the states and countries can be used for clarity of data representation.

So, for any given demographic data item (such as "Population (2002)"), you can display a data map on any one of the above six location dimensions. In other words, if it were to be a command (going back to our hypothetical commands again), an example could be: "Show a Shaded Area Map for *Population (2002)* per *State*," and this command displays 2002 population statistics based on state by using the shaded area data map styles.

Even though the demographic data categories are exposed, the actual data itself is not exposed for direct use. MapPoint 2004 APIs allow you to display demographic data based on location. Each of the previous categories contains statistical data, but the data makes more sense if you can either analyze or visualize it based on location.

Displaying Data Map Using Demographic Data

Our next task is to display a data map using a demographic category based on location. We need three pieces of information to display a data map:

- Data map style
- Data specification
- Data range specification

It makes sense to start with a simple scenario: displaying "Population (2002)" per state in a sized circle map. In this scenario, the map style used is `GeoDataMapType.geoDataMapTypeSizedCircle`, the data field argument value is "Population (2002)," and the show data by argument is `GeoShowDataBy.geoShowByRegion1`. For now, let's leave the data range specifications at their default values.

Displaying a data map

Let's write code to display a data map for these specifications. Assuming that you already have an instance of the MapPoint 2004 ActiveX Control in your Windows form, we will first get the demographic dataset:

```
//Get a reference to the active map
MapPoint.Map map = axMappointControl1.ActiveMap;

//Get the MapPoint demographics dataset
MapPoint.DataSet dataset
    = map.DataSets.GetDemographics(MapPoint.GeoCountry.geoCountryUnitedStates);
```

Now that we have the MapPoint 2004 demographic dataset, define the data field argument:

```
//Define the data field name as a key
object datafieldKey = "Population (2002)";
//Now get the data field from the demographic dataset
object[] datafields = new object[1];
datafields[0] = dataset.Fields.get_Item(ref datafieldKey);
```

You might have noticed that I'm defining the datafields instance as an array of objects. You could also define it as a single object instance as long as you don't need to pass more than one field name.

Next, define a few other arguments, such as color scheme and data range count:

```
//Define the color scheme
//Between 0 and 16; 3 represents orange/red shade
int colorScheme = 3;

//Define data range count
//Between 1 and 8; 3 works for most
int rangeCount = 3;

//Define missing object optional values
object missing = System.Reflection.Missing.Value;
```

Now we have everything we need to display a data map, and the following code snippet shows the actual DisplayDataMap method call:

```
//Now call the display data map for sized circle map
MapPoint.DataMap datamap =
        dataset.DisplayDataMap(MapPoint.GeoDataMapType.geoDataMapTypeSizedCircle,
                datafields, MapPoint.GeoShowDataBy.geoShowByRegion1,
                MapPoint.GeoCombineDataBy.geoCombineByNone,
                MapPoint.GeoDataRangeType.geoRangeTypeDefault,
                MapPoint.GeoDataRangeOrder.geoRangeOrderDefault,
                colorScheme, rangeCount, missing, missing,
                missing, missing, missing);
```

We are using the default values for range type and range order arguments.

Finally, make sure that you have the legend pane open so that you know how to interpret the data map; the following code shows how to set the legend pane state:

```
//Now make sure to display legend pane
axMappointControl1.PaneState = MapPoint.GeoPaneState.geoPaneLegend;
```

When you execute this code, a data map for population statistics per state, shown in Figure 3-11, is created.

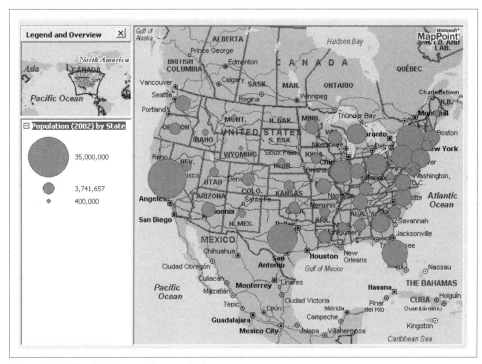

Figure 3-11. Sized circle map for population per state

Remember that we have chosen to use the default data range type for this data map. A little investigation of the resulting datamap object properties (`datamap.DataRanges.DataRangeType`) reveals that MapPoint has chosen `geoRangeTypeContinuousLog` range type, so the resulting data map has three ranges with a low value of 400,000 and a high value of 35,000,000. While this data map does a good job of revealing which state has the largest population (California, with close to 35 million people!) it does not do a very good job indicating the state with smallest population (Wyoming, a quiet 500,000).

Defining data range type and count

It might be useful to expand the data range a little by increasing the data range count to, say, eight (the maximum allowed value). However, changing the data range count to eight also requires a change in the range type (since the default data range does not support range count other than three); to meet this requirement, change the data range type to geoRangeTypeDiscreteEqualRanges. The following code reflects the two changes discussed:

```
//Define data range count
//Between 1 and 8; changing from 3 to 8
int rangeCount = 8;
```

The new method call looks as follows:

```
//Now call the display data map for sized circle map
MapPoint.DataMap datamap =
        dataset.DisplayDataMap(MapPoint.GeoDataMapType.geoDataMapTypeSizedCircle,
            datafields, MapPoint.GeoShowDataBy.geoShowByRegion1,
            MapPoint.GeoCombineDataBy.geoCombineByNone,
            MapPoint.GeoDataRangeType.geoRangeTypeDiscreteEqualRanges,
            MapPoint.GeoDataRangeOrder.geoRangeOrderDefault,
            colorScheme, rangeCount, missing, missing,
            missing, missing, missing);
```

When you execute the code with these new settings, the data map displayed looks like Figure 3-12.

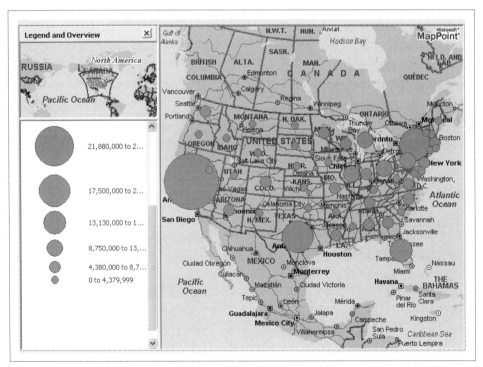

Figure 3-12. Sized circle population using larger data range

Even though the data map has an expanded data range, it's still unclear from the map which state has the smallest population, so you need to use the custom data ranges by specifying custom ranges.

Specifying custom data ranges

In this case, we clearly need a range that starts much lower than the starting range shown in Figure 3-4 (0 to 4,379,999 would be appropriate here). So, define a custom data range as shown below:

```
//Define custom range values
//Since the range count is 8,
//we are defining 9 range objects
object[] arrayOfCustomValues = new object[9];
//Stretch the lower end by defining ranges
//pretty close to each other
arrayOfCustomValues[0] = 250000;
arrayOfCustomValues[1] = 500000;
arrayOfCustomValues[2] = 750000;
arrayOfCustomValues[3] = 1000000;
//Set the maximum value
arrayOfCustomValues[8] = 35000000;
```

In this code, I have just defined the starting range as 250,000 and set the next three ranges in 250,000 increments. What I'm really trying to do here is to stretch the lower end of the data range to have smaller ranges to accommodate better size variation in the circles. I also set the maximum limit for the data to be 35,000,000.

The `DisplayDataMethod` call with this custom data range specification is shown here:

```
//Now call the display data map for sized circle map
MapPoint.DataMap datamap =
        dataset.DisplayDataMap(MapPoint.GeoDataMapType.geoDataMapTypeSizedCircle,
                datafields, MapPoint.GeoShowDataBy.geoShowByRegion1,
                MapPoint.GeoCombineDataBy.geoCombineByNone,
                MapPoint.GeoDataRangeType.geoRangeTypeDiscreteEqualRanges,
                MapPoint.GeoDataRangeOrder.geoRangeOrderDefault,
                colorScheme, rangeCount, arrayOfCustomValues, missing,
                missing, missing, missing);
```

The resulting data map is shown in Figure 3-13.

Now, as you can see, the circle in the state of Wyoming looks smallest of all the circles, so it has the smallest population in all states (only 499,904). Using custom data range specification, we could display both the most and least populous states. While we are at it, we can also customize the legend pane to reflect what we are trying to achieve.

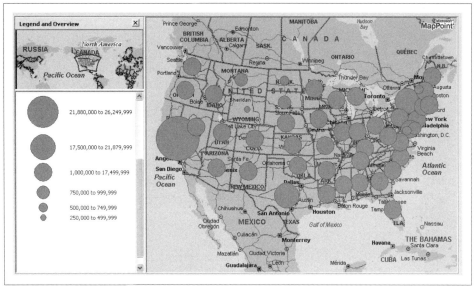

Figure 3-13. Sized circle population chart with custom data range

Customizing the legend pane

You can customize the legend pane names by defining an array of custom names. The number of the custom name array must be equal to the data range count. In our example the range count is set to eight, so we need to define an array of objects of size eight and assign names for each range:

```
//Define custom name array to reflect
//their populations
object[] arrayOfcustomNames = new object[8];
arrayOfcustomNames[0] = "Hello! Anyone home?";
arrayOfcustomNames[1] = "Small and happy!";
arrayOfcustomNames[2] = "Nice and pleasant.";
arrayOfcustomNames[3] = "Have room for some more!";
arrayOfcustomNames[4] = "Just about the right size.";
arrayOfcustomNames[5] = "Still not bad to live here!";
arrayOfcustomNames[6] = "Kind of stuffy here.";
arrayOfcustomNames[7] = "Man, too crowded!";
```

Calling the `DisplayDataMap` method with custom names results in the map shown in Figure 3-14.

The legend pane now contains custom names. They may look (and sound) funny. If you are thinking, "How can you judge whether a state is too crowded based only on population? We're supposed to look at the population density to determine whether it is too crowded or not," these are the exactly right questions to ask. I should display population density (population divided by area of the state) to justify my custom labels. We need to write code to use the `DivideBy` field.

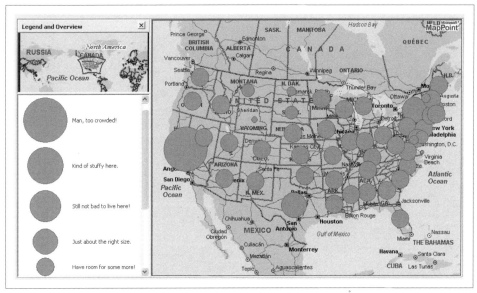

Figure 3-14. Sized circle population map with custom legend pane

Using the DivideBy field

To create a population density map, you need to divide the population by the total area of the corresponding state. The area of the state is available in the demographic data of the "Area in Square Miles" field. To divide the state population with area, we have only to obtain a reference to the "Area in Square Miles" field and pass it as a DivideByField argument:

```
//Define data field indexes
object popIndex = "Population (2002)";
object areaIndex = "Area in Square Miles";

//Get demographic dataset
MapPoint.DataSet dataset =
        map.DataSets.GetDemographics(MapPoint.GeoCountry.geoCountryUnitedStates);

//Get population field
MapPoint.Field datafield = dataset.Fields.get_Item(ref popIndex);
//Get area field
MapPoint.Field divideField = dataset.Fields.get_Item(ref areaIndex);

...

//Define custom range values
//Since the range count is 8,
//we are defining 9 range objects
object[] arrayOfCustomValues = new object[9];
//Set the custom range values
```

```
arrayOfCustomValues[0] = 1;
arrayOfCustomValues[1] = 5;
arrayOfCustomValues[2] = 10;
arrayOfCustomValues[3] = 50;
//Set the maximum value
arrayOfCustomValues[8] = 10000;

...

//Now display Map
MapPoint.DataMap datamap =
    dataset.DisplayDataMap(MapPoint.GeoDataMapType.geoDataMapTypeSizedCircle,
    datafield, MapPoint.GeoShowDataBy.geoShowByRegion1,
    MapPoint.GeoCombineDataBy.geoCombineByNone,
    MapPoint.GeoDataRangeType.geoRangeTypeDiscreteEqualRanges,
    MapPoint.GeoDataRangeOrder.geoRangeOrderHighToLow,
    colorScheme,rangeCount, arrayOfCustomValues, arrayOfcustomNames,
    divideField, missing, missing);

//Set proper legend title
datamap.LegendTitle = "State Population Density";

//Zoom to show compelte data map
dataset.ZoomTo( );
```

As you can see from this code, the divideField is the "Area in Square Miles" field from the demographic dataset. Also, notice that I redefined the custom data range value to accommodate the new data values we'll have after the division process. The new concepts that I have included in this code are setting the LegendTitle property of the data map and zooming to the full data map view by calling the ZoomTo method on the dataset object. The resulting data map is shown in Figure 3-15.

From the data map in Figure 3-15, you can see that Alaska has the lowest population density at about 1.1 people per square mile. When you zoom in to the east coast, you can tell that Washington D.C has the highest population density at about 1,000 people per square mile. There is one more thing you can do with custom data ranges: filter unwanted data from the data map.

Using the custom data range to filter data

By specifying custom data range values, you can show only states with population densities below 100 people per square mile.

```
//Set the range so that you only show
//states with population density
//below 100 people/Sq. Mile
arrayOfCustomValues[0] = 1;
arrayOfCustomValues[1] = 5;
arrayOfCustomValues[2] = 10;
arrayOfCustomValues[3] = 50;
//Set the maximum value
arrayOfCustomValues[8] = 100;
```

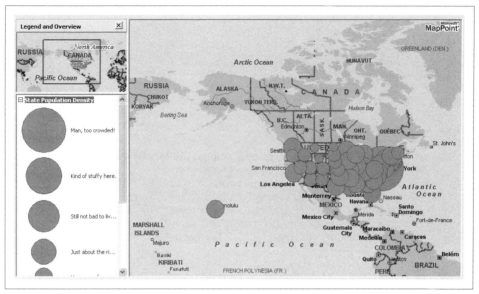

Figure 3-15. Sized circle population density map

You can also specify any other data range count to achieve the same effect.

Finally, to use the Data Mapping Wizard user interface from the MapPoint 2004 product in your application, call the `DataSets.ShowDataMappingWizard` method:

```
MapPoint.DataMap datamap =
        map.DataSets.ShowDataMappingWizard(this.Handle.ToInt32(),
          null, MapPoint.GeoDataMappingPage.geoDataSetPage);
```

This method takes the parent window handle, a `DataSet` instance, if you want to import the data into an existing data set and onto the starting page of the wizard. You can pass null if you want to import the data into a new `DataSet` instance.

Next, let's switch gears and look at how to use your business data to draw data maps.

Working with Your Business Data

Using the MapPoint 2004 APIs, you can import external data (i.e. your business data) and use it to create data maps. MapPoint APIs support variety of data sources for importing data. The data sources supported by MapPoint include, but are not limited to:

- Text (*.TXT*, *.CSV*, *.TAB*)
- Microsoft Excel spreadsheets
- Microsoft Access database
- Any relational database, such as SQL Server or Oracle Server

You can also import Outlook contacts. In this section, I will show how to import data from these data sources and display data maps using the imported data. Then I will show how to integrate your business data with demographic data. You will be able to display data maps rich with both business information and statistical data.

Importing External Data

Importing external data is generally simple using the MapPoint 2004 APIs. You use the DataSets.ImportData method to import external data. This method returns reference to a valid DataSet object upon successfully importing data. The returned DataSet object is also added to the current active map's DataSets collection so that you can use the dataset later; however, once the map is closed, the imported dataset is lost.

Understanding the DataSets.ImportData method

Like the DisplayDataMap method, the ImportData method is also exposed on the DataSets collection, mainly due to the fact that the imported data will be stored as a data set in MapPoint and made available from the DataSets collection for later use. The signature for the ImportData method is as follows:

```
DataSets.ImportData(DataSourceMoniker, ArrayOfFields, Country, Delimiter,
    ImportFlags)
```

Let's discuss each argument in detail.

To import external data into a MapPoint 2004 DataSet, indicate the data source specifics, such as the path to the data source for a text file or an Outlook contacts file moniker, and pass this as the DataSourceMoniker argument. Even though this argument is an Object type, you can pass a string value. However, since there is no direct interface available in MapPoint 2004 to work with relational data bases such as SQL Server, you have to write code to connect to the SQL server and read the data to be imported into a DataSet (which we will see later in this chapter).

The next argument is the ArrayOfFields. This argument is used to import specific fields from the data source. This field is a two-dimensional array of objects. One dimension holds the data field names form the data source, and the other holds the field type specification. The field style specification is defined by using the GeoFieldType enumeration, which provides values such as geoFieldSkipped, geoFieldRegion1, geoFieldData, and so on. Each of these values is used to specify how the data field from the source should be treated in the MapPoint DataSet. The following code snippet shows how to define this argument and cite the field specifications. Say you have a text file that has the following tab-delimited fields:

```
ID  State    Country  Our Sales($) Competitor A Sales($) Competitor B Sales($)
1   Alabama  US       531          2859                 2810
2   Arizona  US       4872         328                  193
```

You can specify the field specification:

```
//Define field specification
object[,] fieldSpecifications = null;

fieldSpecifications = new object[6,2];

//Specify what fields are geographic and what fields are not
fieldSpecifications[0,0] = "ID";
fieldSpecifications[0,1] = MapPoint.GeoFieldType.geoFieldSkipped;

fieldSpecifications[1,0] = "State";
fieldSpecifications[1,1] = MapPoint.GeoFieldType.geoFieldRegion1;

fieldSpecifications[2,0] = "Country";
fieldSpecifications[2,1] = MapPoint.GeoFieldType.geoFieldCountry;

fieldSpecifications[3,0] = "Our Sales($)";
fieldSpecifications[3,1] = MapPoint.GeoFieldType.geoFieldData;

fieldSpecifications[4,0] = "Competitor A Sales($)";
fieldSpecifications[4,1] = MapPoint.GeoFieldType.geoFieldData;

fieldSpecifications[5,0] = "Competitor B Sales($)";
fieldSpecifications[5,1] = MapPoint.GeoFieldType.geoFieldData;
```

The next argument is the country. You have to specify the country enumeration to indicate the data for the country with which you are working. This argument's type is GeoCountry, an enumeration.

The other two arguments are the flags that aid the import process to understand how the data is delimited and data source–specific interfacing. I will discuss these flags later in this section.

Building on this introduction, let's see how to import data from different data sources.

Importing data from a text file

The DataSets.ImportData method can import data from text files with tab, semicolon, and comma delimitation. The following sample code shows how to import a tab-delimited text file with default field settings:

```
//Using the MapPoint Sample Sales data from txt file
//This data file can be found on the companion CD in
//the chapter 03 directory.
string filePath = @"D:\MapPoint\03\Sample Data\Sales.txt";
//Define field specification
//Since we want to import all fields, we can just
//go with default import
object missing = System.Reflection.Missing.Value;

//Import data and create a dataset
```

```
MapPoint.DataSet dataset =
    map.DataSets.ImportData(filePath, missing,
    MapPoint.GeoCountry.geoCountryUnitedStates,
    MapPoint.GeoDelimiter.geoDelimiterTab,
    MapPoint.GeoImportFlags.geoImportFirstRowIsHeadings);
```

When you run this code, each row from the text file is imported into a newly created DataSet, and a pushpin is placed on the map to indicate the location of the record. The new DataSet created with this method is also called a PushpinDataset. You can also call the DataSet.DisplayPushpinMap method to display the contents of a dataset. This method places a pushpin for each record in the corresponding location.

Also, as you might have noticed already, the Delimiter argument in this case is set to geoDelimiterTab, since the source data file has records with tab delimited columns; you can also use the geoDelimiterDefault value. However, in that case MapPoint determines the delimitation based on the filename. By design, MapPoint assumes that the delimitation is a tab for *.txt*, *.asc*, and *.tab* files, while delimitation is a comma for *.csv* files. Finally, The ImportFlags argument is of GeoImportFlags type, an enumeration whose value is set to GeoImportFlags.geoImportFirstRowIsHeadings to indicate that the first row is a header.

After importing the data, you can access the fields in this newly created pushpin dataset as you would access fields in the MapPoint demographic dataset. The following code shows how to access the fields from the imported dataset to display a data map. Say, for example, you have just imported a text file in the following format:

ID	State	Country	Our Sales($)	Competitor A Sales($)	Competitor B Sales($)
1	Alabama	US	531	2859	2810
2	Arizona	US	4872	328	193

Now you can access the data and display a sized pie chart data map to compare your company sales with the other two competing companies. Pie chart maps are great for comparing data side-by-side:

```
//Define data map columns
//These indexes come in the same order as
//the fields in the text file
object oursalesIndex = 4; //Fourth field from the text file
object compAsalesIndex = 5; //Fifth field from the text file
object compBsalesIndex = 6; //Sixth field from the text file

//Now get fields
object[] datafields = new object[3];
datafields[0] = dataset.Fields.get_Item(ref oursalesIndex);
datafields[1] = dataset.Fields.get_Item(ref compAsalesIndex);
datafields[2] = dataset.Fields.get_Item(ref compBsalesIndex);

//Now display datamap
MapPoint.DataMap datamap =
    dataset.DisplayDataMap(MapPoint.GeoDataMapType.geoDataMapTypeSizedPie,
                    datafields, MapPoint.GeoShowDataBy.geoShowByRegion1,
                    MapPoint.GeoCombineDataBy.geoCombineByNone,
```

```
                    MapPoint.GeoDataRangeType.geoRangeTypeDefault,
                    MapPoint.GeoDataRangeOrder.geoRangeOrderDefault,
                    6, 3, missing, missing, missing, missing, missing);
//Set the legend title
datamap.LegendTitle = "Sales by State";

//Set the legend pane
axMappointControl1.PaneState = MapPoint.GeoPaneState.geoPaneLegend;
```

The previous code displays a data map that compares your sales with your competitor company's sales, as shown in Figure 3-16.

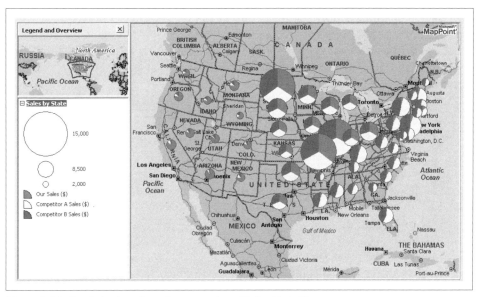

Figure 3-16. Sized pie chart for sales comparison (Color Plate 6)

The map in Figure 3-16 contains a significant amount of information, and there are some immediate conclusions you can draw from it. I have listed a few of them:

- Sales are strong on the West Coast; however, the sales magnitude is less in the West Coast compared to rest of the country.
- Competitor A dominates the market on the East Coast, where the sales magnitude is also large.
- The Midwest seems to be the battle ground among the three companies. They seem to have equal market share. Also, note that the Midwest has the biggest overall market size.

The list of conclusions that can be drawn can go on and on once you get into the details of each market segment, your share of the market segment, your competitor's share, and so on. To get there, though, you can easily import your business data and process that data using location to help you make intelligent and informed business decisions.

You may be wondering, "How does MapPoint understand how each record is linked to a location?" You are right that we haven't specified anything of that nature to tell MapPoint which column is a location column from the text file, neither in the import code nor in the data map display code. So how does it understand? It's actually pretty simple. MapPoint understands keywords like "state," "country," "Zip Code," etc. and maps them to the appropriate geographic region. In this example, MapPoint automatically associated each record with the state location.

So, what happens if you have location data in an obscurely named column, say, "LocX?" Can MapPoint interpret it as a location and map the record to that location? No. That's when you need to help MapPoint understand your data using the `ArrayOfFields` specification argument.

Helping MapPoint understand your text data

When no location column is clearly named or when you have 200 columns of which you want only 10 columns for your data map, you need to specify the field specifications to help MapPoint understand your data. Say, for example, you have a text file as a data source with the following data:

```
ID  LocX     Land   Our Sales($) Competitor A Sales($) Competitor B Sales($)
1   Alabama  US     531          2859                  2810
2   Arizona  US     4872         328                   193
```

Imagine that the requirement is only to import the state field (named LocX) and your sales field (named "Our Sales ($)"), ignoring the rest of the fields. You have to define field specifications:

```
//Define field specification
object[,] fieldSpecifications = null;

//Declare field specifications to indicate about
//each and every field - so we need a total of
//6 fields since we have 6 fields in the txt file
fieldSpecifications = new object[6,2];

//Specify the field name
fieldSpecifications[0,0] = "ID";
//Indicate MapPoint not to import it
fieldSpecifications[0,1] = MapPoint.GeoFieldType.geoFieldSkipped;

//Specify the field name
fieldSpecifications[1,0] = "LocX";
//Indicate MapPoint that this is a State field
fieldSpecifications[1,1] = MapPoint.GeoFieldType.geoFieldRegion1;

fieldSpecifications[2,0] = "Land";
fieldSpecifications[2,1] = MapPoint.GeoFieldType.geoFieldCountry;

//Specify the field name
fieldSpecifications[3,0] = "Our Sales($)";
```

```
//Indicate MapPoint that this is one of the required
//data fields so that MapPoint imports it
fieldSpecifications[3,1] = MapPoint.GeoFieldType.geoFieldData;

//Skip all other fields
. . .

//Now import the data and create a dataset
MapPoint.DataSet dataset =
    map.DataSets.ImportData(filePath, fieldSpecifications,
    MapPoint.GeoCountry.geoCountryUnitedStates,
    MapPoint.GeoDelimiter.geoDelimiterTab,
    MapPoint.GeoImportFlags.geoImportFirstRowIsHeadings);
```

The GeoFieldType enumeration value is used to inform MapPoint about any given field from the data source.

Once you import your data into a dataset, using either a default import or a customized import using the custom field specifications, you can integrate your data with the demographic data and display data map using both datasets.

 For full list of GeoFieldType enumeration values, see the GeoFieldType values topic from the help documentation: *mk:@MSITStore:C:\ Program%20Files\Microsoft%20MapPoint\MapPoint.chm::/ BIZOMVGeoFieldType.htm.*

Displaying Data Maps using your data and demographic data

MapPoint 2004 allows you to draw more than one data map on any given ActiveMap instance meaning that you can display an Annual Average Spending data map using the demographic data set, and then display a data map of your sales on top of the existing data map. The resulting data map contains data from both datasets and gives you an idea of how to make use of demographic data in conjunction with your business data to make intelligent business decisions.

Now that you know how to import data from a text source and how to customize the import using field specifications, let's look at importing data from other data sources.

Importing Data from Microsoft Excel

Importing data from a Microsoft Excel file is no different from importing data from a text file. To use an Excel data source with the MapPoint 2004 API, you need to know how to define an Excel data source moniker. Say you have an Excel file with sales data in the *C:\MapPoint\Data* directory. Also, assume that the actual sales data is in Sheet2 of the Excel book. The data source moniker would be:

```
string filePath = @"C:\MapPoint\Data\Sales.xls!sheet2";
```

Once you have the proper data source moniker ready, importing the data is easy. It is similar to what you have seen in case of a text file:

```
//Define the missing field
object missing = System.Reflection.Missing.Value;
//Import data and create a dataset
MapPoint.DataSet dataset =
    map.DataSets.ImportData(filePath, missing,
    MapPoint.GeoCountry.geoCountryUnitedStates,
    MapPoint.GeoDelimiter.geoDelimiterDefault,
    MapPoint.GeoImportFlags.geoImportExcelSheet);
```

However, if you are importing data from an Excel source, and you want to limit your data to a particular row and column range, the moniker and the data import flag will be different. Table 3-7 shows different data import options, corresponding monikers, and the appropriate data import flags.

Table 3-7. Excel data source monikers and import flag options

Import type	Moniker example	Import flag value
Excel File	C:\MapPointData\Sales.xls	geoImportExcelSheet
Excel Sheet	C:\MapPointData\Sales.xls!Sheet1	geoImportExcelSheet
A1 – Range	C:\MapPointData\Sales.xls! Sheet1!A1:D10	geoImportExcelA1
R1C1 – Range	C:\MapPointData\Sales.xls! Sheet1!R1C1:R10C3	geoImportExcelR1C1
Excel Named Range	C:\MapPointData\Sales.xls!myNamedRange	geoImportExcelNamedRange

The A1 and R1C1 ranges are used to select a particular set of rows and columns from the source Excel sheet.

Importing data from Microsoft Access

Support for importing data from a Microsoft Access database is built into MapPoint 2004 APIs. An import from an Access database differs from any other data source imports that we've seen so far only in terms of defining the data moniker and specifying an appropriate import flag.

For example, if you have a sample sales Access database in the *C:\MapPointData\ Sales.mdb* directory, and if it has a table called *SalesTable* that contains sales information based on location, you can define a moniker as follows:

```
string filePath = @"C:\MapPointData\Sales.mdb!SalesTable";
```

Once you have the right moniker, it is pretty simple to import the data:

```
//Define missing argument for optional argument
object missing = System.Reflection.Missing.Value;
//Import data and create a dataset
MapPoint.DataSet dataset =
        map.DataSets.ImportData(filePath, missing,
        MapPoint.GeoCountry.geoCountryUnitedStates,
        MapPoint.GeoDelimiter.geoDelimiterDefault,
        MapPoint.GeoImportFlags.geoImportAccessTable);
```

Microsoft Access also supports data source monikers in the query form. If you have a query, namely *SalesQuery* in your Access database, you can import data from it using the following moniker and import flag arguments:

```
string filePath = @"C:\MapPointData\Sales.mdb!salesQuery";

//Define missing argument for optional argument
object missing = System.Reflection.Missing.Value;
//Import data and create a dataset
MapPoint.DataSet dataset =
        map.DataSets.ImportData(filePath, missing,
        MapPoint.GeoCountry.geoCountryUnitedStates,
        MapPoint.GeoDelimiter.geoDelimiterDefault,
        MapPoint.GeoImportFlags.geoImportAccessQuery);
```

Next, let's look at how to import data from a SQL database.

Importing data from SQL Server 2000

Unlike the data imports that we have seen so far, MapPoint 2004 does not have any built-in support for importing data from relational databases such as SQL 2000. Using the .NET Framework's ADO.NET base classes, however, you can easily import data. So, in this section, I will show how to import data from SQL into MapPoint. In the following example, I import customer order information from the Orders table in the standard NorthWind database.

Since there is no ImportData method that both supports a SQL data source and creates a resulting DataSet, you need to create a data set yourself in which to import data. The first step is to create a new DataSet instance in the DataSets collection:

```
//See whether there is an existing datasetwith the same name
object datasetName = "NorthWind Orders";
if(map.DataSets.Count > 0 && map.DataSets.get_Item(ref datasetName) != null)
    //If so, delete it
    map.DataSets.get_Item(ref datasetName).Delete();
//Now create a new dataset
MapPoint.DataSet dataset = map.DataSets.AddPushpinSet("NorthWind Orders");
```

I check for an existing DataSet with the name NorthWind Orders and delete it if it already exists. We need to perform this check since you cannot create a dataset with the same name twice in one map session; MapPoint throws an exception when you create a duplicate.

Once you have the DataSet ready to import the data, connect to the SQL Server using the ADO.NET SqlConnection class:

```
//Define a connection string
string sqlConnectionString =
    "server=localhost;database=northwind;User Id=sqluser;Password=password";

//Define a connection object
System.Data.SqlClient.SqlConnection connection
    = new System.Data.SqlClient.SqlConnection(sqlConnectionString);
```

You can also configure your *App.Config* file to read the connection from SQL Server; in either case, make sure to keep your SQL Server user ID and password safe and secure.

Now that your application is ready to connect to SQL Server, the next step is to create a SQL query using the ADO.NET SqlCommand class to get the purchase order records from the orders database:

```
//Define a SQL query
string sqlQueryString = "SELECT CustomerID as ContactName, ShipName as CompanyName,
ShipAddress as Address, ShipCity as City, ShipRegion As Region, ShipPostalCode as
PostalCode, ShipCountry as Country FROM Orders WHERE ShipCountry = 'USA'";

//Define a command object
System.Data.SqlClient.SqlCommand command =
        new System.Data.SqlClient.SqlCommand(sqlQueryString, connection);
```

Since we have the SQL command instance ready, we need to execute the command, read through the records, and import each one of them into the DataSet instance that we have created earlier.

```
try
  {
    //Open the connection
    connection.Open();
    //Get a sql reader from the query
    System.Data.SqlClient.SqlDataReader sqlReader =
            command.ExecuteReader(System.Data.CommandBehavior.CloseConnection);
    if(sqlReader != null)
    {
      while(sqlReader.Read())
        {
          //Get the name of the customer
          string customername = sqlReader["ContactName"] as String;
          //Get the company name
          string companyname = sqlReader["CompanyName"] as String;
          //Get the address string
          string address = sqlReader["Address"] + ", " + sqlReader["City"] + ",
                     " + sqlReader["Region"] + ", " +
                       sqlReader["PostalCode"] + " " + sqlReader["Country"];

          //Find location
          MapPoint.Location location = null;
          try
            {
              //Find the address
              MapPoint.FindResults findrs = map.FindResults(address);
              //If no results found, skip to next record
              if(findrs == null || findrs.Count <= 0)
                  throw new Exception(address);
              //Get the location
              location = findrs.get_Item(ref index) as MapPoint.Location;
```

```
                    //Create a pushpin
                    if(location != null)
                     {
                        MapPoint.Pushpin pushpin =
                              map.AddPushpin(location, companyname);
                        //Assign the contact name
                        pushpin.Note = "Contact : " + customername;
                        //Move to the pushpin dataset
                        pushpin.MoveTo(dataset);
                     }
                }
            catch
                {
                    //Do some logging
                }
        }

        //Close the reader; this will automatically close the connection
        //due to the command behavior setting during the ExecuteReader method
        sqlReader.Close();
    }
  }
catch
    {
        //Do clean up
    }
```

This code loops through the records from the SqlDataReader instance, finding the corresponding location for each ship address in the orders table, adding a pushpin to the map for that location, and, most importantly, at the end, moving that pushpin to the dataset created previously using the Pushpin.MoveTo method.

Upon executing this code, we now have a pushpin DataSet that can be treated like any imported DataSet that we have seen so far in this chapter.

Finally, to use the MapPoint 2004 Import Data Wizard, call the DataSets. ShowImportWizard method.

 You can also import data from a SQL database using a simple UDL file.

So far, we have used MapPoint DataSets to display data maps. There are more powerful business intelligence applications you can build with MapPoint 2004.

A MapPoint DataSet is very versatile—you can build business applications to assist in making intelligent business decisions (similar to the one you have seen at the beginning of this section with pie charts), but now let's take a simple scenario that does not include a data map but still relates to business intelligence and decision making. The DataSet that I will use for this example is the NorthWind Orders dataset that we just created.

Let's tackle a simple form of a supply-chain optimization problem: your company has warehouses on the West Coast where all of the West Coast shipments come from. Considering that the U.S. West Coast is very long, your CEO wants to know whether there is a way to cut transportation costs and boost your company's bottom-line. One simple way to answer his question is by investigating all shipped orders and finding out how many orders are transported from any given warehouse for more than, say, 100 miles. Next, investigate whether there is a possibility of opening another warehouse in a place closer to the customers in that area. Then you could cut down the transportation for the shipments. Can MapPoint 2004 do this? Using the DataSet querying capabilities, absolutely! Let's see how.

Querying a MapPoint DataSet

A MapPoint DataSet object gives you the ability to query the dataset to access the records. These queries can be pure data access queries (using the DataSet. QueryAllRecords method) or geometry- and location-based queries (using the DataSet.QueryCircle, DataSet.QueryPolygon, and so on). In any case, a successful query returns a RecordSet object that you can loop through the records and access the fields and the values contained in that record. With this introduction, let's now look at different ways to query a dataset.

Executing Location Queries Using MapPoint DataSet

You can query a DataSet using specific location queries for which the DataSet object provides methods, such as QueryCircle, QueryPolygon, and QueryShape. I will discuss the QueryCircle and QueryPolygon methods in this section and the QueryShape method shortly after introducing the shape concepts in the next section.

The QueryCircle method allows you to limit your query based on geographic distance. An example of this type of query is, "Find all orders that are being shipped to locations more than 100 miles away from my warehouse." In this query, you would use the QueryCircle method, specify the center of the circle as your warehouse, and set the radius of the circle to 100 miles.

Now, let's get back to our supply-chain optimization problem: imagine that you have a warehouse in Redmond, WA, and you have a database of all orders shipped on the West Coast. You can query the shipment records to find out which orders travel for more than 100 miles from your warehouse in Redmond by following these steps:

1. Import all orders from SQL Server into a dataset:

```
//Create a new dataset
MapPoint.DataSet dataset = map.DataSets.AddPushpinSet("NorthWind Orders");
```

```
//Import orders records from your SQL Server
try
   {
      //Open the connection
      connection.Open( );
      //Get a sql reader from the query
      System.Data.SqlClient.SqlDataReader sqlReader =
                command.ExecuteReader(System.Data.CommandBehavior.
CloseConnection);
      if(sqlReader != null)
       {
          while(sqlReader.Read( ))
           {
              //Get the name of the customer
              string customername  = sqlReader["ContactName"] as String;
              //Get the company name
              string companyname  = sqlReader["CompanyName"] as String;
              //Get the address string
              string address = sqlReader["Address"] + ", " + sqlReader["City"] +
",
                         " + sqlReader["Region"] + ", " +
                          sqlReader["PostalCode"] + " " +
sqlReader["Country"];

              //Find location
              MapPoint.Location location = null;
              try
                {
                  //Find the address
                  MapPoint.FindResults findrs = map.FindResults(address);
                  //If no results found, skip to next record
                  if(findrs == null || findrs.Count <= 0)
                     throw new Exception(address);
                  //Get the location
                  location = findrs.get_Item(ref index) as MapPoint.Location;
                  //Create a pushpin
                  if(location != null)
                   {
                     MapPoint.Pushpin pushpin =
                           map.AddPushpin(location, companyname);
                     //Assign the contact name
                     pushpin.Note = "Contact : " + customername;
                     //Move to the pushpin dataset
                     pushpin.MoveTo(dataset);
                   }
                }
            catch
                {
                  //Do some logging
                }
        }
```

```
        //Close the reader; this will automatically close the connection
        //due to the command behavior setting during the
        //ExecuteReader method
        sqlReader.Close();
      }
    }
  catch
    {
      //Do clean up
    }
```

2. Find the location of your warehouse using the FindResults or FindAddress method:

```
//Now find out how many orders are shipping within 100 miles
//of your warehouse in Redmond, WA
//First step is to find out the warehouse
MapPoint.Location warehouse =
        map.FindResults("1 Microsoft Way, Redmond, WA").get_Item(ref index)
        as MapPoint.Location;
```

3. Define the distance limit (the radius of the circle):

```
//Define the radius of the circle
double radius = 100;
```

4. Query the dataset using the warehouse location and the distance limit:

```
//Now query for records (orders) that fall within 100 miles of distance around
//this warehouse using the QueryCircle method

//Call the Query circle method with warehouse as center and the radius
MapPoint.Recordset orders = dataset.QueryCircle(warehouse, 100);
```

5. Count the number of matching records for this query to get the number of orders shipping from your warehouse in Redmond that travel for distances of 100 miles or more:

```
//Count the orders
int orderCount = 0;
if(orders != null)
{
    orders.MoveFirst();
    while(!orders.EOF)
    {
        orderCount ++;
        orders.MoveNext();
    }
}

MessageBox.Show( orderCount.ToString() + " out of " +
            dataset.RecordCount.ToString() +
            " orders are shipping from Redmond, WA warehouse");
```

Using the standard NorthWind database order data, there are 17 orders out of total 113 being transported for more than 100 miles—that's more than 10% of your company's orders. Now you can extend this code to find out specific locations that are outside the 100-mile radius, find a place at the center of these locations, and recommend it as your new warehouse.

Along the same lines, you can use the QueryPolygon method if you have an array of locations and want to get the records from a dataset that resides within that polygon.

In some cases, you may need to query all the records in a dataset and loop through them. It is possible to accomplish this task with the DataSet object using the QueryAllRecords method.

Querying a Dataset for All Records

You can query a DataSet object for all records using the DataSet.QueryAllRecords method:

```
//Query all records and loop through
    MapPoint.Recordset recordSet = dataset.QueryAllRecords();

    //Move the first record in the cursor
    recordSet.MoveFirst();

    //Loop through the record set and see the values
    while(!recordSet.EOF)
    {
        //Get the row-level values for each field
        foreach(MapPoint.Field field in recordSet.Fields)
        {
            MessageBox.Show(field.Value.ToString());
        }
        //Move to next record
        recordSet.MoveNext();
    }
```

In addition to querying for all records and looping through the records, this code also shows the value for each field contained in the record. Is there a way to query for all records and access fields by their name or index? Yes, using the RecordSet. Fields collection. The following example shows how to access the value of a field selected by the name of the field:

```
//Query all records and loop through
MapPoint.Recordset recordSet = dataset.QueryAllRecords();

//Move the first record in the cursor
recordSet.MoveFirst();

//Define the field name to that we are interested in
object stateField = "State";
```

```
        //Loop through the record set and see the values
        while(!recordSet.EOF)
        {
            MapPoint.Field field = recordSet.Fields.get_Item(ref stateField);
            //Find the corresponding pushpin
            MapPoint.Pushpin pp = map.FindPushpin(field.Value.ToString());
            //For fun show each pushpin detail in a loop
            if(pp != null)
            {
                pp.Highlight = true;
                pp.BalloonState = MapPoint.GeoBalloonState.geoDisplayBalloon;
                System.Threading.Thread.Sleep(1000);
                pp.BalloonState = MapPoint.GeoBalloonState.geoDisplayNone;
                pp.Highlight = false;
            }
            else
            {
                //MessageBox.Show("Field not found!");
            }
            //Move to next record
            recordSet.MoveNext();

        }
```

I'm querying for all records and then for each individual record. I use the value of the location field to find the corresponding pushpin and highlight it. The processing I'm doing in this case (highlighting a pushpin based on a field value) may look trivial, but you need this kind of simple capability when you are building more complex applications like fleet tracking (which we will build in the next chapter). You can also obtain a pushpin corresponding to a dataset record by using the Recordset.Pushpin property.

Now that you have seen how to query a dataset for all the records and use the QueryCircle method, it's time to look at the Shapes and how to query Shapes to explore the power of MapPoint 2004 DataSet APIs.

Working with Shapes

A *shape* in MapPoint 2004 context is an entity that can be drawn on top of a map, queried for location information, or altered in appearance. MapPoint 2004 APIs allow you to draw, query, and alter the shapes on any given map. These shapes include circles, polygons, polylines, text boxes, drivetime zones, and so on. Remember that the circles, pies, series columns, and all other shapes drawn using the DisplayDataMap do not belong to shape category, since there is no way for you to either query or alter the circle shape appearance. Now, let's see how to work with shapes in MapPoint 2004.

Drawing Shapes

MapPoint 2004 APIs expose all shapes on any given map as a Shapes collection (similar to the DataSets collection). Using this Shapes collection, you can add a new shape or retrieve an existing shape. To add a new shape, the Shapes collection offers Add*XXXX* methods (where *XXXX* can be a line, text box, polyline, and so on). Table 3-8 provides a list of these methods and their descriptions:

Table 3-8. Shape-drawing methods exposed on the Shapes collection

Methodname	Notes
AddDrivetimeZone	Adds a freeform closed shape representing the driving distance from a point on the map within a specified amount of time
AddLine	Adds a new line to the map between two points
AddPolyline	Adds a new polyline to the map
AddShape	Adds a new radius circle, oval, or rectangle to the map
AddTextbox	Adds a new text box to the map

When you call one of these Add methods, a shape is created on the map and added to the Shapes collection. The method also returns a reference to the newly created shape as a Shape object. You can also access a shape using the Shapes collection indexer via the shape index or name.

Next, we'll draw a shape using the MapPoint 2004 APIs.

Drawing a circle

Using the AddShape method from the Shapes collection, you can add a circle or oval at any location on the current map. The AddShape method accepts the type of shape, which is of MapPoint.GeoAutoShapeType enumeration, and the location around which to draw this shape at the same height and width. The GeoAutoShapeType enumeration supports drawing ovals, circles, and rectangles. The following example shows how to draw a circle around the location Seattle, WA:

```
//Find a location
object index = 1;
MapPoint.Location location =
        (MapPoint.Location) map.FindResults("Seattle").get_Item(ref index);

//Add a circle with radius = 50 miles
MapPoint.Shape shape =
        map.Shapes.AddShape(MapPoint.GeoAutoShapeType.geoShapeOval,
                        location, 50, 50);
//Zoom to shape
shape.Location.GoTo();
```

To draw an oval, pass a different height and width. What if you want to draw a circle that shows the radius? You'll have to use GeoAutoShapeType.geoShapeRadius as the shape type. You can also draw a rectangle using the same method but passing the GeoAutoShapeType.geoShapeRectangle value for the shape type argument.

Drawing a line

Drawing a line using MapPoint 2004 is very simple. Since a *line* is basically a shape that connects only two locations, pass two locations to this method. So, if you want to draw a line between Seattle, WA, and Los Angeles, CA, use the following code:

```
object index = 1;
//Find Seattle, WA
MapPoint.Location location1 =
    (MapPoint.Location) map.FindResults("Redmond, WA").get_Item(ref index);
//Find Los Angeles, CA
MapPoint.Location location2 =
    (MapPoint.Location) map.FindResults("Los Angeles, CA").get_Item(ref index);

//Now, add a line
MapPoint.Shape shape = map.Shapes.AddLine(location1, location2);
```

Drawing a polyline

While a line connects two locations, a *polyline* connects more than two locations. The AddPolyline method takes an array of locations as an argument and draws a polyline connecting the input locations.

The following example shows how to draw a polyline connecting Redmond, WA, Portland, OR, and Los Angeles, CA:

```
object index = 1;

MapPoint.Location location1 =
  (MapPoint.Location) map.FindResults("Redmond, WA").get_Item(ref index);
MapPoint.Location location2 =
  (MapPoint.Location) map.FindResults("Portland, OR").get_Item(ref index);
MapPoint.Location location3 =
  (MapPoint.Location) map.FindResults("Los Angeles, CA").get_Item(ref index);

//Add a polyline
MapPoint.Shape shape =
map.Shapes.AddPolyline(new MapPoint.Location[] {location1, location2, location3});
```

Drawing a polygon

You can extend the polyline to draw a polygon by closing the polyline to form a polygon. For example, if you have four locations that you are drawing a polyline

with, you can form a polygon using these four locations by connecting the last location with the first location. The following example shows how to create a polygon
using the AddPolyline method:

```
object index = 1;
MapPoint.Location location1 =
   (MapPoint.Location) map.FindResults("Redmond, WA").get_Item(ref index);
MapPoint.Location location2 =
   (MapPoint.Location) map.FindResults("Portland, OR").get_Item(ref index);
MapPoint.Location location3 =
   (MapPoint.Location) map.FindResults("Los Angeles, CA").get_Item(ref index);
MapPoint.Location location4 =
   (MapPoint.Location) map.FindResults("Boise, ID").get_Item(ref index);

//Add a ployline
MapPoint.Shape shape =
    map.Shapes.AddPolyline(new MapPoint.Location[] {
                        location1, location2, location3, location4, location1});
```

Since "location4" is now connected back to "location1," this method draws a polygon that includes the aforementioned four locations as vertices.

Accessing shape vertices

For any non-GeoAutoShapeType shape, you can access vertices/locations at the vertices that make up that shape. You can obtain values for vertices for any shape that is
drawn using AddLine or AddPolyLine methods:

```
//Add a ploygon
MapPoint.Shape shape = map.Shapes.AddPolyline(new MapPoint.Location[]
               {location1, location2, location3, location4, location1});

//Now get the vertices for this polygon
object[] vertices = shape.Vertices as object[];
foreach(object vertex in vertices)
{
    MapPoint.Location loc
        = vertex as MapPoint.Location;
}
```

The vertices are exposed as an array of objects, and you have to typecast them as
Location objects to access the location properties of the vertex.

Sometimes you have to find distance from a given point or location to a shape. In
such cases, since there is no direct API available for this purpose, use the vertices of
the shape to find the nearest vertex to the input location using the Location.
DistanceTo method:

```
//Start with a location object
MapPoint.Location loc;
//Obtain a valid location instance such as Redmond, WA
//and assign it to loc object.
. . .
```

```
//Now get the vertices a polygon from where
//we want to measure distances
object[] vertices = shape.Vertices as object[];
foreach(object vertex in vertices)
{
    MapPoint.Location shapeLoc
        = vertex as MapPoint.Location;
    //Now get distance
    Console.WriteLine(shapeLoc.DistanceTo(loc));

}
```

While this is does not give exactly the nearest location, it provides a workaround for this situation.

Drawing a text box

Finally, the Shapes collection provides a method to draw a text box on the map. This is useful to draw labels that are specific to your business needs. The following example shows how to draw a text box at the center of a circle that indicates your market area:

```
//Find a location
object index = 1;
MapPoint.Location location =
    (MapPoint.Location) map.FindResults("SEA").get_Item(ref index);

//Add a circle
MapPoint.Shape shape =
        map.Shapes.AddShape(MapPoint.GeoAutoShapeType.geoShapeOval,
        location, 150, 150);

//Draw a text box
MapPoint.Shape tBox = map.Shapes.AddTextbox(location, 50, 20);

//Now assign text to the text box
object name = "MarketingAreaTextBox";
//Assign it to the shape
tBox.Name = name.ToString();
//Now assign text by accessing the shape from the collection
map.Shapes.get_Item(ref name).Text = "Marketing Zone A";
```

The shape can be accessed via either the name of the shape or the index of the shape from the Shapes collection.

So far, you have seen how to draw shapes. Next, let's look at how to customize the shape's appearance using the MapPoint 2004 APIs.

Altering Shape Appearance

Using the MapPoint 2004 APIs, you can not only draw shapes but also modify their look and feel. There are some limitations related to the color settings, but I will discuss how to work with the OLE color palette using the .NET colors.

Altering line width

When you draw a shape in MapPoint 2004, the shape is drawn with a default line width and color. However, you can change these attributes by altering the settings available using the `Shape.Line` property, which is a `LineFormat` object. The `LineFormat` object exposes `Width` and `ForeColor` properties to alter the width and color of the line. The properties are `Integer` type. The integer represents the RGB color value of the OLE color format. In order to convert the .NET Color structure to the OLE color structure, use the .NET Framework's `ColorTranslator` class available in the `System.Drawing` namespace. The following example shows how to set the line color and line width of a circle shape:

```
//Add a circle
MapPoint.Shape shape =
    map.Shapes.AddShape(MapPoint.GeoAutoShapeType.geoShapeOval, location, 75, 75);

//Customizing the line format
shape.Line.Weight = 1;
shape.Line.ForeColor = ColorTranslator.ToOle(Color.LightSteelBlue);
```

You can change the visibility of the line using the `LineFormat.Visible` property:

```
//Do not want to show the line
shape.Line.Visible = false;
```

Changing the fill color

You can change the fill color of a shape using the `Shape.Fill` property, which is a `FillFormat` object. The `FillFormat` object exposes properties such as `ForeColor` and `Visible` to change the appearance of the shape. The following sample shows how to change the fill color of a circle shape:

```
//Add a circle
MapPoint.Shape shape =
    map.Shapes.AddShape(MapPoint.GeoAutoShapeType.geoShapeOval, location, 75, 75);

//Customizing a shape look-and-feel
shape.Fill.ForeColor = ColorTranslator.ToOle(Color.LightBlue);
//Set visibility to true
shape.Fill.Visible = true;
```

When I talk about fill color, you may be wondering whether it is possible to fill the shape with alpha blending (or translucency). Actually, OLE fill color does not support alpha blending; however, MapPoint 2004 allows you to create and fill shapes so that the map beneath the shape is still visible.

Simulating translucency

The `Shape` object has a method, `ZOrder`, which you can use to make a shape transparent even with fill color visible. The `ZOrder` method takes an argument of type `GeoZOrderCmd` enumeration, which provides values for sending the shape behind objects (such as roads on the map), bringing it in front of objects, or sending it behind another shape. To make a shape transparent by sending it behind the roads, use the following code:

```
//Add a circle
MapPoint.Shape shape =
    map.Shapes.AddShape(MapPoint.GeoAutoShapeType.geoShapeOval, location, 75, 75);

//Customizing a shape look-and-feel
shape.Fill.ForeColor = ColorTranslator.ToOle(Color.LightBlue);
shape.Fill.Visible = true;
shape.Line.Weight = 1;
shape.Line.ForeColor = ColorTranslator.ToOle(Color.LightSteelBlue);

//Send back to the map
shape.ZOrder(MapPoint.GeoZOrderCmd.geoSendBehindRoads);
```

Toggling shape visibility

Sometimes you have to toggle the visibility of a shape completely. Even though the MapPoint 2004 API provides Visible properties for both line and fill color of shapes, setting them as false does not make the shape disappear completely. You can work around this by moving a shape to an obscure location (such as the North Pole) and bringing it back to its original location when needed. The following steps show how to achieve the visibility toggling effect:

1. Define a Hashtable to hold the shape's original location:

    ```
    //Create a hashtable to store shape ids
    System.Collections.Hashtable hTable = new Hashtable( );
    ```

2. Find a Place and draw a shape around it:

    ```
    //Find a location
    object index = 1;
    MapPoint.Location center
        = map.FindResults("Redmond, WA").get_Item(ref index)
         as MapPoint.Location;
    center.GoTo( );

    //Now add a shape
    MapPoint.Shape shape
      = map.Shapes.AddShape(MapPoint.GeoAutoShapeType.geoShapeOval, center, 5, 5);
    ```

3. Set a unique name for this shape. Having a unique name is important because we will later use it as a key to retrieve the original shape location from the hash table:

    ```
    //Set a unique name
    shape.Name = "Shape1";
    ```

4. Add the original location to the hash table:

    ```
    //Add the shape to the hashtable
    //Persist the location in a hashtable
    hTable.Add(shape.Name, shape.Location);
    ```

5. Make the shape invisible by sending it to the North Pole:

```
//Toggle process
//Find some obsucre location - a pole
MapPoint.Location pole
    = map.GetLocation(0, 0, 2000);

//Send shape to the pole
shape.Location = pole;
```

6. Bring the shape back to the original location when needed:

```
//Get the original location
MapPoint.Location originalCenter
    = hTable[shape.Name] as MapPoint.Location;
//Set original location back
shape.Location = originalCenter;
```

This method works well within a single application session. However, if you want to persist the shape across the application sessions, you may have to persist the shape name and the original location in an external store, such as a config file or a text file.

Now that you know how to draw shapes and customize their look and feel, it's time to explore using the shapes for location information.

Querying Shapes

You can use a shape to query a dataset to find the matching records that reside within that shape. To find out how many records or locations are contained within the specified shape, use the querying shapes technique.

Here is a sample scenario: you have a list of customers spread across the United States. You happen to be in Chicago on a business trip, and you want to find out how many of your customers are within 50 miles of where you are staying so that you can visit them. You create a circle shape with 50-mile radius and query for all customers that are contained within this circle shape. The following code shows this implementation:

```
//Using the MapPoint Sample sales data from mdb file
string filePath = @"C:\MApPointData\Clients.mdb!Addressestable";
//Define missing fields
object missing = System.Reflection.Missing.Value;
//Import data and create a dataset
MapPoint.DataSet dataset =
        map.DataSets.ImportData(filePath, missing,
        MapPoint.GeoCountry.geoCountryUnitedStates,
        MapPoint.GeoDelimiter.geoDelimiterDefault,
        MapPoint.GeoImportFlags.geoImportAccessTable);

//Now Find O'Hare Airport in Chicago (Airport Code ORD) to draw a circle around
//Find a location
```

```
object index = 1;
MapPoint.Location location =
    (MapPoint.Location) map.FindResults("ORD").get_Item(ref index);

//Draw a circle around this location with 50 mile radius
MapPoint.Shape shape  =
    map.Shapes.AddShape(MapPoint.GeoAutoShapeType.geoShapeOval, location, 50, 50);

//Now query for customers that fall within this shape
MapPoint.Recordset records = dataset.QueryShape(shape);

//Customer Name field index from the source file
object fieldIndex = 2;

//Now loop through the records
if(records != null && !records.EOF)
{
    records.MoveFirst();
    while(!records.EOF)
    {
      //Store the address - you need to meet this customer
      . . .
      records.MoveNext();
    }
}
```

This method works well for querying records based on distance (such as the 50-mile radius) constraint. However, don't you think it would be easier if you could query for the records based on time constraints instead of just a distance constraint? You can do this using drivetime zones.

Working with Drivetime Zones

A *drivetime zone* is a free form polygon shape that represents the maximum driving distance from a location on a map within a specified amount of time. In our example, you can modify the query to be: "Find all customers that can be reached within 60 minutes of driving from O'Hare Airport." So, a drivetime zone is essentially a shape that can be added to a map around a prespecified location. You can add a drivetime zone shape using the Shapes.AddDrivetimeZone method:

```
//Add a 60 minute drivetime zone around a location
MapPoint.Shape shape =
   map.Shapes.AddDrivetimeZone(location,
           60 * MapPoint.GeoTimeConstants.geoOneMinute);
```

This method uses the location around which the driving distance is calculated to express the time value in a GeoTimeConstants enumeration. This enumeration provides values for days, hours, and minutes.

A 60-minute drivetime zone is shown in Figure 3-17.

Figure 3-17. A 60-minute drivetime zone around O'Hare Airport (Color Plate 7)

Once you have the drivetime zone, you can use the shape like any other MapPoint shape to find the locations that fall inside that shape using the `DataSet.QueryShape` method.

When thinking of customers all across the United States, it is sometimes helpful to find out which customer falls into which account representative's territory. When you have 20 account representatives, it is a common practice to assign them geographic territories to streamline account management and communication processes. You can use the MapPoint 2004 APIs to display territory maps based on external information.

Working with Territories

MapPoint 2004 provides APIs to generate and display territories based on external data (such as a text file or Access database). As with importing any other location data, the `DataSets` object is used to import territories. The `DataSets` object provides the `ImportTerritories` method to import territories from any source supported by the `ImportData` method.

The following code shows how to create a territory map using the 2004 U.S. presidential election results:

```
//Using the MapPoint Sample Territory data from txt file
string filePath = @"C:\MapPointData\2004Elections.xls";
//Define fields
object missing = System.Reflection.Missing.Value;
//Import data and create a dataset
MapPoint.DataSet dataset =
    map.DataSets.ImportTerritories(filePath, missing,
    MapPoint.GeoCountry.geoCountryUnitedStates,
    MapPoint.GeoDelimiter.geoDelimiterDefault,
    MapPoint.GeoImportFlags.geoImportExcelSheet);

//Zoom to the territory map
dataset.ZoomTo( );
```

The previous code yields the territory map shown in Figure 3-18.

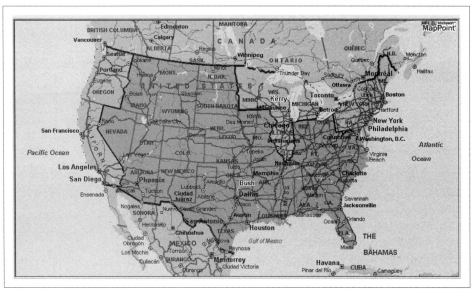

Figure 3-18. U.S. presidential election results as a territory map

Territories are one of the most interesting features of MapPoint 2004; however, they are also a feature that has serious limitations in terms of what you can do with the MapPoint 2004 APIs. For example, if you want to query a location to determine which territory it belongs to, there is no API that can be used for this purpose. However, there is a workaround to achive this.

Determining a Location's Territory

While there is no territory query API available in MapPoint 2004, you can determine a location's territory using a combination of other APIs, specifically Map. ObjectsFromPoint and Dataset.QueryCircle methods, in MapPoint 2004.

Say, for example, you are given the location "Redmond, WA," and now you have to determine whose sales territory it belongs to. In order to do that, you must import the territories into a dataset using the Datasets.ImportData method:

```
//Import territories as Data
//Using the MapPoint Sample Territory data from Xls file
string filePath = @"C:\SampleTerritories.xls";
//Define fields
object missing = System.Reflection.Missing.Value;

MapPoint.DataSet dataset =
    map.DataSets.ImportData(filePath, missing,
    MapPoint.GeoCountry.geoCountryUnitedStates,
    MapPoint.GeoDelimiter.geoDelimiterDefault,
    MapPoint.GeoImportFlags.geoImportExcelSheet);
```

Now that your territories are available in a dataset, find the input location using the Map.FindResults method:

```
//Now find input place
object index = 1;
  MapPoint.Location loc =
      map.FindResults("Redmond, WA").get_Item(ref index)
      as MapPoint.Location;
```

Using this location, use the hit-detection method to find objects from the corresponding point:

```
//Get objects from the given point
MapPoint.FindResults findres =
 map.ObjectsFromPoint(map.LocationToX(loc), map.LocationToY(loc));
```

For each of these objects, see whether there is any territory-representing location present in the dataset that you created at the beginning:

```
//Now for each object see if there is any territory representing
//location in the dataset
for(int i=0; i<findres.Count;i++)
{
  object ind = i+1;
  MapPoint.Location loc1
      = findres.get_Item(ref ind) as MapPoint.Location;
  if(loc1.Type != MapPoint.GeoShowDataBy.geoShowByRegion1)
    continue;
  double radius = 1;
  bool notfound = true;
  object fieldIndex = 2;
  while(notfound)
  {
```

```
    //Query the dataset
    MapPoint.Recordset recs
         = dataset.QueryCircle(loc1, radius);
    while(!recs.EOF)
     {
        //Found territory!
        MessageBox.Show(recs.Fields.get_Item(ref fieldIndex).Value.ToString( ));
        notfound = false;
        i = findres.Count + 1;
        break;
     }
      if(radius > 30)
       {
           //For performance and accuracy reasons
           //Don't search any further
           //Failed to find the territory
           break;
       }
      else
       {
         //Increment the radius and search
         //Dataset again
         radius = radius + 5;
       }
     }
   }
```

All that happens in this code is a query of the dataset around each location (returned by the ObjectsFromPoint method) using the QueryCircle method by increasing the radius until we find a territory or until the radius execeeds 30 miles (a hypothetical value that can be increased or reduced depending on your territory locations). This technique works for most of the territories except when they are too small (for example, if you find multiple territories in a 1-mile radius).

Where Are We?

In this chapter, you have learned how to work with native demographic data and your business data to generate data maps in different map styles. You have also seen how to import data into MapPoint from variety of data source such as text, Excel, Access, SQL, and so on. We also have examined working with shapes, drivetime zones, and territories.

Working with the DataSets and Shapes collections can be among the most interesting tasks of the MapPoint APIs. These two objects provide the core of the location-based business intelligence processing power within MapPoint 2004.

In the next chapter, I will shift the focus slightly from the core MapPoint 2004 to focus on performance, interfacing with other applications by writing Add-Ins, and making MapPoint 2004 work with GPS devices.

CHAPTER 4

Advanced MapPoint 2004 Programming

In the previous chapters, you learned how to use MapPoint 2004 APIs to perform simple location-oriented tasks, business data display, and management tasks. Now it's time to learn how to integrate and extend MapPoint 2004 APIs, as well as how to improve the performance and memory usage of your MapPoint 2004 applications. You'll learn how to:

- Extend MapPoint 2004 by interfacing with a GPS device
- Integrate your applications by writing COM Add-Ins
- Improve your MapPoint 2004 application performance

Sample applications used in this chapter are available in the companion material under the *Chapter04* directory.

Interfacing MapPoint 2004 with a GPS Device

While MapPoint 2004 makes most of its features available via the APIs, there is one feature that you may wish to use that is not available: the ability to interface with a GPS (Global Positioning System) device. Interfacing with a GPS device is fairly independent of any specifics of MapPoint 2004 implementation. The details of Map-Point 2004 interfacing with a GPS device lie in serial port communication and parsing standard NMEA GPS sentence streams. By interfacing them, you can write applications that use MapPoint 2004 and a GPS device to show location in real time.

The first step in building a location tracker application is to understand how GPS works. While it is beyond the scope of this book to discuss it in detail, I want to provide some basics so that it will be easier for those unfamiliar with GPS to understand. If you are already familiar with GPS technology, you can skip the following section.

GPS Basics

GPS is a free radio navigation system built with space satellites launched and managed by the United States Department of Defense. At any given time, there are a minimum of 24 satellites orbiting the Earth 11,000 miles above its surface. The satellites provide GPS receivers on the ground with accurate information about their position, speed, altitude, and direction. *GPS receivers* receive the GPS radio signals, analyze them, and stream the information in ASCII format for our use. A GPS receiver needs clear signals from at least three satellites to calculate valid position information. Usually, GPS receivers stream the data to a computer at 4,800 bits per second (baud rate); however, this speed can vary depending on the GPS receiver device hardware.

In order to allow MapPoint 2004 to work with a GPS receiver device (or simply, GPS device), you must capture the output ASCII stream and parse the data to obtain the necessary information. The ASCII stream can be in many formats, depending on the GPS receiver device hardware manufacturer. The National Marine Electronics Association (NMEA) 0183 format is one of the most popular formats for the ASCII stream. I will be using this format to program with a GPS device in this section.

The NMEA-0183 specification categorizes the GPS ASCII streams into comma-separated text sentences categorized based on the information contained in each sentence. A basic understanding of these sentences is required, since you need to parse these sentences to obtain the location and other information received from a GPS system.

Understanding NMEA GPS Sentences

While NMEA-0183 defines many GPS sentences, you need to understand only a handful to obtain the required information.

 An official copy of NMEA-0183 sentence specification can be obtained from the NMEA web site at *http://www.nmea.org/pub/0183/index.html*.

Table 4-1 shows some of the key NMEA GPS sentences and their use in application programming. We will be using these sentences in the location tracker application that we will build.

Table 4-1. Useful NMEA-0183 GPS sentences

Sentence type	Used for	Notes
Fixed data	Signal validity, location, number of satellites, time, and altitude	This sentence starts with characters `"$GPGGA"`.
		Use this sentence to see whether you are getting valid location information. You can also use this sentence to see the number of satellites that your GPS receiver can access. Examples of this sentence are:
		Invalid Signal: $GPGGA,235947.000,0000.0000,N,00000. 0000,E,0,00,0.0,0.0,M,,,,0000*00
		Valid Signal: $GPGGA,092204.999,4250.5589,S,14718. 5084,E,1,04,24.4,19.7,M,,,,0000*1F
Position and time	Location (lat/long), time, ground speed, and bearing	This sentence starts with characters `"$GPRMC"`.
		Use this sentence to obtain location (latitude, longitude), time, ground speed, and direction (or bearing). This sentence also provides you with information about the validity of the location information. Examples of this sentence are:
		Invalid Signal: $GPRMC,235947.000,V,0000.0000,N,00000. 0000,E,,,041299,,*1D
		Valid Signal: $GPRMC,092204.999,A,4250.5589,S,14718. 5084,E,0.00,89.68,211200,,*25

These sentences may look odd, but they're not difficult to parse. In the following section, I will show how to parse these sentences to obtain location, time, speed, and direction values. If you are not interested in understanding how these sentences are formed, you can simply use the sample assembly (GPS library) packaged with this chapter's information in the companion material, where I also explain how to use this library.

Parsing NMEA Sentences

NMEA sentences are comma-separated lines of text. You need to parse any given sentence using the part index for that sentence. Consider the following fixed data sentence:

```
string sentence =
@"$GPGGA,092204.999,4250.5589,S,14718.5084,E,1,04,24.4,19.7,M,,,,0000*1F"
```

To parse it, use the `String.Split` method to separate the parts within that sentence:

```
string[] parts = sentence.Split(new char[] {','});
```

Now you can access the individual parts by using an index; for example, the first part is always the sentence header, and the value of the fix data sentence header is always "$GPGGA", so you can use the parts in your application:

```
if(parts[0] == "$GPGGA")
{
 //Process values
 //Get latitude from the third word - index 2
 double latitude = this.MyLatConversionRoutine(words[2]);
 . . .
}
```

Since you now know how to parse sentences, let's see how to parse the key fixed data and position/time sentences.

Fields in the Fixed Data Sentence

The fixed data GPS sentence can be used to extract location and other useful information such as time, altitude, and number of satellites. The fields of interest from this sentence are shown in Table 4-2.

Table 4-2. Fields in the fixed data sentence

Index	Name	Example/Value	Notes
0	Sentence ID	"$GPGGA"	Standard header
1	UTC Time	92204.999	Expressed in hhmmss.sss format
2	Latitude	4750.5589	Expressed in degrees, minutes, and decimal minutes format: ddmm.mmmm
3	N/S Indicator	N	N=North (positive), S=South (negative)
4	Longitude	12218.5084	Expressed in degrees, minutes, and decimal minutes format: dddmm.mmmm
5	E/W Indicator	W	E=East (positive), W=West (negative)
6	Position Fix	1	0 = Invalid
			1 = Valid SPS
			2 = Valid DGPS
			3 = Valid PPS
7	Satellites Used	4	Number of satellites being used (0–12)
9	Altitude	19.7	Altitude in meters according to WGS-84 ellipsoid
10	Altitude Units	M	Expressed in meters

Using Table 4-2, you can access the information in a given fixed data sentence:

```
//Split the data to get the parts
string[] parts = sentence.Split(new char[] {','});

//Get Time
//2nd part is the UTC Time
```

```
    if(parts[1].Length > 0)
        time = ConvertToDateTimeExact(parts[1]);

    //Get LatLong
    if(parts[2].Length > 0 &&
        parts[4].Length > 0)
    {
        lat = ConvertDegreeMinuteSecondToDegrees(parts[2]);
        lon = ConvertDegreeMinuteSecondToDegrees(parts[4]);
    }

    . . .
```

There is a problem, however; the words in the sentence are not readily available to be used. Merely extracting the value itself is not useful unless you transform the value into one that is compatible with the application that you are using. In this case, the latitude and longitude must be expressed in degrees using the degrees, minutes, and decimal minutes format used with MapPoint 2004. Similarly, the UTC time expressed in hours, minutes, and seconds must be converted to local time before being displayed in your application. Clearly, we need to convert these values into a format that is understood by our applications. I'll discuss how to make these conversions after we look at the fields in the position and time sentence.

Fields in the Position and Time Sentence

The position and time sentence can be used to extract location information, ground speed information, and bearing information. Table 4-3 shows the fields, along with their indexes, used to extract this information.

Table 4-3. Fields in the position and time sentence

Index	Name	Example/Value	Notes
0	Sentence ID	"$GPRMC"	Standard header
1	UTC Time	92204.999	Expressed in hhmmss.sss format
2	Status	A	A = Valid
			V = Invalid
3	Latitude	4750.5589	Expressed in degrees, minutes, and decimal minutes format: ddmm.mmmm
4	N/S Indicator	N	N = North (+ve)
			S = South (-ve)
5	Longitude	12218.5084	Expressed in degrees, minutes, and decimal minutes format: dddmm.mmmm
6	E/W Indicator	W	E = East (+ve)
			W = West (-ve)
7	Ground Speed	11.39	Speed expressed in knots

Table 4-3. Fields in the position and time sentence (continued)

Index	Name	Example/Value	Notes
8	Ground Course	65.99	Bearing expressed indegrees
9	UTC Date	010105	Date expressed in DDMMYY

Converting NMEA Values

The information in the standard NMEA-0183 sentences needs conversion. For example, ground speed expressed in knots should be converted to either miles per hour or kilometers per hour before it is used in your application, unless you're writing marine applications.

Converting Latitude and Longitude Information

The latitude and longitude information in the NMEA-0183 sentences is expressed in degrees, minutes, and decimal minutes format (dddmm.mmmm) with the direction expressed as a character. To convert this value into decimal degrees, use this formula: degrees = ddd + (mm.mmmm)/60.

The following function performs this conversion:

```
public double ConvertDegreeMinuteSecondToDegrees(string input)
{
  //GPS Sentences input comes in dddmm.mmmm format

  if(input == null || input.Length <=0)
     return 0;

  double inputvalue = Convert.ToDouble(input);
  int degrees = Convert.ToInt32(inputvalue/100);
  return degrees + (inputvalue - degrees * 100)/60;

}
```

The input argument to this function is a string in dddmm.mmmm format. The output is a double value in degrees. There is one additional piece of information you need to add before it is complete: the direction of the latitude/longitude. For NMEA-0183 sentences, the direction is expressed as a character (N, S, E, or W). You can use this character or substitute a plus or minus sign in front of the latitude/longitude in degrees. When the direction is South (S), a negative value is applied to the latitude value; similarly, when the direction is West (W), a negative value is applied to the longitude value.

```
//Get direction for Latitude
if(parts[4] == "S")
  {
     lat = -1 * ConvertDegreeMinuteSecondToDegrees(parts[3]);
  }
```

```
    else
    {
      lat = ConvertDegreeMinuteSecondToDegrees(parts[3]);
    }
. . .
```

Converting the Speed Information

Speed information is expressed as knots in NMEA-0183 sentences; to convert this value into miles per hour, use this formula:

```
milesperhour = knots * 1.151
```

Similarly, to convert the speed into kilometers per hour, use this formula:

```
kmperhour = knots * 1.852
```

This code implements the conversion:

```
public double ConvertKnotsToSpeed(string input, string unit)
{
    if(input == null || input.Length <= 0)
        return 0;

    double knots = Convert.ToDouble(input);
    if(unit == "Kilometers")
    {
      //Return KMPH
      return knots * 1.852;
    }
    else
    {
      //Return MPH
      return knots * 1.151;
    }
}
```

The unit (KMPH or MPH) is expressed as a string value; however, it would be good practice to implement it as a .NET enumeration type (refer to the sample code provided in the companion material for more details on how to implement this).

Converting the Bearing Information

The bearing information is typically used to display the direction of travel on the ground. The bearing information is expressed as degrees, but you need to convert it into a meaningful format that can be understood by your application users. Conversion offers two possible displays:

- A compass image to display the angle of bearing
- The corresponding direction to the text (for example, N or NE)

The following example shows how to convert the bearing angle into text:

```
public static string GetDirectionFromOrientation(double degrees)
{
   string direction = string.Empty;
   //Anything between 0-20 and 340-360 is showed as north
   if((degrees >= 0 && degrees <20) || (degrees <= 360 && degrees > 340))
    {
       direction = "N";
    }
    // degrees in between 70 and 110
   else if(degrees >= 70 && degrees <= 110)
   {
      direction = "E";
   }
   //degrees in between 160 - 200
   else if(degrees >= 160 && degrees <= 200)
   {
      direction = "S";
   }
   //degrees in between 250 and 290
   else if(degrees >= 250 && degrees <= 290)
   {
      direction = "W";
   }
   else if(degrees > 0 && degrees < 90)
   {
      direction = "NE";
   }
   else if(degrees > 90 && degrees < 180)
   {
      direction = "SE";
   }
   else if(degrees > 180 && degrees < 270)
   {
      direction = "SW";
   }
   else if(degrees > 270 && degrees < 360)
   {
      direction = "NW";
   }
   return direction;
}
```

I have assumed a 20 degree range on both sides of the 0, 90, 180, 270, and 360 degree marks to approximate it as the corresponding direction; however, it's not mandatory to use the 20 degree range in your applications. You can extend this logic to approximate the bearing information to suit your application needs.

Converting the UTC Time Information

For our last conversion, let's look at the UTC time information. The NMEA-0183 sentences contain the time information in UTC hhmmssss (hours, minutes, and seconds) format; to convert this time information into your local time, use the .NET Framework's DateTime.ToLocalTime method:

```
private DateTime ConvertToDateTimeExact(string hhmmsssss)
{
    if(hhmmsssss == null || hhmmsssss.Length <= 0)
        return DateTime.MinValue;

    //Extract hours
    int hours = Convert.ToInt32(hhmmsssss.Substring(0, 2));
    //Extract minutes
    int minutes = Convert.ToInt32(hhmmsssss.Substring(2,2));
    //Extract seconds
    int seconds = Convert.ToInt32(hhmmsssss.Substring(4,2));

    DateTime nowInUniversal = DateTime.Now.ToUniversalTime( );
    return new DateTime(nowInUniversal.Year, nowInUniversal.Month,
                        nowInUniversal.Day, hours, minutes,

}
```

The individual hour, minute, and second values are first extracted and then converted to the local time.

Now that you know how to parse and convert the NMEA-0183 GPS sentences, it's time to make your application talk to a GPS receiver device.

Communicating with a GPS device

When you develop your GPS-enabled application, you need to scan the serial communication ports (or simply COM Ports) for a GPS receiver device. Unfortunately, there is no built-in support for serial communication available in the .NET Framework, Version 1.1. There is a shared source Serial Port Communications library available from Microsoft on the GotDotNet samples portal at *http://www.gotdotnet.com/*. Since building a serial port communication is beyond the scope of this chapter, I will be using these sample libraries, with some minor tweaks, for reading the GPS receiver device ASCII streams.

 You can download the Serial Port library sample code from: *http://www.gotdotnet.com/Community/UserSamples/Details. aspx?SampleGuid=b06e30f9-1301-4cc6-ac14-dfe325097c69*

This library (with these tweaks) is also available with full source code in the companion material.

If you are using the .NET Framework, Version 2.0, the serial port communication libraries are built into the Framework class libraries and are available under the System.IO.Ports namespace.

Let's look at the following code to see how to scan for a GPS receiver device connected to your computer on one of the ports from COM ports 1 to 10:

```
string comPortString = string.Empty;
string gpsStream = string.Empty;
bool GPSFound = false;
int comIndex = 1;
while(comIndex < 10)
 {
   comPortString = "COM" + comIndex.ToString();
   System.IO.Ports.SerialPort comport = null;
   try
    {
       comport
          = new System.IO.Ports.SerialPort(comPortString, 4800,
                 System.IO.Ports.Parity.None,
                 8, System.IO.Ports.StopBits.One);
       //Open the port
       comport.Open();

       //Set timer
       comport.ReadTimeout = 5000;

       //Read a line to see if the stream is open
       string  sentence = comport.ReadLine();

      if(sentence != null && sentence.Length > 0)
        {
          GPSFound = true;
          break;
        }
    }
    catch(Exception ex)
    {

    }
    finally
    {
      //Cleanup
      if(comport != null && comport.IsOpen)
      {
         comport.Dispose();
      }
    }
  }
```

In the previous code, I'm scanning for a GPS device from ports 1 to 10. How do you do that? Like any IO process, this task involves three steps: open a port, read the port, and dispose of it at the end. Once you detect a GPS device at any COM port, as long as the GPS device is connected, you can treat that COM port as an infinite data source and keep reading the ASCII streams. Once you have the ASCII streams available to your application, you can parse the NMEA-0183 GPS sentences and extract the location, speed, and direction information as shown earlier in this chapter.

This all sounds easy, right? But if you are careful in reading the above code, you might notice that I set a time-out value of 5 seconds before reading a port. This indicates that the COM port scan routine takes a long time to finish. So, if you are using a single-threaded application, users may get annoyed when the UI freezes on them while the main thread is busy waiting for the GPS response.

Similarly, once you detect a GPS device, reading the ASCII streams continuously may make your application unusable if you use a single-threaded approach because of the amount of time required. An event-driven application with multi-thread support should be built into your application to communicate with the GPS receiver device.

Event-Based Architecture for Reading GPS Sentences

Since a GPS device receives the satellite communication continuously, the ASCII sentences will also be available continuously. However, as we have discussed before, since we are only interested in a couple of sentences (fixed data, position, and time), you can deploy a thread to read the GPS device continuously and fire an event when the thread reads either a fixed data sentence or a position and time sentence. Ideally, you would define the corresponding event arguments to wrap the information (such as location, speed, direction, and so on) received from the GPS receiver.

I have included a sample GPS reader class in the companion material, which implements event-driven architecture and multi-threading. You can use this in your applications if you don't want to deal with implementing your own GPS reader classes from scratch. In the following section, I will give details about how to use the sample GPS reader class.

How to Use the Sample API in Your Applications

The sample GPS utility API that is discussed in this section is available in the companion material under *Chapter 04*.

Follow these steps to use the sample API in your GPS based application (assuming that you have already created a new project):

Add the assemblies *ProgrammingMapPoint.GPSUtil.dll* and *SerialPort.dll* as a reference to your project. These assemblies are provided in the *Assemblies* directory under the root directory.

In your application code, import the GPS utilities namespace:

```
//Add GPS Programming Utilities
using ProgrammingMapPoint.GPSUtilities;
```

Define an instance of the GPSReader class:

```
//Define a GPS Reader
private ProgrammingMapPoint.GPSUtilities.GPSReader gpsreader;
```

Create an instance of the GPSReader class either in either test mode (which reads GPS sentences from a text file) or real mode (which reads GPS sentences from a real GPS device). The following code shows how to create instances in both cases:

- Create an instance in test mode:

```
//TEST MODE - Reads from a file
string filename = @"C:\GPS_Log.txt";
gpsreader = new GPSReader(filename, Units.Miles);
```

- Create an instance in real mode:

```
//REAL MODE
gpsreader = new GPSReader(Units.Miles);
```

The next step is to wire up the events. The GPSReader class exposes the events listed in Table 4-4 that you can use in your application.

Table 4-4. Events exposed by the GPSReader class

Event	Description
ScanCommPortEvent	This event is fired when the GPSReader scans a particular COM port. The argument for this event is ScanCommPortEventArgs class, which includes the COM port name and the scan status.
InitializeCompleteEvent	This event is fired when the GPSReader completes the COM port scan process. The argument for this event is InitializeCompleteEventArgs class, which includes the COM port name if a GPS device is available.
SatelliteInfoEvent	This event is fired when the GPSReader receives a satellite info sentence (which starts with "$GPGSA") from a GPS device. The argument for this event is SatelliteInfoEventArgs class, which includes the information about satellites in view.
LocationInfoEvent!!F020!!	This event is fired when the GPSReader receives a position and time sentence (which starts with "$GPRMC") from a GPS device. The argument for this event is LocationInfoEventArgs class, which includes the information about the location (latitude/longitude) and direction.
GroundSpeedInfoEvent	This event is fired when the GPSReader receives a ground speed information sentence (starts with "$GPVTG") from a GPS device. The argument for this event is GroundSpeedInfoEventArgs class, which includes the information about the ground speed.

You can subscribe to these events as follows:

```
//Wireup for all events
//PortScan Info
gpsreader.ScanCommPortEvent +=
    new ScanCommPortEventHandler(gpsreader_ScanCommPortEvent);
//Loc Info
gpsreader.LocationInfoEvent +=
    new LocationInfoEventHander(gpsreader_LocationInfoEvent);
```

```
//Speed Info
gpsreader.GroundSpeedInfoEvent +=
    new GroundSpeedInfoEventHandler(gpsreader_GroundSpeedInfoEvent);
//Satellite Info
gpsreader.SatelliteInfoEvent +=
    new SatelliteInfoEventHander(gpsreader_SatelliteInfoEvent);
//Initialize complete
gpsreader.InitializeCompleteEvent +=
    new InitializeCompleteEventHandler(gpsreader_InitializeCompleteEvent);
```

The event handler methods such as gpsreader_InitializeCompleteEvent implement the necessary logic to display the information received from the GPSReader class. A word of caution: if you are using this class with a Windows application, and you intend to update the UI using these event handler methods, make sure that your code is thread safe by using the Invoke or BeginInvoke methods of the Windows form (refer to the companion material for sample code on this implementation). Wrap your UI update code in a method and invoke it from the event handler method using the Invoke or BeginInvoke method.

Next, scan all COM ports to see whether there is a GPS device. Call the Initialize method:

```
//Scan for all COM ports by initializing
gpsreader.Initialize();
```

Once the initialization is complete, and if a GPS device is found, the GPSReader class is ready to receive GPS sentences. To start receiving them, call the Start method:

```
//Start receiving GPS sentences
gpsreader.Start();
```

You can also temporarily stop receiving the GPS sentences by calling the Pause method.

Once you start receiving the GPS sentences, the event handler methods take care of updating the location information for your application. When you are done using the GPSReader, make sure to call the Dispose method.

Now that you know how to wire up the GPSReader events and receive the location and speed information, let's look at how you can integrate this information into MapPoint 2004.

Displaying GPS Sentences Using MapPoint 2004

Once you have the location information in latitude and longitude form, you can use the GetLocation method on the MapPoint.Map class. Once you get the MapPoint.

Location instance from this method, you can add a pushpin to display the location on the map:

```
MapPoint.Location loc
    = axMappointControl1.ActiveMap.GetLocation(latitude, longitude,
                            axMappointControl1.ActiveMap.Altitude);

currPushpin
    = axMappointControl1.ActiveMap.AddPushpin(loc, "mylocation");

//Symbol 208 is the icon for "1"
currPushpin.Symbol = 208;
currPushpin.GoTo( );

//Set street level view
axMappointControl1.ActiveMap.Altitude = 4;
//Set Highlight
currPushpin.Highlight = true;
```

Once you create the pushpin on the map to represent your current location, you can keep updating the pushpin location simply by using the `Pushpin.Location` property:

```
//Update the location
currPushpin.Location = loc;
```

Another challenge that you may see coming is how to keep the map centered on the current location.

Centering the Map on the Current Location

If you or the GPS device is moving, your pushpin on the map also moves. So, how do you keep the map centered on the current location indicated by the GPS device?

Centering the map on a location is easy and is done by calling the `Location.GoTo` method. The problem with the `GoTo` method is that it redraws the entire map, making the map flicker each time you call it. To avoid this flickering, (which can happen at the rate of 10 or more times per second) you can define a buffer area (say, an invisible, arbitrary rectangle) around the center of the map and call the `GoTo` method only when the location lies outside that rectangle.

This technique is as follows:

```
//Get X and Y coordinates from the locations
int X = axMappointControl1.ActiveMap.LocationToX(loc);
int Y = axMappointControl1.ActiveMap.LocationToY(loc);

//See if this is outside the 1/3 bounding box
//Simple way of checking this is to calculate
//height (or width) divided by 6;
//which means checking to see if the X or Y
//coord is just 1/3 distance away from either edge.
```

```
if(axMappointControl1.Height/6 > Y)
{
    //Center the map around this location
    axMappointControl1.ActiveMap.Location = loc;
}
else if(axMappointControl1.Width/6 > X)
{
    axMappointControl1.ActiveMap.Location = loc;
}
```

In this code example, we get the x and y coordinates of a location on the screen and see whether they lie within a rectangle one-third of the size of the map, according to our specifications. If the current location is inside the fictitious rectangle, there is no need to re-center the map; if it is not, re-center it by assigning the location to the `Map.Location` property.

You can find this entire implementation in the sample Location Tracker application included in the companion material. The sample application UI is shown in Figure 4-1.

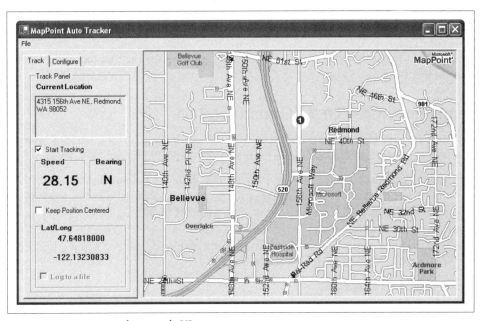

Figure 4-1. Location tracker sample UI

Now that you have seen how to extend MapPoint capabilities by interfacing with a GPS device, let's take another important aspect of advanced MapPoint 2004 programming: integrating your applications with MapPoint 2004 by writing Add-Ins.

Integrating Your Applications with MapPoint 2004

Like any other Microsoft Office application (and also like Visual Studio .NET), Map-Point 2004 supports extensibility architecture, which means that you can develop applications that can plug right into the MapPoint 2004 application. In this section, I will show how to develop Add-Ins for MapPoint 2004.

Before getting into the details of writing Add-Ins, there are two reasons why you need Add-Ins:

Integration

> Add-Ins are great if you want to develop applications that work with MapPoint 2004 and are tightly integrated with MapPoint UI. For example, your company may develop a cool data import application that can be used with MapPoint 2004. If you develop this application as an Add-In, you can potentially sell that application to all MapPoint 2004 customers who could use your application directly from inside the MapPoint 2004 UI.

Performance

> Add-Ins are a way to improve your application performance because MapPoint 2004 runs in its own process space. When you develop an application that runs in a different process space, the data transfer (and associated type conversion, and/or marshalling) between the process spaces causes some serious performance limitations. Developing your application as an Add-In enables MapPoint 2004 to host your application inside its own process space, dramatically reducing the marshalling requirement across the process boundary.

Developing a MapPoint Add-In is no different from developing an Add-In for any other Microsoft Office application. Visual Studio .NET provides you with a project type to develop Add-In applications. The steps below show how to develop a Map-Point Add-In using Visual Studio .NET.

1. Create an extensibility project for a shared Add-In using Visual Studio .NET's New Project dialog, as shown in Figure 4-2.

2. Select the Shared Add-In option to launch a wizard that allows you to select a programming language, as shown in Figure 4-3.

3. Upon selecting a language, the next page of the wizard allows you to select the application host for your Add-In. Since you are developing an Add-In for Map-Point 2004, select Microsoft MapPoint, as shown in Figure 4-4.

4. Once you select the application host, on the next page, enter a name and description for your Add-In (Figure 4-5).

5. After you give your Add-In a name and description, on the next page, set Add-In options, such as loading the Add-In on host application load and installing the Add-In for all users on a computer, as shown in Figure 4-6.

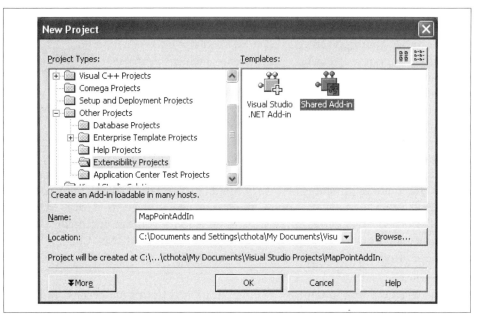

Figure 4-2. Creating an Add-In project

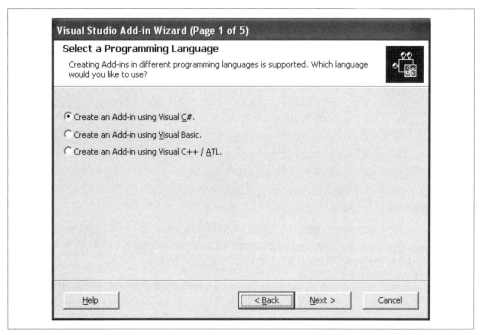

Figure 4-3. Selecting programming language

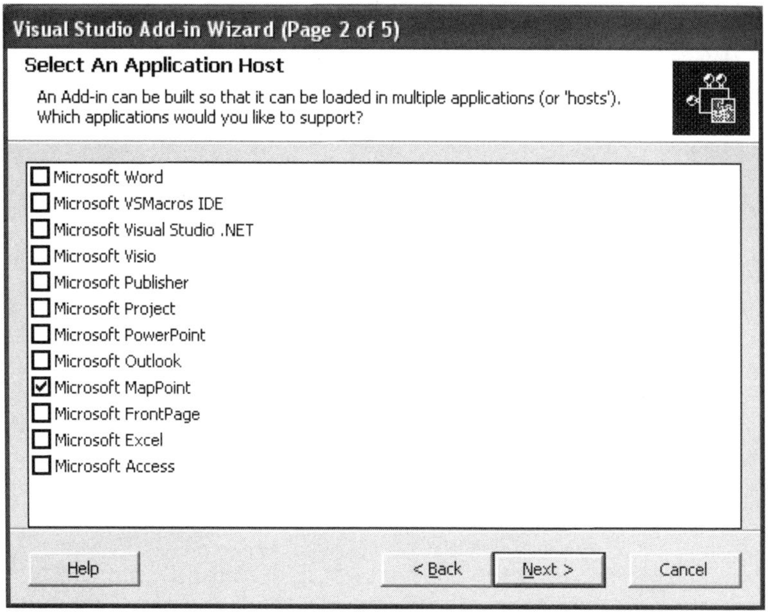

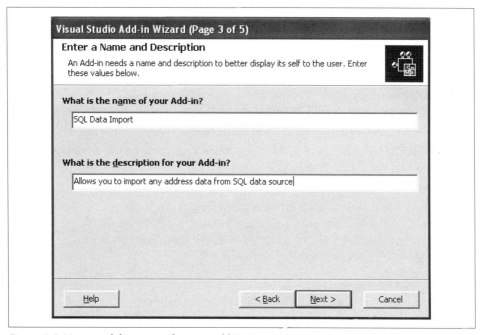

Figure 4-4. Selecting an application host

Figure 4-5. Name and description for your Add-In

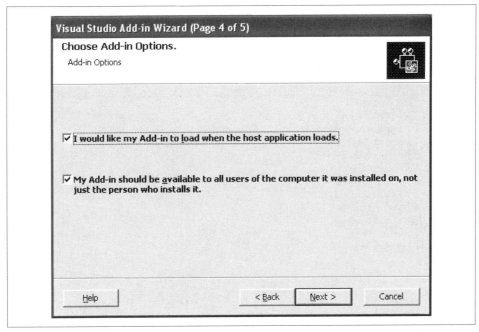

Figure 4-6. Add-In options page

I will leave choosing the installation options to your discretion, but there are a few things to consider about Add-In load options. How do you decide whether you want your Add-In to be loaded at the time of loading the host application? If your Add-In takes a long time to load (because it's waiting for a resource, for example), do not load the Add-In at the time of the host load. Doing so will slow down the entire application load. When this is an issue, you should load the Add-In explicitly, either manually or programmatically, before using it. If your Add-In initialization process is quick, you can choose to load your Add-In when the host application is loaded.

Once you set the Add-In options, the next wizard page presents the summary of your Add-In. When you click Finish, the wizard creates Add-In and setup projects for your Add-In application.

If you take a close look at the Add-In setup project, it includes the file *MPNA82.tlb* (or *MPEU82.tlb* in the European version of MapPoint 2004). This happens to be the type library installed with MapPoint 2004. You must exclude this file from the setup files by right-clicking on it, as shown in Figure 4-7.

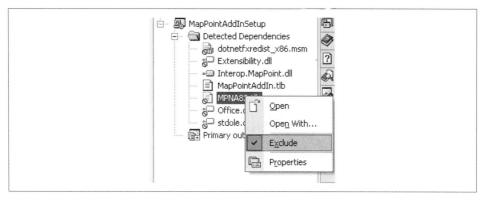

Figure 4-7. Exclude MapPoint type library from setup files

 If you don't exclude this file, when you install the Add-In, the installer looks for this type library on the target machine, and if it does not exist, the installer copies it onto the target machine. The biggest problem comes when you uninstall the Add-In; the installer removes the type library you haven't excluded from the target machine, leaving all MapPoint 2004–based applications broken. The only way to fix this issue once that has happened is to install the MapPoint 2004 product again. To avoid this issue altogether, make sure to exclude the *MPNA82.tlb* from the setup files.

Developing the Add-In

Now we are ready to develop an Add-In. The application logic for your Add-In must go into a *Connect.cs* (or *Connect.vb* if you are working with VB.NET) file. Before you start implementing specifics of your Add-In, add the MapPoint type library to your project as a reference. This way, you can use any of the MapPoint 2004 APIs in your Add-In if you want to.

If you take a close look at the Connect class, it implements the IDTExtensibility2 interface requiring you to implement the extensibility event handler methods, such as OnConnection, OnDisconnection, and so on. However, only implement these methods if you really need them, with one exception: the OnConnection method required to wire up the Add-In with the MapPoint 2004 UI. For example, to add a command button to the MapPoint 2004 application UI, add the following code in the OnConnection event handler method:

```
public void OnConnection(object application,
            Extensibility.ext_ConnectMode connectMode,
            object addInInst, ref System.Array custom)
{
    MapPoint.Application app
            = application as MapPoint.Application;
```

```
    if(app == null)
        return;

    //Add the command
    app.AddCommand("Import NorthWind Customers",
                "ImportNorthWindCustomers", this);
}
```

The `ApplicationClass.AddCommand` method takes the UI display name, the method name, and the type that declares the method name. In the previous code, the `AddCommand` method takes the UI name of Import NorthWind Customers and the method name `ImportNorthWindCustomers` that is implemented in the `Connect` class itself.

If you have the specific initialization code needed for your Add-In, use the `OnStartupComplete` event handler method to implement it. Using this method does not slow down the host application load time due to the Add-In initialization process.

You can also implement other methods in your Add-In as you would do in any other .NET class. If you need a reference to the host `MapPoint.ApplicationClass` to perform any MapPoint related tasks, declare a local field in the `Connect` class that can be assigned to the `MapPoint.ApplicationClass` instance in the `OnConnection` event handler method:

```
//Declare a local field to hold application
//class reference
private object applicationObject;
```

Assign it to the current MapPoint instance using the `OnConnection` method:

```
public void OnConnection(object application,
        Extensibility.ext_ConnectMode connectMode,
        object addInInst, ref System.Array custom)
{
    applicationObject = application;
    . . .
```

Since you have a reference to the host application class (MapPoint 2004 in our case), you can perform any MapPoint 2004-related task in your Add-In using that class instance.

To implement SQL data import Add-In, simply add a method to the `Connect` class that makes use of the `applicationObject` reference:

```
public void ImportNorthWindCustomers()
{
    //Get a reference to the MapPoint Application
    MapPoint.Application app = applicationObject as MapPoint.Application;
    if(app == null)
        return;
```

```
//Get the current map
MapPoint.Map map = app.ActiveMap;

//This sample uses System.Data namespace and standard
//NorthWind sample database that comes with SQL server
//See whether there is an existing dataset with the same name
object datasetName = "NorthWind Orders";
if(map.DataSets.Count > 0 &&
    map.DataSets.get_Item(ref datasetName) != null)
{
    //If so, delete it
    map.DataSets.get_Item(ref datasetName).Delete( );
}

//Now create a new dataset
MapPoint.DataSet dataset
    = map.DataSets.AddPushpinSet("NorthWind Orders");

. . .


}
```

That's it! Once this Add-In is built and installed on a machine, you can invoke the method from the MapPoint UI using the command we added earlier using the `ApplicationClass.AddCommand` method in the `OnConnection` method.

Sometimes, however, you may want to invoke the previous method from another application, especially when you build Add-Ins to improve the application performance. In that case, you can access an Add-In from the `MapPoint.ApplicationClass.AddIns` collection.

Invoking Add-In Methods from an External Application

Suppose you are building a Windows application to import data from the SQL Server North Wind database. Since we have already built the appropriate Add-In, simply create a reference to this Add-In and invoke the `ImportNorthWindCustomers` method.

First, create a new `MapPoint.Application` instance:

```
//Get a reference to the MapPoint Application
MapPoint.Application app = new MapPoint.ApplicationClass( );
```

Next, connect to the SQL data import Add-In that we built earlier in this chapter, if you chose not to load the Add-In when the host application is loaded:

```
//GUID: "E33E751B-0BA4-49D7-B5C8-ED2A539F9803"
app.AddIns.Connect("E33E751B-0BA4-49D7-B5C8-ED2A539F9803");
```

The AddIns collection exposes the Connect method, allowing you to connect to the Add-In that we built earlier. You can either use the GUID or Program ID (also called ProgId) to connect to the Add-In. How do you get this information? When you created the Add-In, the Connect class was created with a GUID and a ProgId:

```
[GuidAttribute("E33E751B-0BA4-49D7-B5C8-ED2A539F9803"),
ProgId("MapPointAddIn.Connect")]
public class Connect : Object, Extensibility.IDTExtensibility2
. . .
```

So, in this case, you can use either the GUID or the ProgId to connect to the Add-In.

Once the Add-In is connected to the application host, get the instance of the Connect class from the Add-In collection:

```
//Get the Add-In instance
object addin = app.AddIns.get_Item(ref index);
```

Now that you have the Add-In instance, invoke the Add-In method using the .NET Framework reflection APIs, which allow you to access and invoke a type's methods at runtime dynamically:

```
//Get the Add-In type
Type t = addin.GetType( );

//Invoke the ImportNorthWindCustomers method
t.InvokeMember("ImportNorthWindCustomers",
               System.Reflection.BindingFlags.InvokeMethod,
               null, addin, null);
}
```

The Type.InvokeMember method call invokes the ImportNorthWindCustomers method on the Add-In instance. Now you know how to invoke a method on a MapPoint 2004 Add-In from your application.

Performance Considerations

When I mentioned that you would be using MapPoint 2004 COM interoperable assemblies from your managed code, you may have been worried about performance. There is reason to worry, mainly because the COM interoperable assemblies add a layer of abstraction that necessitates marshalling across the process boundaries and type conversion between the managed and unmanaged types.

The good news is that you can avoid (or at least minimize) these issues by using:

- Add-Ins to minimize the marshalling across the process boundaries
- Visual C++ (with or without Managed Extensions) to write your client applications, minimizing type conversions

If you are curious about performance gains, here are my findings: when I ran performance tests for SQL data imported from the North Wind database using the C# import process and using the Add-Ins, the Add-Ins method ran 25% faster than the direct application programming with MapPoint types. That's considerable performance improvement.

Along the same lines, using Visual C++ (with or without managed extensions) can improve the speed and reduce memory requirements of your application.

Where Are We?

In this chapter, you have learned how to interface with a GPS device using MapPoint 2004 and how to write Add-Ins. We also discussed how to integrate and improve performance using Add-Ins in your applications.

MapPoint 2004 provides a rich set of APIs to develop windows applications that can work as standalone applications or as Add-Ins that can be integrated into the Map-Point 2004 UI. Yet, we have seen only Windows applications (which could be command line executables as well). So, what are our options if you want to develop applications of other kinds, such as applications for the Web or for other platforms, such as the Pocket PC or SmartPhone? If you are looking to use one of these platforms or application types to develop location-based applications, look at MapPoint Web Service in the next chapter.

PART II

MapPoint Web Service

Programming MapPoint Web Service

MapPoint 2004 offers extensive capabilities for building location applications, but you can only develop Windows desktop applications using MapPoint 2004 APIs. Moreover, map data must be available locally for MapPoint 2004 applications to work. If you want to develop applications for web or mobile devices, MapPoint 2004 is obviously not an option. However, if you want to develop location-based applications for web and mobile devices, you are not out of luck—that's where MapPoint Web Service comes in.

The MapPoint Web Service is a Microsoft-hosted XML web service that is fully compliant with SOAP. The MapPoint Web Service APIs are exposed via the standard Web Service Description Language (WSDL) that can be used to develop applications using any SOAP/XML-aware programming language. Because of that, MapPoint Web Service transcends traditional boundaries to become a platform-agnostic programming tool with which you can develop a variety of location-based applications.

In this chapter, I will explain how the MapPoint Web Service works and how to get started with your development environment. Since the MapPoint Web Service is SOAP protocol-compliant, it is inherently communication protocol-agnostic (working across HTTP, FTP, etc.); however, in this chapter, as well as Chapters 6-8, I will be using the HTTP protocol as the medium of communication.

Finally, before we get into the full details of MapPoint Web Service programming, I want to remind you that the MapPoint Web Service is a subscription-based web service, which means that you will be charged for the usage of the MapPoint Web Service APIs. I strongly recommend reading the end user license agreement (EULA) for more details on the tarrif and details on how the API calls are charged. Don't panic—accessing MapPoint Web Service in the staging environment is absolutely free, so you do not need to pay for accessing the APIs.

How Does MapPoint Web Service Work?

Like any other web service, MapPoint Web Service enables you to develop distributed applications. By invoking MapPoint Web Service methods over the wire, you can perform many location-based tasks, such as finding places, finding addresses, calculating driving directions, rendering maps, and so on. All web service requests that invoke MapPoint Web Service methods must be authenticated using the credentials assigned to your MapPoint Web Service account (I will go into more detail on this subject later in the chapter). Once your request is successfully authenticated, MapPoint Web Service executes the corresponding method using your input parameters and returns an appropriate output wrapped in a valid response. While all this communication happens in SOAP, you do not need to get into the details of SOAP request or response to communicate with MapPoint Web Service; Microsoft .NET framework does a great job of abstracting away the wire-format level specifics.

Figure 5-1 shows how your location-enabled applications communicate with MapPoint Web Service.

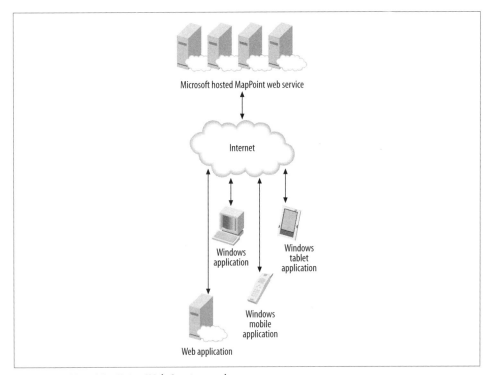

Figure 5-1. How MapPoint Web Service works

As you can see, any application you develop using MapPoint Web Service is a "connected" application, requiring your application to be able to communicate over the wire via the Internet.

So, what are the advantages of a connected MapPoint Web Service-based application? There are many advantages to this model:

Your applications remain lightweight.
Since location-related data and the core processing remains in the cloud, your applications primarily contain your business-specific location processing.

Location data is maintained for you and is always up-to-date.
Since the location data is also hosted by Microsoft, you don't need to worry about keeping the location data up-to-date; this task is abstracted from your program seamlessly.

Building global applications is easy.
Since MapPoint Web Service offers location data for multiple countries/regions of the world, you can write only one application and use many location data sources to work with location data from different countries/regions.

Now that you know how your applications communicate with MapPoint Web Service at a macro level, let's get started programming with MapPoint Web Service.

Getting Started with MapPoint Web Service

In this section, let's look at a step-by-step approach to getting started with MapPoint Web Service. If you have already signed up for MapPoint Web Service, are waiting to receive your credentials, and can't wait to start programming with MapPoint Web Service, use the evaluation credentials provided with the companion material; however, remember that these credentials are shared among all readers of this book and may expire at some point in the future.

Requesting MapPoint Web Service Credentials

The first step in programming with MapPoint Web Service is getting your own credentials to access the MapPoint Web Service APIs. Fill in the account request form available on the MapPoint web site at *http://www.microsoft.com/mappoint/evaluation/ default.aspx*. Once you complete and submit the form, you will receive an email containing your MapPoint Web Service account information that includes a user ID and password to access the MapPoint Web Service APIs and another user ID and password to manage your MapPoint Web Service account. Managing your MapPoint Web Service account is done using their Customer Services site, (also known as the

Extranet), details of which are included in the email. The customer services site can be considered an administrative console where you can manage your account user IDs and passwords, check your MapPoint Web Service usage (i.e., how many requests you have submitted so far), manage your custom data, and so on. Details on the Customer Services site are discussed later in this chapter.

 It is important to remember that the credentials you receive via email only give you access to the staging version of the MapPoint Web Service. The production version of the MapPoint Web Service is accessible only to the customers who actually sign the MapPoint Web Service contract.

The evaluation credentials you have received in the email are only valid for 45 days; after 60 days, these credentials expire, and your application can no longer communicate with MapPoint Web Service. If you are in still in the development phase at that time, however, you can ask the MapPoint Web Service Support to extend the evaluation period.

Accessing the MapPoint Web Service APIs

Now that you have your own set of MapPoint Web Service credentials, let's look at how to access the APIs. The formal WSDL document for the MapPoint Web Service APIs can be found at the following locations:

Staging MapPoint Web Service
   http://staging.mappoint.net/standard-30/mappoint.wsdl
   https://staging.mappoint.net/secure-30/mappoint.wsdl

Production MapPoint Web Service
   http://service.mappoint.net/standard-30/mappoint.wsdl
   https://service.mappoint.net/secure-30/mappoint.wsdl

If you are new to the world of web services, WSDL documents are the "contracts" that publish the web service interfaces, methods, and arguments in XML format. WSDL documents also express the types and their wire formats by defining them in XSD simple and complex types.

You might have noticed that MapPoint Web Service offers a staging environment and a production environment; however, the APIs offered by both environments are exactly the same. So why do you need two different environments? The staging environment is primarily targeted for development and testing purposes, while the production environment should be used for live applications. Moreover, the staging and production environments are physically isolated to ensure the Service Level Agreement (SLA) compliance in terms of availability (99.9%) and API response times. For the staging environment, the SLAs are not applicable (the staging Web Service access is free!); however, the SLAs are fully applicable to the production environment. Again, I recommend that you read the EULA for more details on SLAs related to availability and response time.

If you are either prototyping your MapPoint Web Service application or are still in the development phase, you should use the staging environment; once you are done with the development and testing, move your application to production environment. Note that if you are performing large-scale stress testing, it should be scheduled and worked out with the MapPoint operations team in advance. Moving your application is as simple as changing the service URL within your MapPoint Web Service proxy class, which I'll explain later in this chapter. Finally, MapPoint Web Service APIs are available on both normal (http) and secured (https) channels.

Accessing the Customer Services Site

When you request evaluation credentials to access MapPoint Web Service, you also receive a set of credentials to the Customer Services site, where you can manage your web service account. Figure 5-2 shows the Customer Services site reports page.

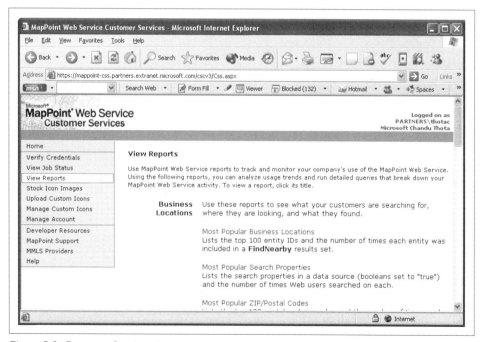

Figure 5-2. Customer Services site

I will discuss managing your custom data later in this chapter.

Preparing Your Development Environment

Now that you know how to get started with MapPoint Web Service, let's look at how to prepare your development environment to develop MapPoint Web Service applications.

Adding a Web Reference

If you are developing managed code applications using Visual Studio .NET 2003 or later, programming with MapPoint Web Service is fairly straightforward; you can access the MapPoint Web Service by using the Add Web Reference option from the project context menu, as shown in Figure 5-3.

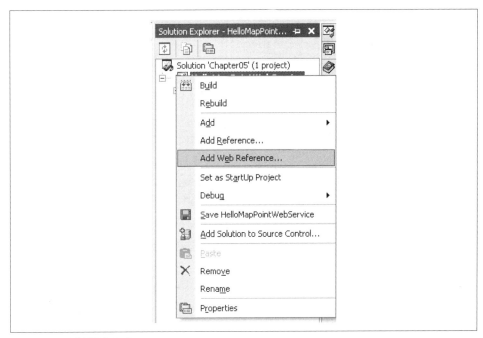

Figure 5-3. Add Web Reference context menu

When you see the Add Web Reference dialog window, type the MapPoint Web Service staging service URL in the URL textbox, as shown in Figure 5-4.

Once you type the staging service URL, and the WSDL document is parsed by Visual Studio, the documentation available within the WSDL document is shown in the preview pane. At this point, you can click the Add Reference button to add the MapPoint Web Service as a web reference to your project. When you click on the Add Reference button, Visual Studio .NET automatically creates a proxy class that can be used to program with MapPoint Web Service. By default, this proxy class is

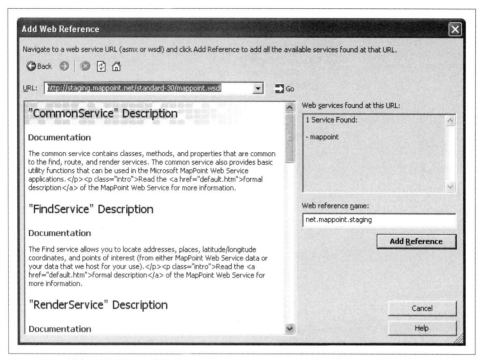

Figure 5-4. Adding MapPoint Web Service staging service as a web reference

named *Reference.cs* (or *Reference.vb*) and is placed within the Web References directory created inside the project's root directory (this file can only be seen when the Show All Files mode is enabled in the Visual Studio .NET solution explorer). The location of the *Reference.cs* file is shown in Figure 5-5.

 If you are developing your applications using VB 6.0/ASP in unmanaged code, you can still use MapPoint Web Service; however, in this case, you need to use either COM Wrappers around the managed code proxy class or the Microsoft SOAP Toolkit.

This class file contains all the C# (or VB.NET) equivalents of the interface definitions in the WSDL document. For example, the MapPoint Web Service WSDL document contains a complex type to represent latitude and longitude:

```
<s:complexType name="LatLong">
  <s:sequence>
    <s:element minOccurs="0" maxOccurs="1" default="0" name="Latitude"
            type="s:double" />
    <s:element minOccurs="0" maxOccurs="1" default="0" name="Longitude"
            type="s:double" />
  </s:sequence>
</s:complexType>
```

Figure 5-5. Proxy class file added by Visual Studio .NET

This type definition is represented as a class in the *Reference.cs* file:

```
public class LatLong {

  /// <remarks/>
  [System.ComponentModel.DefaultValueAttribute(0)]
  public System.Double Latitude = 0;

  /// <remarks/>
  [System.ComponentModel.DefaultValueAttribute(0)]
  public System.Double Longitude = 0;
}
```

As you can see, the previous class is a pure programmatic type representation of the XSD type defined in the WSDL document. You can use this type in your applications as you can any other .NET type. Not all the classes in the proxy file (*Reference. cs* or *Reference.vb*) are pure type definitions with just structure information like Lat- Long class; there are also some classes with methods that you can invoke from your application, including CommonServiceSoap, FindServiceSoap, RouteServiceSoap, and RenderServiceSoap, which are derived from the SoapHttpClientProtocol class from the System.Web.Service.Protocols namespace. Each class has a constructor with the service URL hardcoded within it.

If you are not familiar with service URLs, they are the so-called "service endpoints" of a web service that offer remote methods that can be invoked in a distributed environment. For MapPoint Web Service, there are four service endpoints that map to the service class types specified previously. The service URL and service class type mapping are shown in Table 5-1.

Table 5-1. MapPoint web service endpoints

Service name	Class type	Service URL
Common Service	CommonServiceSoap	*http://findv3.staging.mappoint.net/Find-30/Common.asmx*
Find Service	FindServiceSoap	*http://findv3.staging.mappoint.net/Find-30/FindService.asmx*
Route Service	RouteServiceSoap	*http://routev3.staging.mappoint.net/Route-30/RouteService.asmx*
Render Service	RenderServiceSoap	*http://renderv3.staging.mappoint.net/Render-30/RenderService.asmx*

Each one of the above four types (classes) has a constructor with the service URL hardcoded in the constructor; for example, if you look for the constructor of the FindServiceSoap class in the *Reference.cs* file, you will find the definition as follows:

```
public FindServiceSoap( )
{
    this.Url = "http://findv3.staging.mappoint.net/Find-30/FindService.asmx";
}
```

When you invoke any methods on the FindServiceSoap class, a proxy class for the Find Service, you are remotely invoking methods on the MapPoint Web Service servers. However, if you look closely, the previously stated service URL is pointing to the MapPoint Web Service staging servers. When you want your application to work with the MapPoint Web Service production servers, you must change the URL to point to the production WSDL and recompile the application, which can be an issue if you want to switch between the staging and production environments without re-compiling the application each time you switch. However, it has a very simple workaround—just make the service URL configurable.

Static versus dynamic service URL

After adding a web reference using Visual Studio .NET, you can choose whether to make the service URL dynamic, meaning that the proxy classes are generated such that the service URLs can be configured and managed via the *config* file (*web.config* for web applications and *app.config* for Windows applications). The default option is a static service URL. Figure 5-6 shows the web reference property to change the URL's behavior.

If you look at the FindServiceSoap constructor with the dynamic service URL option, the class constructor looks as follows:

```
public FindServiceSoap( )
{
    string urlSetting =
     System.Configuration.ConfigurationSettings.AppSettings["myapp.CommonService"];
    if ((urlSetting != null))
    {
```

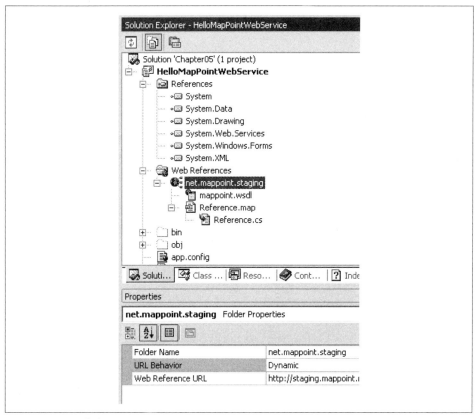

Figure 5-6. URL behavior setting

```
            this.Url = string.Concat(urlSetting, "FindService.asmx");
    }
    else
  {
    this.Url = "http://findv3.staging.mappoint.net/Find-30/FindService.asmx";
  }
}
```

The constructor first tries to obtain the service URL from the configuration file, and when it can't find it in the configuration file, it reassigns the static service URL. It is important to note that only the non-asmx part of the service URL is made configurable, while the asmx (for example, *FindService.asmx*) filename is still hardcoded. To support this dynamic URL behavior, add the following application key in the configuration file to access staging MapPoint Web Service:

```
<appSettings>
    <add key="myapp.CommonService"
        value="http://findv3.staging.mappoint.net/Find-30/"/>
    </appSettings>
</configuration>
```

Along similar lines, add the following value to access the production MapPoint Web Service:

```
<appSettings>
  <add key="myapp.CommonService"
    value="http://findv3.service.mappoint.net/Find-30/"/>
  </appSettings>
</configuration>
```

To enable dynamic service URL behavior, in an ideal world, you would select the Dynamic option for the URL Behavior property from Visual Studio .NET, and you would be all set—except that you aren't. The dynamic URL feature in Visual Studio .NET does *not* work for MapPoint Web Service. In Visual Studio .NET, the static/dynamic service URL feature was designed for web services with one service endpoint per WSDL document, which means there is only class that implements SoapHttpClientProtocol type per *Reference.cs* or *Reference.vb* file. Even if there is more than one service endpoint, the assumption was that the base URL of the service is always the same; however, for MapPoint Web Service, one WSDL actually points to four services that have three physical service endpoints. So, in order to make your MapPoint Web Service proxy class properly enabled with dynamic URL behavior, you need to do the following steps:

First, add the following key to your configuration file:

```
<appSettings>
  <add key="myapp.CommonService"
    value="http://findv3.staging.mappoint.net/Find-30/Common.asmx"/>
  <add key="myapp.FindService"
    value="http://findv3.staging.mappoint.net/Find-30/Find.asmx"/>
  <add key="myapp.RouteService"
    value="http://routev3.staging.mappoint.net/Route-30/Route.asmx"/>
  <add key="myapp.RenderService"
    value="http://renderv3.staging.mappoint.net/Render-30/Render.asmx"/>
</appSettings>
```

Next, modify the service soap class constructors as shown below:

CommonServiceSoap class:

```
public CommonServiceSoap() {
    string urlSetting =
      System.Configuration.ConfigurationSettings.AppSettings["myapp.CommonService"];
    if ((urlSetting != null)) {
        this.Url = urlSetting;
    }
    else {
        this.Url = "http://findv3.staging.mappoint.net/Find-30/CommonService.asmx";
    }
}
```

FindServiceSoap class:

```
public FindServiceSoap() {
    string urlSetting =
        System.Configuration.ConfigurationSettings.AppSettings["myapp.FindService"];
    if ((urlSetting != null)) {
        this.Url = urlSetting;
    }
    else {
        this.Url = "http://findv3.staging.mappoint.net/Find-30/FindService.asmx";
    }
}
```

RouteServiceSoap class:

```
public RouteServiceSoap() {
    string urlSetting =
      System.Configuration.ConfigurationSettings.AppSettings["myapp.RouteService"];
    if ((urlSetting != null)) {
        this.Url = urlSetting;
    }
    else {
        this.Url = "http://routev3.staging.mappoint.net/route-30/RouteService.asmx";
    }
}
```

RenderServiceSoap class:

```
public RenderServiceSoap() {
    string urlSetting =
      System.Configuration.ConfigurationSettings.AppSettings["myapp.RenderService"];
    if ((urlSetting != null)) {
        this.Url = urlSetting;
    }
    else {
      this.Url =
          "http://renderv3.staging.mappoint.net/render-30/RenderService.asmx";
    }
}
```

With this code in place, your application uses the service URL specified in the configuration file; when no configuration setting is found, staging service URLs are used instead.

Before we move to the next section, it is important to note that the modifications that you make to the *Reference.cs* or *Reference.vb* file are not persisted when you refresh the web reference. Be careful when you refresh the MapPoint Web Service web reference.

Storing your credentials securely

You need to secure MapPoint Web Service credentials through proper application configuration. MapPoint Web Service is a subscription-based web service, and each of your MapPoint Web Service requests must be authenticated to obtain a valid

Using WSDL.EXE

If you do not have Visual Studio .NET, you can still create a proxy class using the WSDL.EXE utility that ships with the .NET Framework SDK. You can find this utility in the bin directory of your .NET Framework SDK, and you can generate a proxy class by using the following command line:

WSDL.EXE /l:CS *http://staging.mappoint.net/standard-30/mappoint.wsdl /out:C:\MapPointWebServiceProxy.cs*

To generate a VB.NET proxy class, use the following command:

WSDL.EXE /l:VB *http://staging.mappoint.net/standard-30/mappoint.wsdl /out:C:\MapPointWebServiceProxy.vb*

response; for this purpose, MapPoint Web Service uses digest authentication. When you make a web service method call, you must assign your credentials to the service class.

For example, if you are invoking the `Find` method on the `FindServiceSoap` class, you need to assign your MapPoint Web Service credentials before calling the method:

```
//Create service class instance
FindServiceSoap findservice = new FindServiceSoap();
//Assign credentials - Do not do this!
findservice.Credentials =
      new System.Net.NetworkCredential("yourid", "yourpassword");
//Invoke the method
findservice.find(...);
```

In this code, the credentials are assigned using the `System.Net.NetworkCredential` object by hardcoding the user ID and password. There is a maintenance risk associated with this approach; for security reasons, you are required to change your Map-Point Web Service account password once every 45 to 60 days. When the time comes to change your password, you need to update the password and re-compile. In order to avoid these maintenance headaches, make the user ID and password configurable from a configuration file (*app.config* or *web.config*). Storing the user ID and password in clear text in the configuration file may pose a security threat, so you need to store the credentials in the configuration file in encrypted form.

There are multiple ways of encrypting your MapPoint Web Service ID and password. In any case, you must develop an encryption library using either the Data Protection APIs or Encryption APIs. The simplest way, of course, is to use the Windows Data Protection APIs (DPAPI). The DPAPI support two kinds of entropies: machine store entropy and user store entropy. In both cases, you can also provide private entropy, which adds an additional layer of security.

For a detailed description of DPAPI and Encryption API programming, along with other security recommendations for online web applications, check out the Microsoft Patterns and Practices Guide online: *http://msdn.microsoft.com/library/default.asp?url=/library/en-us/dnnetsec/html/SecNetHT07.asp?frame=true.*

Since the Data Protection APIs are Win32 APIs, you need to build C# wrappers around them. A sample implementation of the DPAPI is included in the companion material (project Chapter05); the DataProtectionCore sample class can be used for encrypting and decrypting the MapPoint Web Service ID and password. The following code shows how to encrypt any given string using the DataProtectionCore sample class:

```
public static string Encrypt(string input)
{
    Chapter05.EncryptionUtil.DataProtectorCore dp
    = new Chapter05.EncryptionUtil.DataProtectorCore(
        Chapter05.EncryptionUtil.Store.USE_MACHINE_STORE);
    byte[] encryptedBuffer =
        dp.Encrypt(System.Text.ASCIIEncoding.ASCII.GetBytes(input),
                null);
    return Convert.ToBase64String(encryptedBuffer);
}
```

Once the user ID and password are encrypted as shown in the previous code, you can store them in the configuration file as follows:

```
<configuration>
    <appSettings>
        <add key="MapPointWebServiceID"
            value="CAAAAAADZgAAqAAAQ....tYt9br2PpFHMOAXJd/tIJ/bbb74="/>
        <add key="MapPointWebServicePassword"
            value="AQAAANCMnd8BFdE ....HTPITIgU6FQcAXJd/tIJXteE8/wQ=="/>
    </appSettings>
</configuration>
```

Now your MapPoint Web Service ID and password are secure in the configuration file; however, your MapPoint Web Service application cannot readily use the encrypted MapPoint Web Service ID and password from the configuration file. You need to write a decrypt routine:

```
public static string Decrypt(string input)
{
    Chapter05.EncryptionUtil.DataProtectorCore dp
    = new Chapter05.EncryptionUtil.DataProtectorCore(
        Chapter05.EncryptionUtil.Store.USE_MACHINE_STORE);
    byte[] decryptedBuffer = dp.Decrypt(Convert.FromBase64String(input)
                        , null);
    return System.Text.Encoding.ASCII.GetString(decryptedBuffer);
}
```

In this routine, the input string is decrypted back to the original ASCII text. Once you have this decrypt routine, you can always read the encrypted MapPoint Web Service ID and password, decrypt them, and pass them to the MapPoint Web Service:

```
//Create a find service instance
FindServiceSoap find = new FindServiceSoap();
//Assign credentials
find.Credentials = new System.Net.NetworkCredential(
Decrypt(ConfigurationSettings.AppSettings["MapPointWebServiceID"]),
Decrypt(ConfigurationSettings.AppSettings["MapPointWebServicePassword"]));
. . .
//Find places
FindResults results = find.Find(spec);
```

The Encrypt and Decrypt methods are available in the companion material in the Chapter05 class.

Preauthenticate requests for performance gains

Finally, for performance reasons, always assign the PreAuthenticate property on the service SOAP class to True so that your application can avoid any extraneous round-trips to the server just for authentication. For example, on FindServiceSoap service class, set the value as shown:

```
findservice.PreAuthenticate = true;
```

Now that you know how to prepare your development environment for MapPoint Web Service application development, let's get into the MapPoint Web Service object model before we start programming.

Understanding MapPoint Web Service Object Model

MapPoint Web Service consists of four core services (or engines) that work with an array of map data sources. The core services depend on the data sources for location-oriented tasks, such as finding a place, finding an address, and so on. The data sources provide the necessary data to perform location-based tasks. In MapPoint Web Service, the data sources are organized based on geographic coverage; for example, the data source that contains the map data for all North American regions is MapPoint.NA. Figure 5-7 summarizes this discussion pictorially.

Along with the predefined MapPoint data sources, you can also add your business-specific data as custom data source. With this introduction, let's look at services and data sources in detail. If you recall from our earlier discussion, MapPoint Web Service consists of four integral service components, including:

- Common service
- Find service

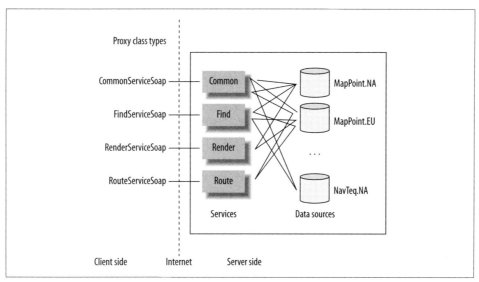

Figure 5-7. MapPoint Web Service core services

- Render service
- Route service

Let's look at each service in detail to understand more.

Common Service

The *common service* contains classes, methods, and properties that are common to the other three services (find, route, and render) or are basic utility functions, such as getting the version of the MapPoint Web Service, obtaining data source information, and calculating great circle distance.

This service is programmatically represented by the CommonServiceSoap class.

Find Service

The *find service* offers core find functionality, such as finding places, addresses, nearby points of interests, latitude/longitude coordinates, and geographic entities (such as parks, airports, and so on).

Some of the find methods only work with MapPoint Web Service data, and a few methods in the find service are designed to work only with your business-specific data (I will discuss this more later).

This service is programmatically represented by the FindServiceSoap class.

Render Service

The *render service* allows you to render maps of found places or addresses and routes, using your custom business data as pushpins. You can also use it to customize the map visualization, size, label font size, and so on.

This service is programmatically represented by the `RenderServiceSoap` class.

Route Service

The *route service* offers methods to calculate driving directions, routes, and route map views. Using this service, you can calculate the driving directions among any given waypoints.

This service is programmatically represented by the `RouteServiceSoap` class.

I will discuss these core services in detail in Chapters 6, 7, and 8, but for now let's look at another important concept in programming with MapPoint Web Service: data sources.

MapPoint Web Service Data Sources

Data sources are the essential building blocks on which the MapPoint Web Service functionality largely depends. At a macro level, data sources are simply stores that contain map data, geographic entity information, and point of interest information; this data is made accessible to the MapPoint Web Service via several APIs.

Data sources in MapPoint Web Service can be broadly categorized into two categories: MapPoint data sources and customer data sources. MapPoint data sources are compiled (created), hosted, and maintained by Microsoft; an example would be the geographic coverage map data source for North America, `MapPoint.NA`. A customer data source contains business specific data (such as Company A's 40 store locations in North America) compiled and maintained by customers (your company or you) but hosted by MapPoint Web Service. Next, let's look at each one of these data source types in detail.

MapPoint data sources

MapPoint Web Service makes more than 45 data sources available for you to program with. These 45 data sources can be broadly categorized into three types of data sources:

- Map data sources
- Point of interest data sources
- Icon data sources

Let's look at each data source type in detail.

Map data sources. Map data sources contain the geographic data used to perform location-oriented tasks, such as finding places and addresses, calculating routes, and rendering maps. All these data sources support *entities*, which represent the physical existing "things" in the real world, such as airports, coffee shops, libraries, roads and so forth. Table 5-2 shows the Map Data Sources available in MapPoint Web Service.

Table 5-2. Data sources and coverage areas

Data source name	Geographic coverage
MapPoint.NA	North America
MapPoint.EU	Europe
MapPoint.BR	Brazil
MapPoint.AP	Asia Pacific
MapPoint.World	World
MapPoint.Moon	Moon

 For a detailed list of entities supported by these data sources, check Microsoft's online documentation at *http://msdn.microsoft.com/library/ default.asp?url=/library/en-us/mappointsdk/html/index.asp*.

Point of interest data sources. MapPoint Web Service provides more than 35 point of interest data sources containing information about millions of businesses and organizations in several countries and regions in Europe and North America. The data contained in these data sources is organized by Standard Industry Code (SIC) and includes properties such as location and contact information. You can use these data sources to find businesses either by searching attributes (such as store names, cities, etc.) or by performing a proximity search around a given latitude and longitude (such as a store-locator).

Almost all point of interest data are provided by external data vendors (such as NavTeq or Acxiom) to Microsoft, so these data sources are named after their vendor's name. For example, if you want to use the point of interest data in the North American region provided by NavTeq, use the NavTeq.NA data source.

Along with the vendor-supplied point of interest data sources, MapPoint Web Service also provides one sample point of interest database for a fictitious company called Fourth Coffee Company. The data source for this company, MapPoint. FourthCoffeeSample, contains fictitious coffee shops across North America and Europe. This data source can be used as an example of how your business data can be uploaded as point of interest data to the MapPoint Web Service servers.

For a full list of point of interest data sources and the entity types supported by them, check Microsoft's online documentation at *http:// msdn.microsoft.com/library/default.asp?url=/library/en-us/mappointsdk/ html/index.asp.*

Icon data sources. MapPoint Web Service provides one icon data source, `MapPoint.Icons`, which contains over 900 icon images that you can use with the `Pushpin` object when rendering a map. Each icon image in the icon data source is indexed with either text or numbers that can be used in your application to indicate to use of a pushpin. Identify the icon data source for the pushpin image, and then render that pushpin using one of the map data sources.

 You can see a full list of icons in Microsoft's online documentation at *http://msdn.microsoft.com/library/default.asp?url=/library/en-us/ mappointsdk/html/mpn35devTablesIcons.asp*

Now that you know what MapPoint data sources are, let's look at customer data sources in detail.

Customer data sources

Customer data sources are created and maintained by customers that use MapPoint Web Service; however, the actual data is hosted on MapPoint Web Service servers. For example, if your company wants to show your office locations on MapPoint Web Service-rendered maps, you need to upload your office location data to Map-Point Web Service servers. The uploaded data is geo-coded and stored in a data source specifically associated with your MapPoint Web Service account. This data source is only accessible by you, and no other MapPoint Web Service customer can read or write to this data source.

You will be automatically assigned a custom data source with a pre-assigned name when you sign up for the MapPoint Web Service, but you can also create your own data sources apart from the pre-assigned one. For example, if your company name that is registered with MapPoint Web Service account is CompanyXyz, and your MapPoint Web Service ID is 6909, your default data source name will be CompanyXyz.6909, and any new data sources that you create will contain this name as their first part. If you want to create a new data source to store only your office locations with the name Office, the data source name will be CompanyXyz.6909.Office.

You can create new data sources either manually by using the Customer Services web site (*https://mappoint-css.partners.extranet.microsoft.com/cscv3/*) or programmatically by using the Customer Data Service API (see Chapter 8 for more details).

MapPoint Web Service currently supports only point of interest data and icon data for customer data sources, which means that you can only upload points of interests and your own icons to use in your MapPoint Web Service applications.

With so many data sources available in MapPoint Web Service, if you are wondering how to remember which data source performs each location-oriented task, you can find out the capabilities of any data source programmatically in MapPoint Web Service.

MapPoint Web Service data source capabilities

Each data source in the MapPoint Web Service environment supports certain location-oriented and non-oriented tasks. The data source capabilities define which data source supports each task.

The *data source capabilities* are the metadata defined for each data source, which you can use to find out which tasks that data source can support. For example, to find out what all the tasks that can be performed by the data source MapPoint.NA are, query the capabilities metadata using the CommonServiceSoap API. The data source capabilities are programmatically represented as the DataSourceCapability flagged-enumeration whose values are shown in Table 5-3.

Table 5-3. Data source capabilities enumeration

Name	Flag	Function
CanDrawMaps	1	Used to render maps
CanFindAddress	16	Used to find addresses
CanFindNearby	4	Used for proximity searching and attribute searching
CanFindPlaces	2	Used for finding places
CanRoute	8	Used for calculating driving directions and creating routes
HasIcons	32	Used for setting pushpin icons

Data source capabilities can be grouped by their basic functionality, such as find, render, and route, which we will look at in detail in the next couple of chapters; also remember that one single data source can support more than one of these capabilities. For example, the MapPoint.NA data source supports CanDrawMaps, CanFindAddress, CanFindPlace, and CanRoute.

Finally, before we wrap up our discussion on data sources, you need to be familiar with which languages these data sources support.

Language support in data sources

Although MapPoint Web Service currently supports 10 languages, not every data source currently supports all 10 languages. The core geographic coverage data sources,

`MapPoint.NA`, `MapPoint.EU`, `MapPoint.BR`, and `MapPoint.AP`, support the nine languages shown in Table 5-4.

Table 5-4. Languages supported in data sources

Language (Country/Region)	Language code	LCID
Dutch	nl	19
English	en	9
English—United States	en-US	1033
French	fr	12
German	de	7
Italian	it	16
Portuguese	pt	22
Spanish	es	10
Swedish	sv	29

The data sources `MapPoint.Moon` and `MapPoint.World` support all of these languages as well as Japanese (language code ja and LCID 1041).

It is also important to note that the `MapPoint.Icons` data source and all MapPoint point of interest data sources are available only in United States English.

Language preference in MapPoint Web Service is exposed via the `CultureInfo` object using the `UserInfoHeader` class, which you can use to set a desired culture Name or Lcid value from the previous table. The following code shows how to request a culture specific setting during a `FindService` call:

```
//Create a Find Service proxy class instance
FindServiceSoap find = new FindServiceSoap( );
//Assign Credentials
. . .
//Set culture specific settings
//Create the user info header instance
find.UserInfoFindHeaderValue = new UserInfoFindHeader( );
//Initialize culture value and set italian
find.UserInfoFindHeaderValue.Culture = new CultureInfo( );
find.UserInfoFindHeaderValue.Culture.Name = "it";
//Assign data source name and invoke find method
. . .
```

When you set a specific culture for the Find Service, the find results returned by the service are expressed in the culture requested. For example, if you try finding Redmond, WA with "en-US" as your culture information, you get Redmond, Washington, United States as the display name of the found entity, but the same find request returns the "Redmond, Washington, Stati Uniti d'America" when you set the culture info as "it" to get return results in Italian culture format.

Where Are We?

So far, we have looked at several aspects of MapPoint Web Service programming, such as getting started with MapPoint Web Service, understanding the core service components, security and configuration implications, MapPoint data sources and customer data sources, and data source capabilities and languages.

With this introduction as a background, the next chapter will take an in-depth look at MapPoint Web Service Find APIs.

CHAPTER 6

MapPoint Web Service Find APIs

The Find Service is one of the four core components of the MapPoint Web Service, allowing you to find places, addresses, points of interest around a given place or address, locations based on entity types, and so on. In this chapter, we'll take an in-depth look at the MapPoint Web Service Find APIs.

Understanding Find APIs

If you remember from our discussion in Chapter 5, the Find Service endpoint is located at the FindService.asmx, and the APIs available for Find Service are exposed via the FindServiceSoap class in the Web Service proxy (*Reference.cs* or *Reference.vb*). The FindServiceSoap class contains a number of find-related methods used for finding places, addresses, nearby points, and so on. Table 6-1 shows the methods exposed on the FindServiceSoap class.

Table 6-1. Methods available on the FindServiceSoap class

Method	Description
Find	Finds geographic locations in a specified data source based on a place name.
	Returns an array of results as a FindResults object. Maximum returned values is 500. Default number of returned results is 25.
FindAddress	Finds geographic locations in a specified data source based on an address.
	Returns an array of possible results as a FindResults object. Maximum returned values is 100. Default number of returned results is 25.
FindByID	Finds points of interest based on entity ID. The found results are returned as a FindResults object.
FindByProperty	Finds points of interest based on predefined or custom properties. This method is independent of the location information such as distance and latitude/longitude. The found results are returned as a FindResults object.

Table 6-1. Methods available on the FindServiceSoap class (continued)

Method	Description
FindNearby	Finds points of interest within a specified distance of a given latitude and longitude coordinate; returns an array of found points of interest ordered by proximity to a selected point as a FindResults object. Maximum returned values is 500. Default number of returned results is 25.
FindNearRoute	Finds points of interest within a specified distance from a route. The found results are returned as a FindResults object.
FindPolygon	Finds polygons in a specified data source, based on a FindPolygonSpecification object. The found results are returned as a FindResults object.
GetLocationInfo	Finds geographic entities and addresses for a specified latitude and longitude coordinate (also known as *reverse geocoding*). Returns an array of locations (Location objects). Maximum returned values is 250.
ParseAddress	Parses a specified address string and returns an Address object.

In this chapter, we will go over these methods in detail; first, let's look at some basic concepts.

The Anatomy of Find Methods

The FindServiceSoap class contains the methods related to find functionality, such as Find (place), FindAddress, FindNearby, and so on. Choose the appropriate find method based on your application's needs. All find methods share a common signature pattern as shown in the following example, where **XXX** can be an address or a nearby entity):

```
FindResults FindXXX( FindXXXSpecifiction )
```

A find method, no matter what type of find it is, always returns the results in the form of the FindResults instance, which tells you how many matches are found for your find query along with the actual location matches. The actual location matches are represented as an array of FindResult class instances, each of which contains an instance of matched location as a Location object that provides information such as latitude/longitude, address, entity type, and the confidence score of the location match. It is important to note that Location instances in MapPoint Web Service expose the actual latitude and longitude information of the physical location and a corresponding best possible map view associated with it.

Unlike the consistent output returned by all find methods, the input argument is unique to each find method type, so the specification corresponding to each find type is represented by specific types. For example, if you are using the FindAddress method, use the FindAddressSpecification object as an input argument; if you are using the FindNearby method, use the FindNearbySpecification object as an input argument. Each input specification object contains three core parts:

Color Plate 1 (Figure 3-2). Shaded area map

Color Plate 2 (Figure 3-5). Multiple symbol map

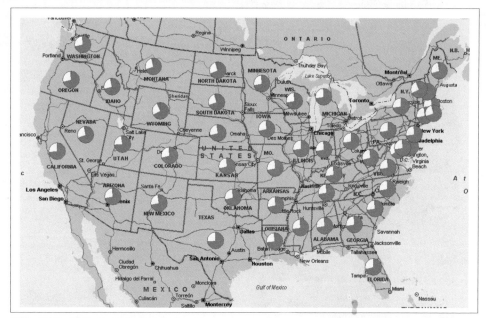

Color Plate 3 (Figure 3-6). Pie chart map

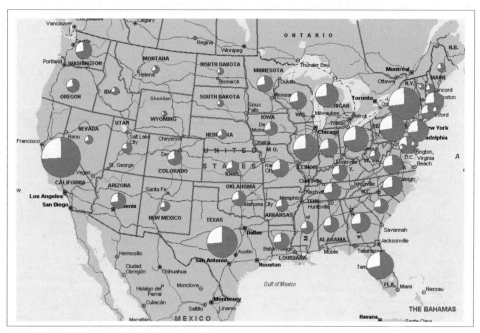

Color Plate 4 (Figure 3-7). Sized pie chart map

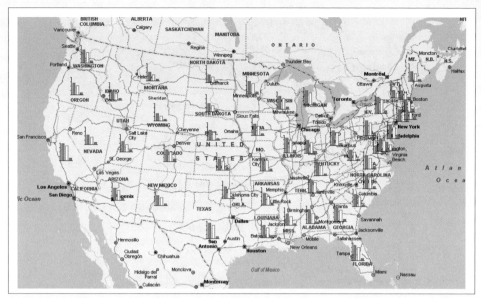

Color Plate 5 (Figure 3-8). Column chart map

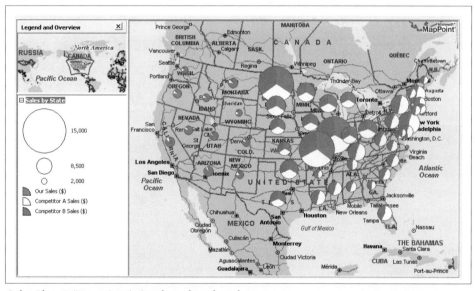

Color Plate 6 (Figure 3-16). Sized pie chart for sales comparison

Color Plate 7 (Figure 3-17). A 60-minute drivetime zone around O'Hare Airport

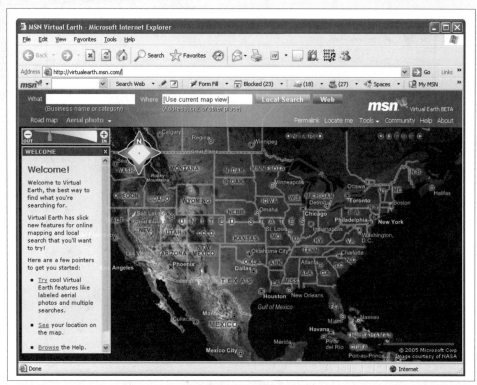

Color Plate 8 (Figure 11-1). Virtual Earth map

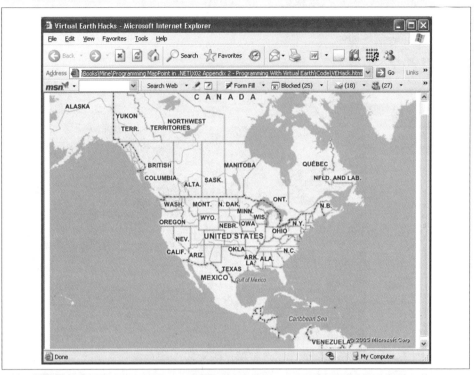

Color Plate 9 (Figure 11-2). Map Control: Absolute positioning in the body

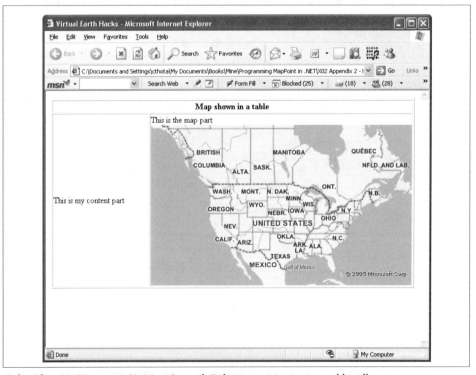

Color Plate 10 (Figure 11-3). Map Control: Relative positioning in a table cell

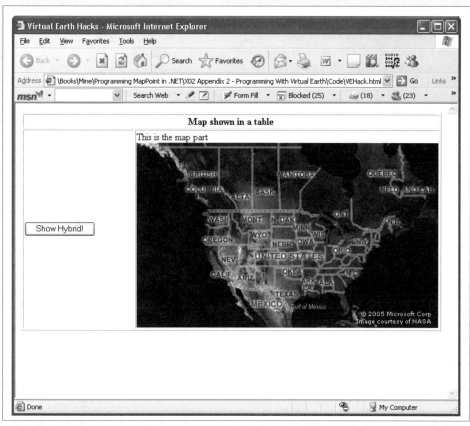

Color Plate 11 (Figure 11-4). Switch map style using the SetMapStyle method

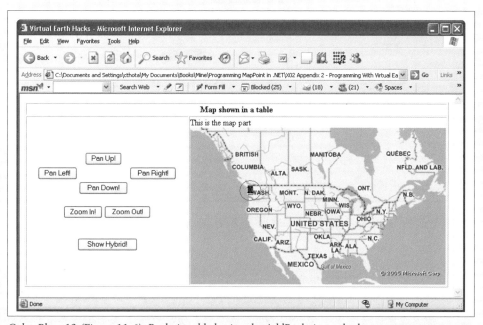

Color Plate 12 (Figure 11-6). Pushpin added using the AddPushpin method

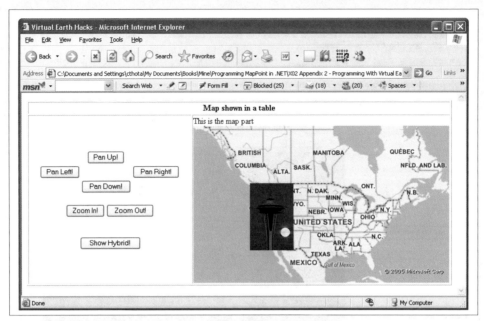

Color Plate 13 (Figure 11-7). The Space Needle shown as an icon over Seattle

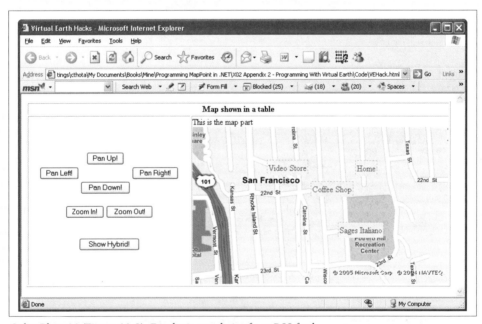

Color Plate 14 (Figure 11-8). Displaying pushpins from RSS feed

Data source name

This field is found across all specification objects for all find methods and indicates which data source to use for the find.

Find-type specific arguments

This field is unique to each find method and includes arguments such as input address for an address search, place name for a place search, and so forth.

Optional FindOptions *object*

This field is found across all the specification objects for all find methods and can be used to control the output behavior.

For example, the FindAddressSpecification object, which is passed to the FindAddress method to find an address, contains the following three fields:

DataSourceName

A string value that represents the data source to be used for the address search (such as MapPoint.NA and MapPoint.EU).

InputAddress

An instance of the Address class that represents the input address to be used in the search.

Options

An instance of the FindOptions class that can be used to control the behavior of the results returned by any find method. This argument is optional.

Any specification object used in the find method is consistently modeled in this format.

By now, I'm sure you are wondering how the FindOptions object can alter the behavior of the results returned by the find method. Let's look briefly at this object so that you understand its purpose. The FindOptions object contains the following fields:

Range

This field can be used to control the number of returned matches and the starting index of the returned results. For example, if you are searching for a place and your search yields 200 matches, you can request to return only the top 10 results. Along the same lines, you can also request a range of results starting with any valid index (such as from 21 to 30), which is very useful if you are displaying the search results from multiple pages (the typical pagination feature for displaying data). This field is of type FindRange.

ResultMask

By default, all find methods return latitude/longitude, entity type information, address, and best map view information for each matched location of the input query. You can use this field to mask the unwanted information returned from a find method. For example, if you are searching for a place and looking only for latitude/longitude information, you can prevent the find method from returning any other information using this mask. The ResultMask field is of type FindResultMask and is an enumeration.

SearchContext

This field indicates the entity ID within which you want to perform your search. In this case, the entity ID represents a geographic area to which you want to limit your search. Assigning an entity to provide a search context returns more relevant matches faster. This field is of type `Integer`.

ThresholdScore

Each result returned by any find method contains a score indicating the level of confidence in the match. Using this field, you can filter out the low-confidence results below the specified `ThresholdScore`. This field is of type `Double`, and the valid values are between zero and one (low confidence to high confidence).

Using the `FindOptions` object, you can tailor the results returned by the find method according to your application's needs. There is one more interesting tidbit you may want to know about the `FindOptions` object: when you use it in your find method calls, you actually positively impact the performance (and possibly the economics) of your application. I will discuss the details at the end of this chapter in the section on optimizing your find calls performance.

Now that you know the anatomy of the Find Service, let's look briefly at entities and the entity relationships model in MapPoint Web Service before we get into coding aspects of the Find Service.

Understanding Entities and Entity Relationships

Entities in MapPoint Web Service represent real *things* (e.g., countries, cities, landmarks, schools) that exist in the real world. All entities are first-class citizens in the world of MapPoint Web Service; they have type definitions, carry their own identities, enjoy entity-level find capabilities, maintain relationships, and in some cases even persist their identity across different versions of MapPoint Web Service.

Before I get into too many details, here is an example to help you understand this concept. Consider the United States: in MapPoint Web Service, the country is an entity with entity ID 244; the states contained within it are represented as children entities to the United States entity. Counties, cities, and towns within these states are represented as the children entities to the state entities; this parent-child relationship continues down to things like bridges, roads, parks, and schools. Figure 6-1 summarizes this discussion by showing the entity relationships for the town of Redmond, WA.

How do all the entities and entity relationships defined in MapPoint Web Service help you? The short answer is that you can issue smarter and more focused find queries to find things that suit your needs. Many applications require you to drill down into the subgeographic areas starting with a larger coverage. To continue with our United States example, you may want to develop an application where your customers start with the United States, go to the 50 states in the United States, pick a state

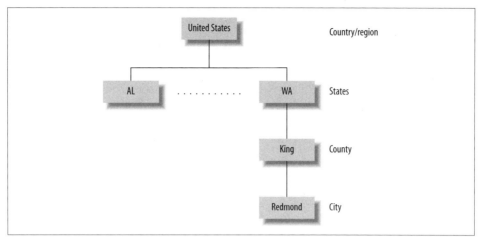

Figure 6-1. Entity parent-child relationships

and get all counties, pick a county and get all cities, and pick a city and get all interested entities within it. Entities are used to issue queries with limited geographic context (such as all states within the United States). You can also add your own custom entity types (or points of interest) that allow you to find places using the entities and entity relationships.

Programmatically, all entities are represented by the `Entity` class, and the definition of an entity type is represented by the `EntityType` class. The `EntityType` objects define the schema of an entity type, including the name, parent, and valid properties of an entity type.

Each physical entity represented using the `Entity` class has an ID, a `DisplayName`, which is a long descriptive name, and a common short `Name`. An `Entity` object also indicates the type of entity using the `TypeName` field (which is a `string`); this type name maps to a corresponding `EntityType` object. Finally, an `Entity` object exposes a collection of properties specific to that entity type as an array of `EntityPropertyValue` objects. The `EntityPropertyValue` object is a simple name value pair that gives you the name and value of the property. If you know an entity's properties, you can issue queries to find entities by their properties—we will look at this concept later in this chapter.

If you find the concepts of `EntityType` and `Entity` confusing, think of it this way: an `EntityType` defines the schema, and an `Entity` represents the instance of a "thing" with that schema (similar to the difference between a class and an object). For example, the entity type `PopulatedPlace` defines the schema and parent-child relationships for geographic entities such as cities, towns, and villages; the entity type `PopulatedPlace` is represented by the `EntityType` class programmatically. The city of Paris is an entity of type `PopulatedPlace`, so the actual city is represented by an `Entity` object programmatically with a `TypeName` of `PopulatedPlace`.

Data Sources and Entity Types

Because entities in MapPoint Web Service are real things, they are contained in corresponding data sources for any given geographic extent. For example, if you consider the North American map data source MapPoint.NA, entities within the United States, Canada, Mexico, and Puerto Rico are contained in this data source. The only way to get to these entities is by knowing which entity types are supported by a particular data source. To find out which entity types are supported by a given data source, use the CommonServiceSoap method to get a list of the entity types supported by different data sources.

Getting all supported entity types within a data source

You can get a list of entity types supported by a specific data source using the CommonServiceSoap.GetEntityTypes method, which takes the data source name as an input argument and returns an array of EntityType objects. The following code snippet shows how to get all entity types defined in the MapPoint.NA data source:

```
//Define an instance of CommonServiceSoap class
CommonServiceSoap commonService = new CommonServiceSoap();
//Assign credentials
. . .
//Define a local entitytypes array
EntityType[] entityTypes;
//Datasource in question
string datasource = "MapPoint.NA";
//Get all entity types using the GetEntityTypes method
entityTypes = commonService.GetEntityTypes(datasource);
//Now loop through each entity display the name, parent
foreach(EntityType et in entityTypes)
{
    Console.WriteLine(et.Name);
    Console.WriteLine(et.Definition);
    Console.WriteLine(et.ParentName);
}
```

Along the same lines, you can also get all entity type definitions for all data sources in MapPoint Web Service environment:

```
//Create an instance of common service soap
CommonServiceSoap commonService = new CommonServiceSoap();
//Assign credentials
. . .
DataSource[] dataSources;
dataSources = commonService.GetDataSourceInfo(null);
foreach (DataSource ds in dataSources)
{
    String datasource = ds.Name;
    //Now get entity type info for this data source
    //Define a local entitytypes array
    EntityType[] entityTypes;
    //Datasource in question
```

```
//Get all entity types using the GetEntityTypes method
entityTypes = commonService.GetEntityTypes(datasource);
//Now loop through each entity display the name, parent
foreach(EntityType et in entityTypes)
{
   Console.WriteLine(et.Name);
   Console.WriteLine(et.Definition);
   Console.WriteLine(et.ParentName);
}
}
```

I use the `CommonServiceSoap.GetDataSourceInfo` method to get a list of data sources and then the `CommonServiceSoap.GetEntityTypes` method to get a list of entity types defined in each data source.

Once you know the names of the entity types, you can use the Find APIs, which we will see in detail later in the chapter, to customize the find queries to find only particular entity types.

Data Sources and Countries/Regions

Just as each data source in MapPoint Web Service supports different entity types, there is country/region level mapping to each MapPoint data source. The geographic extent (or the geographic coverage) of each data source is predefined by MapPoint Web Service. For example, the data source `MapPoint.NA` has a geographic extent of the United States, Canada, Mexico, and Puerto Rico. In the same way, other data sources have different supported country listings. You don't need to remember which data source needs to be used for each country name—you can use the `CommonServiceSoap` class for this purpose as well.

Countries/Regions and Their Entity IDs

Before we get into the details of how to query data source geographic extents and how to map a country to a supported data source programmatically, you need to understand how the countries/regions are managed in MapPoint Web Service Data sources. Each country/region is given an entity ID, which is a unique integer number. Each country/region also holds an ISO2- and ISO3-compatible code associated with that country. All of this information is represented as the `CountryRegionInfo` object, which exposes several properties, such as `EntityID`, `FriendlyName`, `Iso2`, `Iso3`, and `OfficialName`. If you take the United States, for example, the country region information is organized as follows:

`Entity ID`	244
`FriendlyName`	United States
`Iso2`	US
`Iso3`	USA
`OfficialName`	United States of America

An instance of the CountryRegionInfo class that represents a valid country/region also includes the centroid latitude/longitude of the country. The entity ID for the United States is 244, and it does not change across different versions of the MapPoint Web Service, so you can safely hardcode this ID into your applications for any United States–specific find queries.

To get the country/region information using MapPoint Web Service, use the CommonServiceSoap.GetCountryRegionInfo method:

```
//Create Common Service SOAP Class instance
CommonServiceSoap commonsoap = new CommonServiceSoap( );
//Assign credentials
. . .

//Get country region info
CountryRegionInfo[] countryregioninfos =
        commonsoap.GetCountryRegionInfo(null);

//Do some processing
foreach(CountryRegionInfo crinfo in countryregioninfos)
{
  . . .
}
```

The GetCountryRegionInfo method takes an array of entity IDs as integers; however, in the previous code example, I'm passing null in order to get country/region information for all the countries listed in MapPoint Web Service. Similarly, if you want only country/region information for the United States, your call would look like this with 244 entity ID as an input argument:

```
//Get country region info
CountryRegionInfo[] countryregioninfos =
        commonsoap.GetCountryRegionInfo(new int[] {244});
```

You get only one CountryRegionInfo object (that corresponds to the United States) back from this method.

Note that since the list of county/region information does not change that frequently, it is good idea to store it in an in-memory data structure (such as a Hashtable with the entity ID as the key) in your applications to avoid round trips to the MapPoint Web Service.

Querying for Geographic Extent for a Data Source

Now that you know how the country/region information is organized in MapPoint Web Service, let's look at how to get a list of countries supported by different data sources.

The geographic extent of the countries supported by a particular data source is defined using the EntityExtent field of the DataSource object. The DataSource.

EntityExtent field is an array of integers that represent the corresponding country entity IDs. The following code snippet shows how to get the geographic extent of the data source MapPoint.NA:

```
//Create Common Service SOAP Class instance
CommonServiceSoap commonsoap = new CommonServiceSoap( );
//Assign credentials
. . .

//Get Data Source Info for MapPoint.NA
DataSource[] datasources =
        commonsoap.GetDataSourceInfo(new string[] {"MapPoint.NA"});
//Get entity extent
int[] extents = datasources[0].EntityExtent;
```

The geographic extent is expressed using the country/region entity IDs discussed in the previous section. To get the name of the country that each entity ID corresponds to, call the CommonServiceSoap.GetCountryRegionInfo method.

Programmatically Mapping a Country/Region to a Data Source

So far, I have shown how to get supported countries given a MapPoint Web Service data source. A common application scenario would be the other way around: choosing an appropriate data source for a given country. To programmatically map a country/region to a data source, you need to identify the task for which you need the data source, deciding whether you want a data source to find a place, find an address, calculate a route, or render a map. You can use the DataSourceCapability enumeration discussed in Chapter 5. Once you have the DataSourceCapability figured out, you can get an appropriate MapPoint Web Service data source name using the following code:

```
private string[] GetDataSources(string countryRegionName,
                                DataSourceCapability capability)
{
    if(countryRegionName == null || countryRegionName.Length <= 0)
        throw new Exception(
          "Invalid country/region name; country/region
             name cannot be null or empty.");

    ArrayList datasourceList = new ArrayList( );

    //Now loop through the list of data sources and
    //see what data source fits the purpose
    foreach(DataSource datasource in datasources)
    {
      if(((int)datasource.Capability & (int)capability) != 0)
       {
          //OK, this data source has the capability, but does it support the
          //entity extent (the country that we need a data source for?)
          int[] entityextent = datasource.EntityExtent;
```

```
        //Now loop through each entity extent and compare the input name
        foreach(int entityid in entityextent)
         {
           //Now look up using the entity id to see if the input
           //country/region name matches any entity extent
           //in this case I'm country region information
           //cached in a Hastable
           if(this.countryRegionsTable[entityid] as string
                        == countryRegionName.Trim())
            {
              //Found a match for both requirements
              //Return the name
               datasourceList.Add(datasource.Name);
               break;
            }
         }
     }
   }

   if(datasourceList.Count <= 0)
      throw new Exception(
         "No data source found to match your needs for this country.");

   //Return a sorted list
   datasourceList.Sort();

   return datasourceList.ToArray(typeof(String)) as string[];
}
```

The previous function returns an array of suitable MapPoint Web Service data source names. The countryRegionsTable is a Hashtable containing cached country/region information indexed on the entity IDs. The algorithm used in this function is pretty simple: first, find a data source with matching capability, and then get the geographic extent for that data source and see whether there is a match with the input country/region name. You can also find the code for this function, along with other functionalities discussed in this section, in the Chapter 6 solutions on the companion material.

With this introduction to find methods, entity types, and data source relationships, let's look at how to perform various spatial queries using Find Service.

Working with Find Methods

MapPoint Web Service Find Service is programmatically exposed as part of the FindServiceSoap class, which has many find methods including Find, FindAddress, FindNearby, and FindById. Choose an appropriate find method based on your application's requirements. In this section, let's look in detail at each find method offered by the MapPoint Web Service Find Service.

Finding Places

To find geographic entities and places by their names, use the FindServiceSoap.Find method. This method takes the FindSpecification as an input argument and returns the FindResults object as a return value. The FindSpecification wraps several values, including the input place name as a string, the data source to be used for searching the place, and an array of entity type names to find. Table 6-2 shows the fields of the FindSpecification class.

Table 6-2. Fields of the FindSpecification class

Field	Description
DataSourceName	A string representing the name of the data source in which to search for a place. For example, MapPoint.NA is the data source used for finding places in North America.
EntityTypeNames	An array of strings representing the names of the entity types to find.
InputPlace	The place name to find.
Options	The search options (FindOptions object), which includes the range of results, the threshold score of results returned, the search context, and a flag to identify which objects are desired in the returned results.

The data source used for the Find method must have the CanFindPlaces capability. The FindResults return value indicates the number of matches for the input place query using the FindResults.NumberFound field; when no results match your query, the NumberFound field is set to zero. All matches are exposed via the FindResults. Results field as a collection of FindResult objects; each FindResult object returned as a match contains a Location object that wraps the location information and a score indicating the level of confidence in the match. A valid Location object provides one or all of the following: address information, entity information, latitude/longitude information, and best map view information.

Next, let's look at the Find method details: the following code shows how the Find API can be used to find all places named Redmond:

```
//Create find service soap
FindServiceSoap findsoap = new FindServiceSoap();
//Assign credentials
. . .

//Create FindSpecification
FindSpecification findspec = new FindSpecification();
//Assign data source
findspec.DataSourceName = "MapPoint.NA";

//Assign input place to search
findspec.InputPlace = "Redmond";

//Now call find
FindResults findresults = findsoap.Find(findspec);
```

```
//Assign found count
foreach(FindResult findresult in findresults.Results)
{
    //Display results
    . . .
}
```

With options set at their defaults, this query returns the following seven places named Redmond:

```
Redmond, Washington, United States
Redmond, Oregon, United States
Redmond, Western Australia, Australia
Redmond, Larimer, Colorado, United States
Redmond, Butler, Pennsylvania, United States
Redmond, Sevier, Utah, United States
Redmond, Mason, West Virginia, United States
```

Finding more default matches

These results include places from both the United States and Australia. By default, the find threshold score is set to 0.85, which means that any find match with a confidence score of less than 0.85 is not returned. So, to get more results for this query, you can simply decrease the threshold score using the FindOptions.ThresholdScore field:

```
//Create find options
findspec.Options = new FindOptions();

//Set threshold score to zero
findspec.Options.ThresholdScore = 0;
```

With the threshold score set to zero, the same query for Redmond yields 32 results of which only the following first 25 are returned:

```
Redmond, Washington, United States
Redmond, Oregon, United States
Redmond, Western Australia, Australia
Redmond, Larimer, Colorado, United States
Redmond, Butler, Pennsylvania, United States
Redmond, Sevier, Utah, United States
Redmond, Mason, West Virginia, United States
Redmond Fall City Road Park (park), Washington, United States
Redmond Park (park), Cedar Rapids, Iowa, United States
Redmond Park (city park), Yonkers, New York, United States
Redmond Branch Library (library), Redmond, Oregon, United States
Redmond Chamber of Commerce (tourist information office), Redmond, Oregon, United
States
Redmond Chamber of Commerce (tourist information office), Redmond, Washington, United
States
Redmond City Hall (city hall), Redmond, Oregon, United States
Redmond City Hall (city hall), Redmond, Washington, United States
Redmond Community Cemetery (cemetery), Redmond, Washington, United States
Redmond Corner, Oneida, New York, United States
```

```
Redmond Cut (pass), California, United States
Redmond District Court (courthouse), Redmond, Washington, United States
Redmond Elementary School (school), Redmond, Washington, United States
Redmond High School (school), Redmond, Washington, United States
Redmond Junior High School (school), Redmond, Washington, United States
Redmond Memorial Cemetery (cemetery), Redmond, Oregon, United States
Redmond Municipal Court (courthouse), Redmond, Oregon, United States
Redmond Municipal Court (courthouse), Redmond, Washington, United States
```

Returning more find results

By default, MapPoint Web Service always returns only 25 results at once, but you can get a maximum of 500 results using the FindOptions.Range field:

```
//Create find options
findspec.Options = new FindOptions();
//Set result count
findspec.Options.Range = new FindRange();
//Set to the maximum count
findspec.Options.Range.Count = 500;
```

After adding this code to the Find code, you get all 32 results returned by the Find method.

Selectively finding entity types

Notice that this list includes all kinds of entities, such as city halls, parks, libraries, and schools in the result list. Imagine for now that you need only a list of cities named after Redmond—you need to tell MapPoint Web Service that you are only looking for city entity matches to your query. You can do this using the FindSpecification.EntityTypeNames field. The EntityTypeNames field is an array of strings that represents the entity type names that the Find method needs to look for. Since you are only interested in cities named Redmond, pass the entity type name PopulatedPlace:

```
//Assign entities to search
fndspec.EntityTypeNames = new string[] {"PopulatedPlace"};
```

A call to the Find method with this addition returns the following nine cities named Redmond:

```
Redmond, Washington, United States
Redmond, Oregon, United States
Redmond, Western Australia, Australia
Redmond, Larimer, Colorado, United States
Redmond, Butler, Pennsylvania, United States
Redmond, Sevier, Utah, United States
Redmond, Mason, West Virginia, United States
Redmond Corner, Oneida, New York, United States
Redmondville, Iron, Missouri, United States
```

Even though your threshold score is 0 and there are 500 returned results requested, by assigning specific entity type, the find is narrowed down to 9 results from the original 32 results.

Limiting search to a geographic area

Notice that the above list contains cities from both the United States and Australia. If you are looking only for cities in the United States and need to instruct MapPoint Web Service to limit the search within a geographic boundary, using the FindOptions.SearchContext field you can limit the search to a particular geographic area. The SearchContext field is an integer value that represents the entity ID of a specific geographic area. Since you are specifically looking for cities named Redmond in the United States, the context ID should be set to the United States country entity ID 244. The following code shows the addition of search context to the find request:

```
//Assign country context for United States
findspec.Options.SearchContext = 244;
```

With this addition, the search now only returns the following 8 results:

```
Redmond, Washington, United States
Redmond, Oregon, United States
Redmond, Larimer, Colorado, United States
Redmond, Butler, Pennsylvania, United States
Redmond, Sevier, Utah, United States
Redmond, Mason, West Virginia, United States
Redmond Corner, Oneida, New York, United States
Redmondville, Iron, Missouri, United States
```

The list now includes only cities in the United States.

Finding geographic entities with no input place name

The Find method is very powerful because it allows you to find geographic entities without actually specifying a place name. Example queries include: "Find all states in the United States" and "Find all airports in Australia." You can perform these queries based on entity type names, geographic contexts, or by assigning the input place name a null value. The following code shows how to get all state names in the United States:

```
//Create find service soap
FindServiceSoap findsoap = new FindServiceSoap();
//Assign credentials
. . .

//Create FindSpecification
FindSpecification findspec = new FindSpecification();
//Assign data source
findspec.DataSourceName = "MapPoint.NA";
```

```
//Assign null to input place
findspec.InputPlace = null;

//Create find options
findspec.Options = new FindOptions( );
//Set result count
findspec.Options.Range = new FindRange( );
//Set to the maximum count
findspec.Options.Range.Count = 500;

//Set threshold score to zero
findspec.Options.ThresholdScore = 0;

//Assign state entity type to search
fndspec.EntityTypeNames = new string[] {"AdminDivision1"};

//Now call find
FindResults findresults = findsoap.Find(findspec);
//Assign found count
foreach(FindResult findresult in findresults.Results)
{
    //Display results
    . . .
}
```

This search results in 51 entities (50 states and Washington D.C.).

To explore more on data sources, entity types, and entity based finds, I have included an application, MapPoint Web Service Data Source Browser, on the companion material as part of the Chapter06 sample solution. Figure 6-2 shows a screenshot of the application with results for the query "Find all airports in Australia."

Finally, it is important remember that, due to performance reasons, for any find query, the maximum number of results returned (FindResult objects) is 500; you cannot issue a find query such as "Find all cities in the world," but if you do have such a requirement, I recommend breaking down the query to get a manageable result set that is less than or equal to 500 each time. An example of such implementation would be to provide a browse functionality where your customers can select a country first, a state second, a county third, and then find all cities within that county without hitting any maximum result count issues, since you are confining your query to a smaller, limited geographic area.

Finding Addresses

While the FindServiceSoap.Find method works well for finding places and geographic entities in general, it doesn't offer any help to find addresses; use the FindServiceSoap.FindAddress method for that purpose.

Like any FindServiceSoap.Find method, the FindServiceSoap.FindAddress method takes a specification object of type FindAddressSpecification and inputs a data

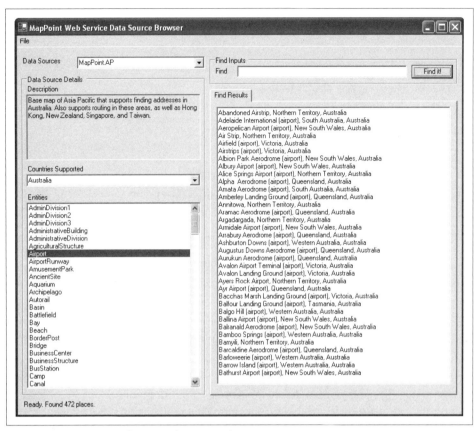

Figure 6-2. MapPoint Web Service data source browser

source name field of type String and an Options field of type FindOptions as input fields to expose an InputAddress field of type Address. Table 6-3 shows the fields exposed on the FindAddressSpecification object.

Table 6-3. Fields exposed in the FindAddressSpecification class

Field	Description
DataSourceName	A string representing the name of the data source in which to search for the address. Example: MapPoint.NA.
InputAddress	The input address to be found. This field is of type Address class.
Options	The search options (FindOptions object), which include the range of results, the threshold score of results returned, and a flag to identify which objects are desired in the returned results.

To use a data source to find addresses, it must have the CanFindAddress capability. An address in MapPoint Web Service is always represented as a valid instance of the Address object; the Address class provides fields such as AddressLine, PrimaryCity, SecondaryCity, Subdivision, PostalCode, CountryRegion to represent a valid address for all countries/regions. When used as input, the address line information of an address is optional. When an address is returned as an output, the address object also provides a formatted address string via the FormattedAddress field.

Say you want to find the following address:

```
1 Microsoft Way
Redmond, WA 98052
US
```

First, you need to create an Address object:

```
//Create an address object
//And assign address values
Address address =  new Address();
address.AddressLine = "1 Microsoft Way";
address.PrimaryCity = "Redmond";
address.Subdivision = "WA";
address.PostalCode = "98052";
address.CountryRegion = "US";
```

Once the Address object is ready, you can find the address information (such as latitude/longitude, best map view information, etc.) using the FindServiceSoap. FindAddress method:

```
//Create a find address specification object
FindAddressSpecification findAddressSpec = new FindAddressSpecification();
//Assign input address
findAddressSpec.InputAddress = address;
findAddressSpec.DataSourceName = "MapPoint.NA";

//Call the find address method
FindResults foundAddressResults =
            findService.FindAddress(findAddressSpec);

//Process found results
if (foundAddressResults.NumberFound > 0)
{
    if(foundAddressResults.Results[0].FoundLocation.LatLong != null)
      {
        //Process latitude/longitude information
        . . .
      }
}
```

The previous code snippet assumes that you have the FindService object available with proper credentials assigned.

The FindAddressSpecification also exposes the Options field so that you can control the behavior of the locations returned by this method using the FindOptions class; the FindOptions behavior that we have looked at in the Find method still holds true for this method except that you can only get a maximum of 100 results instead of 500.

Finding Points of Interest Around a Location

To find points of interest around a given location, use the `FindServiceSoap.FindNearby` method. The `FindNearby` method works only with data sources that have the `CanFindNearby` capability. As a general rule of thumb, only the point of interest data sources supplied by data vendors such as `NavTeq` and `Acxiom` have this capability; data sources such as `MapPoint.NA` and `MapPoint.EU` do not support the `FindNearby` method.

Like any other find service method, the `FindNearby` method also takes a specification of type `FindNearbySpecification` class. The `FindNearbySpecification` object takes information such as the data source name, input location around which you want to find points of interest (as a latitude/longitude), distance to be covered around the original location to find points of interest, and entity types you want to find. Table 6-4 gives an idea of the fields presented in the `FindNearbySpecification` object.

Table 6-4. Fields in a FindNearbySpecification object

Field	Description
DataSourceName	Data source name as a string.
Distance	The distance from the `LatLong` property.
Filter	The filter (`FindFilter` object) to apply to the results. In other words, it is the specific entity type, properties, and values that the returned results must match.
LatLong	The latitude and longitude coordinate (`LatLong` object) of the point around which the search is made.
Options	The search options (`FindOptions` object), which include the range of results and a flag to identify which objects are desired in the returned results.

To find all ATMs around the address 1 Microsoft Way, Redmond, WA, get the latitude and longitude information using the `FindServiceSoap.FindAddress` method, and call `FindServiceSoap.FindNearby` with one of the point of interest data sources (in this case, I chose to use `NavTech.NA`) and the entity type name for ATM, `SIC3578`:

```
//Create find service soap instance
FindServiceSoap findService = new FindServiceSoap( );
//Assign credentials
. . .

//Define findnearby specification
FindNearbySpecification findNearbySpec  = new FindNearbySpecification( );
//Assign a data source
findNearbySpec.DataSourceName = "NavTech.NA";
//Since you are looking for ATMs, assign ATMs entity type
findNearbySpec.Filter = new FindFilter( );
//Assign entity type for ATMs
findNearbySpec.Filter.EntityTypeName = "SIC3578";
```

```
//Set the distance in miles
findNearbySpec.Distance = 1;
//Assign the location around which you want to find ATMs
findNearbySpec.LatLong = new LatLong( );
findNearbySpec.LatLong.Latitude = 47.6;
findNearbySpec.LatLong.Longitude = -122.33;

//Call findnearby method
FindResults foundResults;
foundResults = findService.FindNearby(findNearbySpec);
//Process the results
foreach(FindResult fr in foundResults.Results)
{
  . . .
}
```

The previous code finds ATMs around the specified address within one mile using the NavTech.NA data source; of course you could have also used other points of interest data sources from Acxiom.

Next, say that you are working for a banking company and building an ATM locator application; obviously you would display your company's ATMs around any specified address. It is possible to display your ATMs with the FindNearby method, but since none of the MapPoint data sources or vendor data sources (NavTech, Acxiom, and so on) know about your bank's ATMs specifically, you need to provide a data source for MapPoint Web Service to use with the FindNearby method. That's when the customer data sources come into the picture.

 If you do not want to upload your data to MapPoint servers due to security reasons, you can implement your own FindNearby functionality using SQL Server—see Appendix C for more details.

Customer data sources—displaying your data

When you sign up for MapPoint Web Service, you are assigned space on MapPoint servers to upload your business data (such as points of interest and icons) to use with the FindNearby method. Using this space, you can create a maximum of 25 data sources on the MapPoint Web Service servers. For example, if your company has banks and ATMs, you would create two data sources with one assigned to each entity type. So, with multiple data sources, you can use different data source files for different types of data. Having said that, there are certain requirements for creating your own data sources:

- The combined size of all your data sources cannot exceed 2 gigabytes.

- Each data file that you upload (that contains a number of location records) cannot exceed 100 megabytes.

- Each data source and the entities it contains must have an entity type, which is a user-defined alphanumeric string, and an entity id, which is an integer.
- The total number of searchable non-Boolean cells (or entity properties) per data source cannot exceed 8.75 million.

Every entity (or location record) has three required properties (EntityID, latitude, and longitude) and six additional properties created by the MapPoint Geocoder sevice, including `MatchCode`, `MatchedAddress`, `MatchedMethod`, `EditedLocationUTC`, `EditedPropertyUTC`, and `InputModified`. All of these properties are treated as searchable non-Boolean cells, so the number of entities contained in a single data source cannot exceed 972,222 (8.75 million cells divided by 9 non-Boolean, searchable properties per row). The number of Boolean cells per entity in a data source cannot exceed 200.

There are additional requirements applicable for entity property types in MapPoint Web Service, such as number of characters per field and type of characters per field.

 For more information on the customer data formatting requirements, see the "Requirements for Custom Location Data" section from the MapPoint Web Service Customer Services site help documentation.

There are two options for uploading and downloading your entities to and from the customer services site: you can either use the Customer Services site web UI, or programmatically upload and download using the Customer Data Service Web Service, which is discussed in detail in Appendix A. Once you upload your custom data, you can use the `FindServiceSoap.FindNearby` method to use it against your own data.

Finding Points of Interest Along a Route

To find points of interest along a given route, use the `FindServiceSoap.FindNearRoute` method. The `FindNearRoute` method works only with data sources that have the `CanFindNearby` capability. As with the `FindNearby` method, only the point of interest data sources supplied by data vendors such as `NavTeq` and `Acxiom` have this capability; data sources such as `MapPoint.NA` and `MapPoint.EU` do not support the `FindNearRoute` method.

 You can read more about calculating routes using `RouteServiceSoap` in Chapter 7.

Like any other find service method, the `FindNearRoute` method also takes a specification of type `FindNearRouteSpecification` class. The `FindNearRouteSpecification` object takes information, such as the data source name, input route (as a `Route` object) around which you want to find points of interest, and distance to be covered along the route, and uses it to find points of interest and entity types you want to find. Table 6-5 gives an idea of the fields presented in the FindNearRouteSpecification object.

Table 6-5. Fields in a FindNearRouteSpecification object

Field	Description
DataSourceName	The data source name as a string
Distance	The distance from the Route property
Filter	The filter (FindFilter object) to apply to the results; that is, the specific entity type, properties, and values that the returned results must match
Route	The route from which the points of interest are searched
Options	The search options (FindOptions object), which include the range of results and a flag to identify which objects are desired in the returned results

Say you want to find all the coffee shops along the route that you are planning for a road trip. First, calculate your route using the RouteServiceSoap class; next, call the FindServiceSoap.FindNearRoute with one of the point of interest data sources (I chose to use MapPoint.FourthCoffeeSample) and the entity type name for coffee shops, FourthCoffeeShops, as follows:

```
FindServiceSoap findService =
                new FindServiceSoap();
findService.Credentials =
            new System.Net.NetworkCredential(myMapPointUserId,
                                        mySecurePassword);

RouteServiceSoap routeService = new RouteServiceSoap();
routeService.Credentials =
            new System.Net.NetworkCredential(myMapPointUserId,
                                        mySecurePassword);

//Route between two locations
LatLong[] latLongs = new LatLong[2];
latLongs[0] = new LatLong();
latLongs[1] = new LatLong();
latLongs[0].Latitude = 52.5;
latLongs[0].Longitude = 13.1;
latLongs[1].Latitude = 52.51;
latLongs[1].Longitude = 13.11;

//Calculate route
Route myRoute =
routeService.CalculateSimpleRoute(latLongs,
                        "MapPoint.EU",
                        SegmentPreference.Quickest);

//Create near route specificiation
FindNearRouteSpecification findnearroutespec =
                        new FindNearRouteSpecification();
```

```
findnearroutespec.DataSourceName = "MapPoint.FourthCoffeeSample";
findnearroutespec.Filter = new FindFilter();
findnearroutespec.Filter.EntityTypeName = "FourthCoffeeShops";
findnearroutespec.Distance = 20;
findnearroutespec.Route = myRoute;

FindResults foundResults;
foundResults = findService.FindNearRoute(findnearroutespec);

//Process the results to display on a map
...
```

This code finds the coffee shops around the specified route within 20 miles from the beginning of the route using the MapPoint.FourthCoffeeSample data source; you could use different point of interest data sources from Acxiom or NavTech or even your own data source.

Finally, note that the distance must always be greater than 0.1 miles (0.160934 kilometers) and less than 25 miles (40.2336 kilometers).

Finding Custom Entity Types

MapPoint Web Service has a certain set of methods that find entities using their identities and properties, but these methods can only be used with the custom data uploaded to the MapPoint servers. These methods are particularly useful for queries that depend on nonspatial attributes. For example, if you upload all your ATMs to MapPoint servers and you want to display all ATMs in the city of Chicago, or only the ATM that has the unique identity of 13324, these methods can be either simple non-spatial queries or spatial queries. In this section, let's look at these find methods that can be used with your custom data.

Find entity by identity

You can use the FindServiceSoap.FindByID method to find entities using their entity IDs. Like any other find method, this method takes a specification object of type FindByIDSpecification and returns a FindResults object. The FindByIDSpecification object takes up to 500 IDs as input parameters. Table 6-6 shows the fields exposed on the FindByIDSpecification object.

Table 6-6. Fields exposed in the FindByIDSpecification object

Field	Description
DataSourceName	Data source name as a string
EntityIDs	Array of unique entity IDs; only points of interest with matching entity IDs are returned, while the rest are ignored

Table 6-6. Fields exposed in the FindByIDSpecification object (continued)

Field	Description
Filter	The filter (FindFilter object) to apply to the results, which includes the specific entity type, properties, and values that the returned results must match
Options	The search options (FindOptions object), which may include the range of results and a flag to identify which objects are desired in the returned results

The following code shows how to use the FindByID method:

```
//Create a Find Service proxy
FindServiceSoap findService = new FindServiceSoap();
//Assign credentials
. . .

//Define find by id specification
FindByIDSpecification findbyidspec = new FindByIDSpecification();

//Assign a data source name
findbyidspec.DataSourceName = "MapPoint.FourthCoffeeSample";

//Apply a filter for entity name
findbyidspec.Filter = new FindFilter();
findbyidspec.Filter.EntityTypeName = "FourthCoffeeShops";

//Now assign the entity IDs to find
int[] arrayID = {-21835, -21836};
findbyidspec.EntityIDs = arrayID;

//Call FindById method
FindResults foundResults;
foundResults = findService.FindByID(findbyidspec);
```

The found entities are returned in the same order that the entity IDs are passed in, but you can override this sorting behavior using the FindFilter.SortProperties. Assuming that you want to sort the ATMs in the previous FindByID method by their associated bank name (assuming that there is a property called ParentBankName), the method call looks as follows:

```
//Create a Find Service proxy
FindServiceSoap findService = new FindServiceSoap();
//Assign credentials
. . .

//Define find by id specification
FindByIDSpecification findbyidspec = new FindByIDSpecification();

//Assign a data source name
findbyidspec.DataSourceName = "MapPoint.FourthCoffeeSample";

//Apply a filter for entity name
findbyidspec.Filter = new FindFilter();
findbyidspec.Filter.EntityTypeName = "FourthCoffeeShops";
```

```
//Specify what properties to be used to sort the found results
SortProperty[] sortproperties = new SortProperty[1];
sortproperties[0] = new SortProperty();
//Assign the property name to be sorted on
sortproperties[0].PropertyName = "ParentBankName";
//Specify the sort direction: Ascending or Descending
sortproperties[0].Direction = SortDirection.Descending;

//Assign sort specification to the find filter
findbyidspec.Filter.SortProperties = sortproperties;

//Now assign the entity ids to find
int[] arrayID = {-21835, -21836};
findbyidspec.EntityIDs = arrayID;

//Call FindById method
FindResults foundResults;
foundResults = findService.FindByID(findbyidspec);
```

As you can see, the SortProperties method is an array, so you can sort the resulting entities by more than one attribute if needed.

It is important to remember that the points of interest entity identities are not persisted from one version of the MapPoint Web Service to another, so if you hardcode the point of interest entity IDs into your application, when you upgrade to a newer MapPoint Web Service, your application may break. To make it easy to distinguish between positive and negative IDs, all negative entity IDs (such as entity ID -21835 for a coffee shop) are not persisted across versions, while the positive IDs are (such as entity ID 244 for the United States).

Finding entity by properties

Many times, you want to query for entities based on their properties—for example, finding all ATMs in the city of Chicago, or all coffee shops that accept credit cards. In this case, the query is based solely on the entity properties, and you should use the FindServiceSoap.FindByProperty method for this purpose. The FindByProperty method takes a specification object of type FindByPropertySpecification, which takes the queries to find entities using their properties. Table 6-7 shows the fields exposed on the FindByPropertySpecification object.

Table 6-7. Fields in the FindByPropertySpecification object

Field	Description
DataSourceName	Name of the data source as a string
Filter	The filter (FindFilter object) to apply to the results; that is, the specific entity type, properties, and values that the returned results must match
Options	The search options (FindOptions object), which may include the range of results and a flag to identify which objects are desired in the returned results

The following code shows how to use these expressions to find entities using the FindByProperty method:

```
//Create a find service soap proxy class
FindServiceSoap findService = new FindServiceSoap();
//Assign credentials
. . .

//Create find by property specification
FindByPropertySpecification findbypropspec = new FindByPropertySpecification();

//Define find by property specification
findbypropspec.DataSourceName = "MapPoint.FourthCoffeeSample";
//Assign a filter
findbypropspec.Filter = new FindFilter();
//Specify the entity type that you are looking for
findbypropspec.Filter.EntityTypeName = "FourthCoffeeShops";

//Now define and assign the expression
findbypropspec.Filter.Expression = new FilterExpression();
findbypropspec.Filter.Expression.Text = "PrimaryCity = {0} AND IsWiFiHotSpot";
findbypropspec.Filter.Expression.Parameters = new object[] {"Chicago"};

FindResults foundResults;
foundResults = findService.FindByProperty(findbypropspec);
```

The resulting expression from this code is "PrimaryCity = 'Chicago' AND IsWiFiHotSpot", which means to return only coffee shops in the city of Chicago that have WiFi Hotspots available. Even though the filter expressions look and behave like SQL expressions, there are limitations that you need to be aware of:

- The expression text should never contain the values that are being compared, but the text must provide the placeholders for all non-Boolean value types. Placeholders are represented by "{nn}" where n is an integer between 0 and 9.

- The comparison operators LIKE and NOT LIKE support only the "Starts with" condition.

- Maximum length of the expression text is limited to 2,000 characters.

- No more than one level of nesting (parenthesis) is allowed.

- A maximum of 10 non-Boolean comparisons and a maximum of 10 sub-clauses are allowed.

- A maximum of 50 total comparisons per expression is allowed.

Next, let's look at an example expression: you want to find all coffee shops in the *city of Chicago* that have *a seating capacity greater than 20* or *that are open 24 hours a day* whose names *start with the letter C*. The expression to pass for the FindByProperty method would be: (City={0} AND SeatingCapacity>{1}) OR (StoreType={2} AND Name LIKE {3}) with the arguments Chicago, 20, Open 24 Hours and C.

Now that you know how to use the find service APIs, let's look at some of the common service methods that are relevant to the finding places, addresses, and entities.

Finding Polygons

With the find methods, you have seen how to find places, addresses, and points around a place or address, but all you have been finding so far are points (latitude and longitude coordinates). You may have a requirement to find polygons in situations with queries such as: "find all polygons that contain a point (latitude/longitude)" or "find all polygons that have spatial relationship with a rectangle." In order to accomplish such tasks, use the FindServiceSoap.FindPolygon method.

 To learn more about polygons, refer to Appendix B.

Like any find method in Find Service, the FindPolygon method takes the FindPolygonSpecification object as an argument and returns a valid FindResults object. The FindPolygonSpecification object provides a way for you to specify arguments such as data source name and spatial filter. Table 6-8 shows the fields exposed by the FindPolygonSpecification class.

Table 6-8. Fields of the FindPolygonSpecification class

Field	Description
DataSourceName	Name of the data source as a string
Filter	The filter (FindFilter object) to apply to the results, including the specific entity type, properties, and values that the returned results must match
Options	The search options (FindOptions object), which may include the range of results and a flag to identify which objects are desired in the returned results
SpatialFilter	The spatial filter (SpatialFilter object) to apply to the results

One interesting field from Table 6-8 is the SpatialFilter field; this field is of type SpatialFilter class, and it defines the spatial relationship between polygons, points, and rectangles. The SpatialFilter class is an abstract class, and there are two classes that derive this abstract class to define two specific spatial relationships:

LatLongSpatialFilter

Defines a spatial filter that returns only polygons that include the point specified by the LatLong object. This is used in specifying a spatial filter to find polygons that contain a certain point. This class has only one field that takes the target point as a LatLong object. The following code shows how to specify a LatLongSpatialFilter to find polygons that contain a given set of latitude and longitude coordinates:

```
//Create a new instance of LatLongSpatialFilter
LatLongSpatialFilter filter = new LatLongSpatialFilter();
//Assign the given latitude and longitude values
Filter.LatLong = new LatLong();
Filter.LatLong.Latitude = 47.44;
Filter.LatLong.Longitude = -122.55;
```

LatLongRectangleSpatialFilter

Defines a spatial filter that returns polygons related to the LatLongRectangle specified via the BoundingRectangle field. The relation between the polygons and the rectangle is determined by the PolygonRectangleRelation field. This field is of type SpatialRelation enumeration and has two values that are shown in Table 6-10. The LatLongRectangleSpatialFilter class is used in defining a spatial filter to find polygons that fall within or touch a rectangle. The following code shows how to define this spatial filter to find all polygons that fall within a rectangle:

```
//Define a new instance of LatLongRectanglSpatialFilter
LatLongRectangleSpatialFilter rectangleFilter =
                new LatLongRectangleSpatialFilter();

//Define a bounding rectangle with north east and south west
//corners
LatLongRectangle boundingRectangle = new LatLongRectangle();
boundingRectangle.Northeast = new LatLong();
boundingRectangle.Northeast.Latitude = 47.44;
boundingRectangle.Northeast.Latitude = -122.56;

boundingRectangle.Southwest = new LatLong();
boundingRectangle.Southwest.Latitude = 41.44;
boundingRectangle.Southwest.Latitude = -119.56;

//Now assign bounding rectangle to the filter
rectangleFilter.BoundingRectangle = boundingRectangle;
//Define the spatial relationship to be
//"find polygons inside the rectangle"
rectangleFilter.PolygonRectangleRelation =
                SpatialRelation.WithinArea;
```

Now that you know how to define spatial filters, let's look at the FindPolygon method in action, using the relations shown in Table 6-9.

Table 6-9. SpatialRelation enumeration

Item	Description
WithinArea	Returns all polygons contained entirely within the specified rectangle
TouchesArea	Returns all polygons that come into contact with the specified rectangle

Use the FindPolygon method to find Polygons that either contain a specified point or are spatially related to a rectangle. The y method takes the FindPolygonSpecification object as an argument, as shown in the following code:

```
//Create an instance of FindServiceSoap and assign
//Credentials
FindServiceSoap findService
                    = new FindserviceSoap( );
//Assign your credentials
. . .

//Create an instance of FindPlygonSpecification
FindPolygonSpecification findPolySpec
                    = new FindPolygonSpecification( );

//Create a new instance of LatLongSpatialFilter
LatLongSpatialFilter filter = new LatLongSpatialFilter( );
//Assign the given latitude and longitude values
Filter.LatLong = new LatLong( );
Filter.LatLong.Latitude = 47.44;
Filter.LatLong.Longitude = -122.55;

//Assign the spatial filter to the find polygon specification
findPolySpec.SpatialFilter=filter;

//Assign your polygon data source
findPolySpec.DataSourceName="your polygon data source";

//Define what kind of entities you are looking for
FindFilter findfilter = new FindFilter( );
findfilter.EntityTypeName = "your entity name";
findPolySpec.Filter = findfilter;

//Call Find Polygon
FindResults findResults = findService.FindPolygon(findPolySpec);
//Now get the polygon entities
foreach(FindResult findResult in findResults.Results)
{
    //Get polygons that matched the query
    Console.WriteLine(String.Format(
                    "Polygon Entity Matched with ID: {0}",
                     findResult.FoundLocation.Entity.ID)
                );
}
```

Now that you have the entity IDs of polygons that match your spatial filter criteria, you can use that information either to render the polygons (covered more in Chapter 8) or to perform any other processing to suit your business needs.

Getting Entities from Latitude/Longitude

We have looked at find service methods that take place names and addresses and return the corresponding latitude/longitude and other entity information. To find entity (or address) information for any given latitude/longitude, use the FindServiceSoap.GetLocationInfo; it gives you entity information for any given latitude and longitude. The GetLocationInfo method takes the GetInfoOptions object as an argument, along with a latitude/longitude and a data source name as a string. The GetLocationInfo object gives you control to decide which entity types you want using the GetInfoOptions.EntityTypesToReturn field; you also have the option to obtain addresses for a given latitude/longitude (if available) using the GetInfoOptions. IncludeAddresses flag. The following code shows how to use the GetLocationInfo method:

```
//Create a find service soap proxy
FindServiceSoap findService = new FindServiceSoap( );
//Take an example lat long information that you want to
//find using GetLocationInfo
LatLong latlong = new LatLong( );
latlong.Latitude = 47.682;
latlong.Longitude = -122.132;

//Define get info options object
GetInfoOptions options = new GetInfoOptions( );
//I'm looking only for cities
options.IncludeAllEntityTypes = false;
options.EntityTypesToReturn = new string[] {"PopulatedPlace"};

//Define a field to hold returned locations
Location[] returnedLocations;
//Call GetLocationInfo with "MapPoint.NA" data source
returnedLocations = findService.GetLocationInfo(latlong, "MapPoint.NA", options);
//Get entity information
for(int i = 0; i < returnedLocations.Length; i++)
{
    Console.WriteLine(returnedLocations[i].Entity.DisplayName);
}
```

When I'm querying for corresponding entities for the latitude/longitude, I limit my query to a city (the entity name PopulatedPlace) using the EntityTypesToReturn field; it is important to remember that you must set the IncludeAllEntityTypes to false when you request specific entities.

This method is not a direct inverse to the FindServiceSoap.FindAddress method, so if you call the FindServiceSoap.FindAddress method to obtain latitude/longitude for an address and pass that latitude/longitude to the FindServiceSoap.GetLocationInfo method, the resulting address won't match your original address because of the internal representation of the address data; in MapPoint data sources, addresses are stored in address range blocks along the streets, and the interpolation algorithms are used to calculate the address for a given latitude/longitude and vice versa. So, the addresses returned by the `FindServiceSoap.GetLocationInfo` are approximations of the original address; in fact, this method returns an array of four possible addresses for any given latitude/longitude in increasing order of the distance from the given latitude/longitude.

Parsing Addresses

We have seen various capabilities of Find Service to find places, addresses, nearby entities, and points of interest, but what happens if you have an address in an unstructured or unformatted form? What if you want to create an application where your users can type their address in a textbox without worrying about the formatting? How do you parse the address field to understand various parts of the address? You can use the `FindServiceSoap.ParseAddress` method for these purposes. The `ParseAddress` method takes two arguments, input address as a string and an optional country/region name, and returns an `Address` object for valid addresses. For example, if you have the address 1 Microsoft Way, Redmond, WA in string format, you can use the `ParseAddress` method to parse it into an `Address` object:

```
//Create a web service proxy
FindServiceSoap findService  = new FindServiceSoap();
//Assign credentials
. . .

//Parse a string into a valid address object
Address address =
    findService.ParseAddress("1 Microsoft Way, Redmond", "United States");
```

One of the greatest advantages of this method is that you can implement one user interface that can perform both find place and find address depending on what users input without having to design two different UIs for two different purposes.

Asynchronous Programming with Find Service

When developing applications using Web Service, keep in mind that you are making a network round-trip with every method call, which has serious implications on your application's performance in terms of responsiveness. For example, since calls over the network take a long time to return, you don't want to block the UI thread for your Windows application. This is where the asynchronous programming patterns come to the rescue. Using the .NET framework, it is easy to call Web Service methods asynchronously. So, let's see how you would implement a `FindServiceSoap.Find` method call asynchronously.

Asynchronous Programming for Windows Applications

When you generate the MapPoint Web Service proxy class using Visual Studio .NET, it also generates the necessary methods for asynchronous programming. For example, if you look for the `FindServiceSoap.Find` method, you also find the `FindServiceSoap.BeginFind` and `FindServiceSoap.EndFind` methods in the proxy class. The Begin and End method pairs enable the asynchronous programming patterns for your web service client applications. Using these methods is really easy; in a synchronous scenario, your Find call looks like the following code:

```
//Call the Find Method
FindResults findresults = findsoap.Find(findspec);
//Now display find results
DisplayFindResults(findresults);
```

If this code is running on the UI thread, it does not get to the `DisplayFindResults` method until the Find method call completes and returns the `findresults` value; during this period, users of your application may find it unresponsive. To avoid this situation, create a worker thread and call the Find method using it so that your UI thread is free during this long network round-trip. In fact, that's exactly what the `BeginFind` and `EndFind` methods do behind the scenes. To implement the previous code using asynchronous methods, you would do something similar to the following:

First, define a callback method for your asynchronous method calls:

```
private void FindServiceCallback(IAsyncResult ar)
{
   FindServiceSoap findSoap
      = ar.AsyncState as FindServiceSoap;
   if(findSoap == null)
      return;
   FindResults findresults = findSoap.EndFind(ar);
   DisplayFindResults(findresults);
}
```

Next, modify your find call to become an asynchronous `BeginFind` call:

```
//Async call to find
AsyncCallback callback = new AsyncCallback(FindServiceCallback);
findsoap.BeginFind(findspec, callback, findsoap);
```

The `BeginFind` invokes the Find method on a different (worker) thread and passes a pointer to the `FindSeviceCallback` method as a callback method; when the Find method returns a `FindResults` instance, the callback delegate is invoked so that the `FindServiceCallback` method gets executed on the UI thread again. In the `FindServiceCallback` method, you need to obtain the `FindResults` returned by the Find method by calling the `EndFind` method and displaying them. Keep in mind that the HTTP session is kept alive during this asynchronous operation behind the scenes—this pattern is asynchronous at your application thread level but not at the HTTP communication level.

Asynchronous Programming for Web Applications

Multithreaded programming works well for Windows applications if you are calling web services, but wouldn't it be nice to adopt this asynchronous programming model for web applications as well? Wouldn't it be convenient to develop more responsive applications without doing a complete page refresh? You can do these things with a combination of JavaScript and `Msxml2.XMLHTTP` ActiveX control. The use of JavaScript with asynchronous XML messaging is called *Asynchronous JavaScript and XML*, or simply *AJAX*. While AJAX terminology is fairly new to web application development, the use of JavaScript and XMLHTTP is not. In this section, I will go over some scenarios where AJAX can be used in your web applications to improve the overall user experience.

AJAX-Enabling Your Web Applications

In theory, AJAX is no different from any other web application that uses HTTP request and response—however, adding asynchronous calls from your web page to the web server that uses JavaScript dramatically improves the user's experience.

To understand how to leverage AJAX in your MapPoint Web Service web applications, you need to understand how AJAX works, which is explained in the following section.

For AJAX to work, you need three core components:

- A web page (*htm*, *aspx*, etc.) that hosts JavaScript containing asynchronous calls to the web server
- XMLHTTP ActiveX control enabled from the client web browser
- A server-side component that can process HTTP GET requests using the query string parameters

All three of these components together make an AJAX implementation. Usually, the server-side component is an HTTP Handler, since it renders only the script instead of conventional HTML. An HTTP Handler is similar to an ISAPI extension, and you need to implement the IHTTPHandler interface to develop an ASP.NET HTTP Handler. These concepts are shown pictorially in Figure 6-3.

Since designing a web page and writing JavaScript are straightforward tasks, let me delve into the server-side components that are required for AJAX.

For example, you want to develop a web application that implements "Find a place" functionality; in this application, when users search for a place, generally MapPoint Web Service comes back with a list of possible matches to be displayed for disambiguation. Conventionally, you would implement this process using the following series of actions:

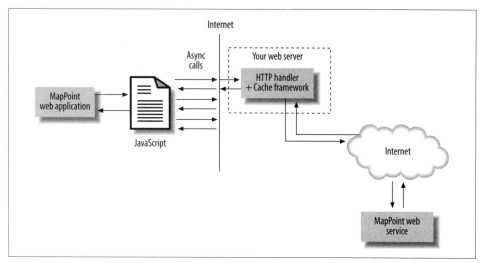

Figure 6-3. AJAX architecture for MapPoint Web Service applications

1. Have the user type in a place and click a button to find it.

2. Post the request to the server page that invokes the MapPoint Find Service calls to find the place.

3. If there is more than one match to the input string, display them in a list box where the user can select the place that he is looking for.

4. Post that selection back to the server page that invokes MapPoint Render Service to get a map.

The same application can be implemented with AJAX to improve the overall user experience:

1. As the user types each character into the input place textbox, make an asynchronous call to the server to fetch matching places and display them in a dynamic drop-down list.

2. Have the user select the place she is looking for.

3. Post that selection back to the server page to display a map.

An implementation of this application results in the user interface shown in Figure 6-4.

The experience of using the application is far richer with AJAX when compared to a traditional MapPoint find web application. Next, let's see how to implement this application.

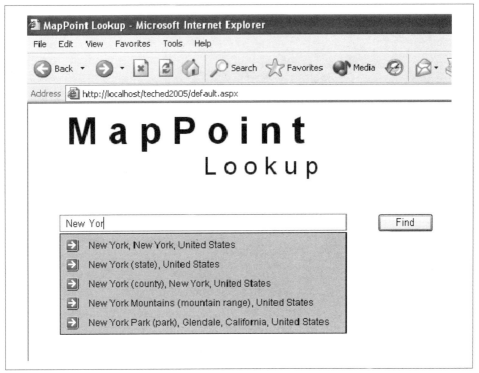

Figure 6-4. Place lookup using MapPoint Web Service and AJAX

Implementing MapPoint Lookup AJAX Application

The implementation of this application consists of developing the following:

- The web page that hosts JavaScript that makes async calls to the server
- An HTTP Handler that processes async requests and returns proper JavaScript
- JavaScript that makes async calls.

Let's look at each step in detail.

Developing the web page. In this step, simply create an ASPX page that has the input place textbox with the following event wired up:

```
<input id="place" onkeyup="DoLookup()" type="text" size="56">
```

The input textbox "place" has the onkeyup event wired up to the DoLookup( ) method, which will be called each time the user types in a character.

Also define a div element to hold the results; this element acts as a dynamic list box to show results. If no results are found, the div is hidden as an invisible element on the page, and if search results are found, the div is visible for the user to select the desired find result:

```
<div id="placepanel" UNSELECTABLE='on' style="VISIBILITY: hidden;"></div>
```

The next step is to implement the HTTP Handler that processes find requests on HTTP GET.

Developing the HTTP Handler. To develop an HTTP Handler, you need to implement the System.Web.IHttpHandler interface, which requires overriding the ProcessRequest method that handles the incoming request.

 You can read more about implementing HTTP Handlers on MSDN at *http://msdn.microsoft.com/library/default.asp?url=/library/en-us/cpref/ html/frlrfsystemwebihttphandlerclassprocessrequesttopic. asp?frame=true.*

In this method, you check an incoming request's query string to see whether there is any place name; if a place name exists, make a FindServiceSoap.Find method call to return matching find results. The results need to be formatted so that the calling JavaScript can understand and display the contents. So, I decided to do the result formatting on the server side in the HTTP handler and simply return the find results that are display-ready. The following code shows the ProcessRequest method implementation:

```
public void ProcessRequest(HttpContext context)
{
    //See incoming place query string parameter
    string input = context.Request["place"] as string;

    if(input == null || input == string.Empty)
    {
        context.Response.Write("var invalidInputFound = 0;");
        return;
    }

    //If there is a valid input call MapPoint Web Service
    try
    {
        //See if this has a cache item:
        string response = context.Cache[input] as string;
        if(response != null)
        {
            context.Response.Write("ShowLocation(" + response + ");");
            return;
        }
        else
        {
            String[] findings = null;
            //Call MapPoint Web Service and get the place names into
            //the findings string array
            . . . .

            //Now write back appropriate JavaScript
            if(findings == null || findings.Length == 0)
            {
```

```
            context.Response.Write("var novalidOutputFound = 0;");
            return;
        }

        System.Text.StringBuilder sb = new System.Text.StringBuilder();
        int count = findings.Length;
        sb.Append("\"");
        for(int i =0; i< count; i++)
        {
            //Open div and add id
            sb.Append("<div id='findresult_" + i.ToString() + "' ");
            //Add unselectable = on
            sb.Append(" UNSELECTABLE='on' ");
            //Add findresult content
            sb.Append("<img align=absmiddle src=arrow.gif border=0> " +
                        findings[i].Trim().Replace("'", "\'"));
            //close div
            sb.Append("</div>");
        }
        sb.Append("\"");

        //Write back the necessary JavaScript and
        //add this entry to cache so that we don't have to hit MapPoint
        //Web Service
        if(sb.Length > 5)
        {
            //Write JavaScript
            context.Response.Write("ShowLocation(" + sb.ToString() + ");");
            //Add to cache
            context.Cache.Add(input, sb.ToString(), null,
                            System.DateTime.MaxValue,
                            TimeSpan.FromHours(6),
                            System.Web.Caching.CacheItemPriority.Default,
                            null);
        }
        else
        {
            context.Response.Write("var zeroOutputFound = 0;");
        }
    }

    return;

}
catch(Exception ex)
{
    context.Response.Write("var errorMesage = '" + ex.Message + "';");
}
}
```

This HTTP handler writes appropriate JavaScript back to the client as a response to
any incoming request. For example, an incoming request such as the following:

```
http://yourHTTPHandlerUrl?place=New%20York
```

---

results in the following JavaScript being sent back as response:

```
ShowLocation("<div id='findresult_0'  UNSELECTABLE='on' ><img align=absmiddle
src=arrow.gif border=0> New York, New York, United States</div><div id='findresult_1'
UNSELECTABLE='on'><img align=absmiddle src=arrow.gif border=0> New York (state),
United States</div><div id='findresult_2'  UNSELECTABLE='on'><img align=absmiddle
src=arrow.gif border=0> New York (county), New York, United States</div><div
id='findresult_3'  UNSELECTABLE='on'><img align=absmiddle src=arrow.gif border=0> New
York, Santa Rosa, Florida, United States</div><div id='findresult_4'
UNSELECTABLE='on'><img align=absmiddle src=arrow.gif border=0> New York, Wayne, Iowa,
United States</div>");
```

You can also simply return an array of strings in JavaScript and let the client code do the formatting for the display, but I chose to implement it on the server side since it simplifies the JavaScript implementation.

The next step is to develop the JavaScript to glue these pieces together.

Developing the JavaScript. You might have noticed a couple of JavaScript functions that I have been using so far:

DoLookup
> Captures the user's key inputs and sends an asynchronous call to the HTTP Handler.

ShowLocation
> Displays the find match results to the user in a dynamic drop-down list.

Let's see how to implement these two functions.

The DoLookup function uses XMLHTTP functionality to send the request that we developed in the previous step asynchronously to the HTTP handler; a simplified version of DoLookup is shown in the following code:

```
//Define a global variable to hold http request
//object
var xmlhttp=null;

Function DoLookup()
{
    //Create a valid url with user typed place value
    var url = "your http handler url"? + place.value;

    //Create an instance of xmlHttp
    xmlhttp=new ActiveXObject("Msxml2.XMLHTTP");
    if(xmlhttp)
    {
        //Now open a request and assign callback
        xmlhttp.open("GET",url,true);
        xmlhttp.onreadystatechange=FindPlaceRequestCallBack;
        //Send the request
        xmlhttp.send(null);
    }
}
```

A callback function, FindPlaceRequestCallBack, is assigned to handle the response and any other state changes in the input request; the implementation of the FindPlaceRequestCallBack is as follows:

```
function FindPlaceRequestCallBack()
{
  if(xmlhttp)
  {
    if(xmlhttp.readyState==4&&xmlhttp.responseText)
    {
      //Get the response content
      var placecontent = xmlhttp.responseText;
      //Just execute the response content
      eval(placecontent);
      xmlhttp = null;
    }
  }
}
```

The callback function receives the response text from the HTTP handler and executes the resulting JavaScript using the eval method. The resulting JavaScript is nothing but the ShowLocation function call with Find result matches for the input place. Next, we need to implement the ShowLocation function:

```
function ShowLocation(findResults)
{
    if(!findResults)
    {
        return;
    }

    //Display results
    if(document.getElementById(displayplanelname))
    {
      document.getElementById(displayplanelname).style.visibility="visible";
      document.getElementById(displayplanelname).innerHTML = findResults;
      document.getElementById("place").focus();
    }
}
```

In this function, the results are assigned to the div element to be displayed to the user. Your AJAX application for place lookup is now ready. With minimal effort, you can AJAX-enable your MapPoint Web Service web application to provide a great user experience.

Obviously, you can extend these functions more to optimize your client-server communication by limiting the requests to strings more than three characters in length. Also, you can implement more features such as scroll enabling with arrow keys, and mouse-select enabling in JavaScript to add more depth to the application. The sample application included in the companion material has all these features implemented in JavaScript.

Finally, because you are charged a fee for each MapPoint Web Service Find call, you need to evaluate this design appropriately; a more cost-effective variation to this implementation might be to do a lookup asynchronously when the user clicks Enter, instead of performing a lookup for each character typed.

Optimizing Find Call Performance

One of the advantages of working with web services is that you can invoke methods over the wire using XML, but due to the remote nature of this method and XML's inherent behavior to bloat the packet size, it may pose performance and end user experience issues. For example, say you are building a mapping application for a handheld device that depends on GPRS for connectivity; usually the users of these connected handheld devices pay the network service provider for the data plans (the number of bytes downloaded over the air using the GPRS connections).

To find a place, your MapPoint Web Service application sends a request SOAP XML message and receives the response SOAP XML message from the Web Service. Because the XML bloats the size of the request and response packet, this could cost your application users a lot of money. Not only could having large request and response messages slow down your application for network transfer, but it also may result in poor end user experience. There are multiple ways to optimize your Map-Point Web Service applications for SOAP XML size and response speed; let's look at them in detail.

Optimizing the SOAP Response Size

Always write your applications to receive only the information you need and filter out all unnecessary noise. There are three elements you can limit to do this:

Result-set size

> If you are looking for a place and are certain of its name, request only one find result using the FindRange object:

```
//Create a FindServiceSoap object.
FindServiceSoap findservicesoap = new FindServiceSoap( );
//Assign credentials go here.
. . .
//Create a FindSpecification object.
FindSpecification findspecification = new FindSpecification( );
//Assign a valid data source name.
findspecification.DataSourceName = "MapPoint.NA";
//Specify a place to find.
findspecification.InputPlace = "Redmond, WA";
//Create a FindOptions object.
findspecification.Options = new FindOptions( );
//Create a Range object.
findspecification.Options.Range = new FindRange( );
```

```
//Assign the Range StartIndex and the result count to be returned.
findspecification.Options.Range.StartIndex = 0;
findspecification.Options.Range.Count = 1;
//Invoke the Find method.
FindResults findresults =
        findservicesoap.Find(findspecification);
```

Result information

Usually, all find methods return FindResult objects with location, entity, and best map view information, leaving it up to you to pick and choose what information you need and don't need. If you are looking only for latitude/longitude information for one particular place, get only that information by filtering all other information using the FindResultMask enumeration:

```
//Create a FindServiceSoap object.
FindServiceSoap findservicesoap = new FindServiceSoap( );
//Assign credentials go here.
. . .
//Create a FindSpecification object.
FindSpecification findspecification = new FindSpecification( );
//Assign a valid data source name.
findspecification.DataSourceName = "MapPoint.NA";
//Specify a place to find.
findspecification.InputPlace = "Redmond, WA";
//Set ResultMask to retrieve only map view information.
findspecification.Options.ResultMask = FindResultMask.BestMapViewFlag;
//Invoke the Find method.
FindResults findresults =
        findservicesoap.Find(findspecification);
```

Limit entity information

Even though this is only applicable to point of interest methods, such as FindNearby, FindById, FindByProperty, and FindNearRoute, it is always a good practice to request entity attributes using the FindFilter object. This object has a property, PropertyNames of type string array, that allows you to define which attributes you want to see on returned entities. If an entity (such as a coffee shop) has 200 properties and you plan to use only 2 properties (say, Name and PhoneNumber), you can specify that in your FindNearby request using the FindFilter.PropertyNames so that your response SOAP XML contains only 2 properties instead of all 200. The only caveat to this approach is that your definition for property names must also include the names used in filter expression in the FindFilterExpression.Expression object. The following code snippet shows the usage of the FindFilter.PropertyNames property:

```
//Declare a find nearby specification object
//and assign all required information
FindNearbySpecification findNearbySpec  = new FindNearbySpecification( );
findNearbySpec.DataSourceName = "MapPoint.FourthCoffeeSample";
findNearbySpec.Distance = 1;
findNearbySpec.LatLong = new LatLong( );
findNearbySpec.LatLong.Latitude = 47.6;
findNearbySpec.LatLong.Longitude = -122.33;
```

```
findNearbySpec.Filter = new FindFilter();
findNearbySpec.Filter.EntityTypeName = "FourthCoffeeShops";
//Minimize the properties on returned entities by
//specifying the property names field
//Define the properties you plan to use
//in your application
string[] returnProperties = new string[2];
returnProperties[0] = "Name";
returnProperties[1] = "Phone";
//Assign it to find nearby specification
findNearbySpec.Filter.PropertyNames = returnProperties;

FindResults foundResults;
foundResults = findService.FindNearby(findNearbySpec);
```

Applying Proper Metadata for Faster Searches

Whenever possible, try to apply proper metadata for your find queries, including applying proper entity type information and adding search contexts. For example, if you are searching for Redmond, WA in the United States, you can improve your application's performance by adding the entity type information of PopulatedPlace (using the entity type name for cities means that you are looking only for a city) and a context of 244 (the entity ID of the United States narrows your search to the United States) during your find call:

```
//Create a find specifications object
FindSepcification findspecification = new FindSepcification();

//Assign the EntityTypeNames value
findspecification.EntityTypeNames = new string[] {"PopulatedPlace"};

//Assign search context
findspecification.Options = new FindOptions();
//Add context for United States
findspecification.Options.SearchContext = 244;
```

Use Asynchronous Programming Patterns

Since any web service call involves a network round-trip, using asynchronous programming improves the user's experience dramatically. With MapPoint Web Service Find Service, you can use asynchronous programming paradigms provided by Microsoft .NET Framework. If you are building a web or Windows application using MapPoint Web Service, you can use the MapPoint Web Service asynchronous methods to perform tasks such as Find or FindAddress; however, in order to use asynchronous methods, you use the Begin and End pair methods instead of the actual method itself. For example, to call the Find method in asynchronous patterns, use the BeginFind and EndFind methods, which internally use the SoapHttpClientProtocol object's BeginInvoke and EndInvoke methods.

When you are building an enterprise-level application using MapPoint Web Service, obviously performance is not the only thing you need to keep in mind; you also need to think about supporting multiple languages and cultures, so globalizing your applications to support local languages is an essential part of your application. In the next section, let's see how to leverage some of the MapPoint Web Service features to build global applications

Globalizing Find

MapPoint Web Service currently supports 10 different languages, meaning that when you use the Find Service with a desired (and supported) language, the Find results are returned in that language. It is important to note that in the case of the Find service, only city names and other entity information are localized to display in that specific language.

Table 6-10 shows the list of languages currently supported in MapPoint Web Service:

Table 6-10. Languages supported in MapPoint Web Service

Language	Language Code	Lcid
Dutch	nl	19
English	en	9
English-United States	en-us	1033
French	fr	12
German	de	7
Italian	it	16
Portuguese	pt	22
Spanish	es	10
Swedish	sv	29

The data sources `MapPoint.Moon` and `MapPoint.World` support all of these languages as well as Japanese (language code ja and LCID 1041).

To send your desired language information to the MapPoint Web Service during your Find Service calls, MapPoint Web Service provides SOAP Headers. With Find Service, these settings use the `FindServiceSoap.UserInfoFindHeaderValue` field. The `UserInfoFindHeaderValue` is of type `UserInfoFindHeader`, and it and provides fields to set values for the location search context (the `UserInfoFindHeader.Context` field), user preferred culture (the `UserInfoFindHeader.Culture` field), and default distance unit as either miles or kilometers (the `UserInfoFindHeader.DefaultDistanceUnit` field). To use Find Service with a search context for Canada (whose country entity ID is 39) with a preferred language of French (name fr), you would have to provide the user information header to the FindServiceSoap:

```
//Create a find service soap object
FindServiceSoap findService = new FindServiceSoap();
//Create a user header
UserInfoFindHeader userInfoFindHeader  = new UserInfoFindHeader();
//Set the country context to Canada
userInfoFindHeader.Context = new CountryRegionContext();
userInfoFindHeader.Context.EntityID = 39;

//Set the language preference
userInfoRenderHeader.Culture = new CultureInfo();
userInfoRenderHeader.Culture.Name = "fr";

//Then assign the header to the find service proxy
findService.UserInfoFindHeaderValue = userInfoFindHeader;
```

The entity ID and language name are assigned to the find header before making any find calls. To set the desired culture information, you could also use the Lcid ID for French instead of using the language name. One thing to remember while using the user information header to obtain localized information from Find Service is that the addresses returned by the FindServiceSoap.FindAddress method are never localized.

Where Are We?

Find Service is one of the core components of the MapPoint Web Service, providing many features such as finding places, addresses, and points of interest around a given location. Find Service also provides a way to convert any latitude/longitude information to an entity that contains the geographic information about that given point; it also provides necessary tools to parse addresses to see whether a given string is a place or an address so that you can call the appropriate method to find information.

Since Find Service methods are web service methods, it is important to think about performance optimization and asynchronous programming patters where applicable. Finally, Find Service also provides a way to get information in a specific localized language (among the 10 supported languages).

In the next chapter, we'll look at MapPoint Web Service Route and Render Service components.

CHAPTER 7

MapPoint Web Service Route APIs

Like Find Service, Route Service is one of the four core components of the MapPoint Web Service, allowing you to calculate routes, driving directions, and itineraries between places or addresses. In this chapter, we'll take an in-depth look at the Map-Point Web Service Route APIs.

Understanding Route APIs

The Route Service end point is located at RouteService.asmx, and the APIs available for Route service are exposed via the RouteServiceSoap class in the Web Service proxy (*Reference.cs* or *Reference.vb*).

RouteServiceSoap class contains methods related to route functionality, namely CalculateRoute and CalculateSimpleRoute. Either of these two methods can be used to calculate routes between places, addresses, or latitude/longitude coordinates; however, there are some differences that you need to be aware of when using these methods, which we will get to later in this chapter. Table 7-1 shows the methods offered by the RouteServiceSoap class.

Table 7-1. Methods available on the RouteServiceSoap class

Method	Notes
CalculateRoute	Calculates and returns a route (Route object) based on identified route segments and specifications
CalculateSimpleRoute	Calculates and returns a route (Route object) based on an array of latitude and longitude coordinates

Before I get into the details of using the route-related methods, let's look at how a route is represented in MapPoint Web Service APIs.

Anatomy of a Route

In MapPoint Web Service, a *route* is made up of two or more *waypoints*, each of which indicates a starting point, ending point, or stopping point along the route. Each waypoint is associated with a *route segment*, which connects two waypoints but contains information about only one of them. To understand this better, see Figure 7-1.

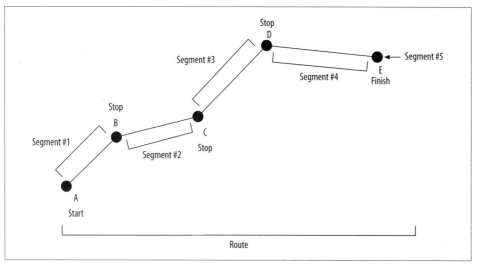

Figure 7-1. Sample route with segments and waypoints

Figure 7-1 shows with five waypoints and five associated segments. The starting point (waypoint A) and other stopping points (waypoints B, C, and D) in this route are connected via four route segments (1, 2, 3, and 4); the last segment represents the finish point, waypoint E, with its own route segment, 5. In MapPoint Web Service APIs, each segment contains information about the beginning waypoint, the segment distance, and directions for the segment.

Next, let's see how the route in Figure 7-1 morphs into programmatic types.

Representing a Route Programmatically

In MapPoint Web Service APIs, a valid route is always represented by a Route object. A Route object contains the following instances:

- A RouteItinerary class that represents the textual driving directions
- A RouteSpecification class that represents the specifications such as starting point, ending point, stopping points, and driver's profile
- A CalculatedRouteRepresentation class that contains a cached version of the route for rendering purposes

When a route is calculated using `RouteServiceSoap.CalculateRoute` with an instance of the `RouteSpecification` class, both `RouteItinerary` and `CalculatedRouteRepresentation` are returned by default. However, you can change this behavior and mask the unnecessary information depending on your needs using `RouteResultMask` enumeration.

A valid `RouteItinerary` object contains information about the route itinerary and map view representations. The itinerary information is represented as an array of `Segment` objects. Each `Segment` object contains a `Waypoint` object that denotes the starting point for that segment in the route, and an array of `Direction` objects that indicate driving directions for the current segments. Each `Direction` object contains detailed textual driving directions, as well as other information such as bearing, latitude/longitude of the directions' starting point, and formatted text instruction. Finally, each `Waypoint` object contains the location information for the starting point of the corresponding `Segment` object.

A valid `RouteSpecification` object defines a route in terms of a segment collection using an array of `SegmentSpecification` objects in conjunction with a `DriverProfile` that sets the driving time preferences. Each `SegmentSpecification` object contains specifications for an individual route segment by setting the waypoint (the starting point for the segment) and other segment preferences indicating what type of segment the current segment needs to be—such as a shortest segment or a quickest segment. Table 7-2 shows the fields exposed on the `RouteSpecification` class.

Table 7-2. Fields exposed on the RouteSpecification class

Field	Notes
DataSourceName	Name of the data source as a string.
DriverProfile	The time to start and end driving each day (`DriverProfile` object).
ResultMask	Indicates, as a `RouteResultMask` enumeration, whether a returned route should include driving directions, a calculated route representation, or both.
Segments	The specification of each segment that makes up the route as an array of `SegmentSpecification` objects. The order of the array is the order of the stops on the route.

Table 7-3 shows the fields of the `SegmentSpecification` object:

Table 7-3. SegmentSpecification fields

Field	Notes
Options	The route preference and map view options (`SegmentOptions` object) for the specified segment of the route
Waypoint	The waypoint (`Waypoint` object) for the route segment; the beginning of the segment

When you are calculating a route, a `RouteSpecification` object is passed to the `RouteServiceSoap.CalculateRoute`, and the resulting `Route` object automatically inherits these route specifications as an instance of the `RouteSpecification` object, so you never actually assign a `RouteSpecification` instance to a `Route` object.

Finally, the `CalculatedRouteRepresentation` object is a cached representation of a calculated route; this object is useful only in rendering a route on top of a map, so a valid instance of this object contains an array of bytes that represents the calculated route, which can later be used in rendering a map using the MapPoint Web Service route service.

This discussion is summarized in Figure 7-2.

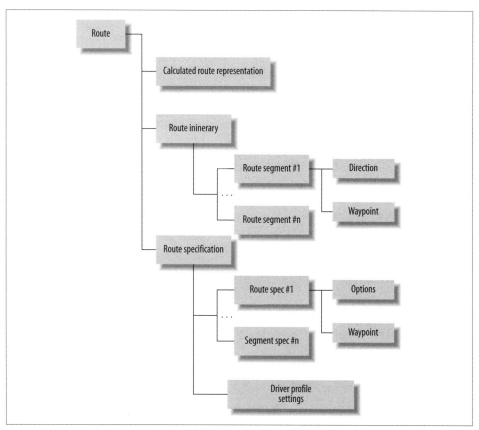

Figure 7-2. Programmatic representation of a route using MapPoint Web Service types

With this introduction, let's look at how to create `Route` objects using the `RouteServiceSoap` APIs.

Calculating a Route

A valid route consists of a starting point and an ending point; sometimes a route can also have one or more stops between its starting and stopping points. To calculate a route, you need to have at least two waypoints expressed in terms of LatLong objects. Depending on how much control you need in calculating a route, MapPoint Web Service offers two methods: RouteServiceSoap.CalculateSimpleRoute and RouteServiceSoap.CalculateRoute.

Calculating a Route Using the CalculateSimpleRoute Method

The RoutServiceSoap.CalculateSimpleRoute method calculates a route using latitude/longitude coordinates. This method uses an array of latitude/longitude coordinates, a map data source name (such as MapPoint.NA), and a SegmentPreference enumeration to indicate whether the route should be calculated using the SegmentPreference.Quickest option (yielding the route with minimal travel time) or the SegmentPreference.Shortest option (yielding the route with minimal travel distance). The following example shows how to use the RouteServiceSoap.CalculateSimpleRoute method with latitude/longitude pairs:

```
//Define waypoints
LatLong[] latLongs = new LatLong[2];

//Seattle, WA
latLongs[0] = new LatLong();
latLongs[0].Latitude = 47.6034;
latLongs[0].Longitude = -122.3295;

//Redmond, WA
latLongs[1] = new LatLong();
latLongs[1].Latitude = 47.6785;
latLongs[1].Longitude = -122.1308;

//Now create a route service proxy
RouteServiceSoap routeService = new RouteServiceSoap();

//Assign credentials
routeService.Credentials = new System.Net.NetworkCredential(userid, password);

//Calcuate Route
Route route = routeService.CalculateSimpleRoute(latLongs,
                    "MapPoint.NA", SegmentPreference.Quickest);
```

Keep in mind that if your route exceeds 50,000 kilometers, an error is thrown, but you can pass a maximum of 50 latitude/longitude pairs to this method. Despite this apparent flexibility, it does not offer much control over the route service behavior, such as setting the driving starting time and ending time, requesting only route itinerary without a calculated route representation cache, and so on. This method tends to be inefficient when you just want to calculate route itinerary without returning a calculated route representation; however, that's exactly the level of control that the RouteServiceSoap.CalculateRoute method offers.

Calculating a Route Using the CalculateRoute Method

The RouteServiceSoap.CalculateRoute method takes a valid RouteSpecification object as an input parameter and returns a Route object. The RouteSpecification object allows you to specify your route using Waypoint objects and Segment objects. One of the advantages of this approach is better control over the route calculation process; using a RouteSpecification object, you can control the segment level routing settings, such as shortest versus quickest and driving times.

A Waypoint object is a wrapper around a location that is part of a route. To define a Waypoint object, you need to have an associated latitude/longitude pair (or a LatLong object). Once you have the Waypoints outlined for a route, you can assign them to Segment objects to create an array of route segment specification. This route segment specification array is used in calculating the route when the RouteServiceSoap.CalculateRoute method is called.

The following example shows how to call this method using a RouteSpecification object:

```
//Now create a route service proxy
RouteServiceSoap routeService = new RouteServiceSoap();
//Assign credentials
routeService.Credentials = new System.Net.NetworkCredential(userid, password);

//Now define RouteSpecifications

//Define segments
SegmentSpecification[] routeSegmentsSpec = new SegmentSpecification[3];

//Define start segment
routeSegmentsSpec[0] = new SegmentSpecification();
routeSegmentsSpec[0].Waypoint = new Waypoint();
routeSegmentsSpec[0].Waypoint.Name = "Start";
//Seattle, WA
routeSegmentsSpec[0].Waypoint.Location = new Location();
routeSegmentsSpec[0].Waypoint.Location.LatLong = new LatLong();
routeSegmentsSpec[0].Waypoint.Location.LatLong.Latitude = 47.6034;
routeSegmentsSpec[0].Waypoint.Location.LatLong.Longitude = -122.3295;
//Set this segment to be the quickest
routeSegmentsSpec[0].Options = new SegmentOptions();
routeSegmentsSpec[0].Options.Preference = SegmentPreference.Quickest;

//Define stop segment
routeSegmentsSpec[1] = new SegmentSpecification();
routeSegmentsSpec[1].Waypoint = new Waypoint();
routeSegmentsSpec[1].Waypoint.Name = "Stop";
```

```
                //Redmond, WA
                routeSegmentsSpec[1].Waypoint.Location = new Location( );
                routeSegmentsSpec[1].Waypoint.Location.LatLong = new LatLong( );
                routeSegmentsSpec[1].Waypoint.Location.LatLong.Latitude = 47.6785;
                routeSegmentsSpec[1].Waypoint.Location.LatLong.Longitude = -122.1308;
                //Set this segment to be the shortest
                routeSegmentsSpec[1].Options = new SegmentOptions( );
                routeSegmentsSpec[1].Options.Preference = SegmentPreference.Shortest;

                //Define to segment
                routeSegmentsSpec[2] = new SegmentSpecification( );
                routeSegmentsSpec[2].Waypoint = new Waypoint( );
                routeSegmentsSpec[2].Waypoint.Name = "Finish";
                //Portland, OR
                routeSegmentsSpec[2].Waypoint.Location = new Location( );
                routeSegmentsSpec[2].Waypoint.Location.LatLong = new LatLong( );
                routeSegmentsSpec[2].Waypoint.Location.LatLong.Latitude = 45.5118;
                routeSegmentsSpec[2].Waypoint.Location.LatLong.Longitude = -122.6755;

                //Now create a Route Specification and assign segments
                //and data source to be used
                RouteSpecification routeSpec = new RouteSpecification( );
                routeSpec.DataSourceName = "MapPoint.NA";
                routeSpec.Segments = routeSegmentsSpec;

                //Set the itinerary only mask
                routeSpec.ResultMask = RouteResultMask.Itinerary;

                //Calculate Route
                Route route = routeService.CalculateRoute(routeSpec);
```

In this example, I define three segments from Seattle, WA to Portland, OR with a
stop at Redmond, WA. The real advantage to using the CalculateRoute method can
be seen in how I set the segment preferences; I have set the first segment of my route
from Seattle to Redmond as the quickest segment:

```
                //Set this segment to be the quickest
                routeSegmentsSpec[0].Options = new SegmentOptions( );
                routeSegmentsSpec[0].Options.Preference = SegmentPreference.Quickest;
```

This guarantees that when my route is calculated, I get the directions that can take
me from Seattle to Redmond in the minimal amount of time; then, I set the second
segment as the shortest segment:

```
                //Set this segment to be the shortest
                routeSegmentsSpec[1].Options = new SegmentOptions( );
                routeSegmentsSpec[1].Options.Preference = SegmentPreference.Shortest;
```

This setting guarantees that the route contains the directions that travel the minimal
distance to go from Redmond, WA to Portland, OR. Finally, you can also reduce the
SOAP payload by requesting the "itinerary only" route object by setting the following RouteResultMask to the RouteSpecification object:

```
                //Set the itinerary only mask
                routeSpec.ResultMask = RouteResultMask.Itinerary;
```

The CalculateRoute method provides considerably more control than the CalculateSimpleRoute method; however, keep in mind that only 50 waypoints are allowed with this method. Finally, as with the CalculateSimpleRoute method, if your route exceeds 50,000 kilometers, an error is thrown.

Controlling the driving times

Before we get into the details of getting the route object information returned by the previously discussed methods, there is one more setting you can set to the RouteSpecification object to control the driving times, the DriverProfile object.

By default, MapPoint Web Service considers the valid driving times in a day to be from 9:00 a.m. to 5:00 p.m. When you calculate a route without setting any specific driver profile settings, routes are calculated using these default times. However, if you want to drive from 10:00 a.m. to 3:00 p.m., use the DriverProfile object.

To set specific starting and ending driving times in a day, use the DriverProfile object; this object has two fields, DayStartTime and DayEndTime, using which you can set the starting time and ending time in a day. These two values are always expressed in minutes elapsed since the day has started at 12:00 a.m. (except for the default values of -1 and -1).

To set a DayStartTime at 10:00 a.m., use the following code:

```
//Create a driver profile object
DriverProfile driverProfile = new DriverProfile();
//Start driving every day at 10 AM in the morning
driverProfile.DayStartTime = 10 * 60;
```

Similarly, you can set the DayEndTime at 3:00 p.m. as follows:

```
//End driving every day at 3 PM in the evening
//3 PM = 12 + 3 = 15 hours since 12:00 AM
driverProfile.DayEndTime = 15 * 60;
```

To set this DriverProfile object to the RouteSpecification object to put the new driving day start and end times into effect while calculating your route, use the following code:

```
//Assign Driver's profile
routeSpec.DriverProfile = driverProfile;
```

Keep in mind that setting the driver's profile with custom driving start and end times changes the total trip time as well as the driving directions accordingly.

Setting default distance units

Depending on where you are actually driving, sometimes it makes sense to see the driving directions and distances in the units that are used locally; for example in the United States, the distance is measured in miles, while in the United Kingdom, the distance is measured in kilometers. MapPoint Web Service allows you to set your distance preference for route calculations via the UserInfoRouteHeader object. This object is set to the RouteServiceSoap instance before calling the CalculateRoute or CalculateSimpleRoute methods:

```
//Create an instance of user info route header
UserInfoRouteHeader routeHeader = new UserInfoRouteHeader( );

//Set distance unit to Miles
routeHeader.DefaultDistanceUnit = DistanceUnit.Mile;

//Assign it to Route Service instance
routeService.UserInfoRouteHeaderValue = routeHeader;

//Calculate Route
route = routeService.CalculateRoute(routeSpec);
```

Depending on what the default distance unit is set to, the route object contains the information about the total route distance and segment distance accordingly. The default distance unit always starts out as kilometers, and you need to change that if you want miles.

Setting the default culture

You can also use the UserInfoRouteHeader object to obtain the driving directions in any of the supported languages; to get driving directions in French, use the following code:

```
//Create an instance of user info route header
UserInfoRouteHeader routeHeader = new UserInfoRouteHeader( );

//Create Culture Info
routeHeader.Culture = new CultureInfo( );
//And set it to French
routeHeader.Culture.Name = "FR";

//Assign it to Route Service instance
routeService.UserInfoRouteHeaderValue = routeHeader;

//Calculate Route
route = routeService.CalculateRoute(routeSpec);
```

This code results in driving directions in French. For a full list of languages supported by MapPoint Web Service, refer to Chapter 5.

Now that we have seen how to calculate a route with different options, it's time to look at the itinerary details contained within a route.

Displaying Details of a Route

A Route object contains several details about a calculated route, including the total driving time, trip time, distance traveled, and detailed segment level driving directions, distance, and time.

Displaying the Route Summary

Route summary information contains the details, such as the amount of time the entire trip took, total time spent driving, and total distance traveled. This information can be obtained from the RouteItinerary object instance. A valid route exposes the RouteItinerary object via the Itinerary field, and the RouteItinerary object provides several fields, such as Distance, TripTime, and DrivingTime, to provide information about total distance traveled, total trip time, and time spent driving, respectively. The following code shows how to access this information from a Route object:

```
//Getting the Route Summary

//Get total distance
string distance = route.Itinerary.Distance.ToString("#.##");

//Get total drive time
string totalDriveTime = String.Format("Total drive time: {0} Hours",
        (Convert.ToDouble(route.Itinerary.DrivingTime)/
                        (60 * 60)).ToString("#,##"));

//Get total trip time
string totalTripTime = String.Format("Total trip time: {0} Hours",
        (Convert.ToDouble(route.Itinerary.TripTime)/
                        (60 * 60)).ToString("#.##"));
```

The distance is expressed in kilometers by default unless you set it otherwise as shown in the previous section. The trip and drive times are expressed in seconds, and in this example, I convert them into hours.

A route summary with the previous example's formatting looks as follows:

```
Total Distance: 198.42 (Miles)

Total drive time: 3.94 Hours

Total trip time: 3.94 Hours
```

You might notice that the trip and drive times are the same in this case; however, if you set the driving day start and end timings and your route spans across multiple days, you see a difference between the trip time and the drive time (since trip time is the amount of time spent both driving and resting).

Displaying Route Details

Route details include the segment-level driving instructions along with the bearing and distance. These can be obtained from the Segment array in the RouteItinerary. Segments field.

Each Segment object contains a collection of Direction objects, distance traveled, driving time, trip time, and a LatLong object. Each Direction object contains information such as driving directions, driving instructions, and bearing directions that are used to display detailed driving directions.

The following example shows how to use the RouteItinerary.Segments to display detailed driving directions:

```
//Get the directions
foreach(Segment segment in route.Itinerary.Segments)
{
    //Get segment distance
    if(segment.Distance > 0)
    {
        string segmentDistance = segment.Distance.ToString("#.##");
        //Display segment distance
        Console.WriteLine(segmentDistance.ToString());
    }

    //Get directions for each segment
    foreach(Direction direction in segment.Directions)
    {

        //Simple use
        //string instruction = direction.Instruction;

        //Complex use
        //See whether we need this direction as a specific entry
        switch(direction.Action)
        {
            case DirectionAction.Depart:
            case DirectionAction.Arrive:
                //Display instruction
                //Ex: Arrive Finish
                Console.WriteLine(direction.Instruction);
                break;
            case DirectionAction.Other:
                //State Borders etc
                //Display only as needed
                //Ex: Entering Oregon
                Console.WriteLine(direction.Instruction);
                break;
            default:
                if(direction.Towards != null &&
                    direction.Towards != string.Empty)
                {
```

```
            //Display instruction along with "towards" text
        //Ex: Take Ramp (LEFT) onto I-405 [I-405 / Renton]
            Console.WriteLine(
            String.Format("\t\t {0} [{1}]\r\n",
                        direction.Instruction,
                        direction.Towards));
            */
        }
        else
        {
            //Display instruction along with no "towards" text
            //Ex: Take Ramp (LEFT) onto I-405
            Console.WriteLine(
            String.Format("\t\t {0} \r\n",
                        direction.Instruction));
        }
        break;
    }
  }
}
```

As you can see, each Direction instance contains a DirectionAction enumeration that you can use to identify what kind of information the current instance contains. In this example, I have considered only a couple of actions such as Arrive, Depart, and Other, but you can add more custom driving directions display logic around the rest of the direction action enumerations.

Where Are We?

In this chapter, you have seen how a route is represented programmatically using MapPoint Web Service APIs. You learned that to calculate routes, you use the RouteServiceSoap.CalculateSimpleRoute and RouteServiceSoap.CalculateRoute methods. When a route is calculated, it contains route segments, and each segment contains a collection of directions. You can change the route distance units and the language used in describing driving directions using the UserInfoRouteHeader object. When displaying driving directions, you learned to use the DirectionAction enumeration to understand the type of directions contained in a Direction object.

In the next chapter, we will learn how to render routes.

CHAPTER 8

MapPoint Web Service Render APIs

The Render Service is another of the four core components of the MapPoint Web Service, allowing you to render maps with places/addresses, routes, pushpins and more. In this chapter, we'll take an in-depth look at the MapPoint Web Service Render APIs.

Understanding Render APIs

The Render Service end point is located at the RenderService.asmx, and the APIs available for it are exposed via the RenderServiceSoap class in the Web Service proxy (*Reference.cs* or *Reference.vb*).

The RenderServiceSoap class contains methods related to render functionality, namely GetMap, GetBestMapView, ConvertToLatLong, and ConvertToPoint, which can be used to get maps, get map views, and to convert a point on a map to a pixel coordinate or vice versa. Table 8-1 describes the methods of the RenderServiceSoap class.

Table 8-1. RenderServiceSoap methods

Method	Description
ConvertToLatLong	Converts pixel coordinates on a given map to latitude and longitude coordinates. Returns an array of LatLong objects from a given array of PixelCoord objects.
ConvertToPoint	Converts latitude and longitude coordinates to pixel coordinates. Returns an array of PixelCoord objects from a given array of LatLong objects.
GetBestMapView	Creates a single best map view for displaying a set of locations. A *best map view* is the largest scale map that can be centered over the set of locations while displaying the entire location along with a small buffer. This method returns a MapViewRepresentations object for a specified Location object or array of Location objects.
GetMap	Creates one or more rendered images of a map. Returns a MapImage object or an array of MapImage objects based on a specified map view or array of map views.
GetLineDriveMap	Renders a line-drive map and returns an array of LineDriveMapImage objects.

Before getting into the details of using the render-related methods, let's look at the essential basics to understand in rendering maps.

Introduction to Views

A *view* defines a specific area that needs to be rendered on a map and can be expressed in four ways using MapPoint Web Service.

View by bounding locations

In this case, a map view is defined using a set of locations, and the map is rendered to contain all of the locations on the map. Programmatically, this view is represented by the ViewByBoundingLocations class, which takes an array of Location objects to define the map view. All input Location objects must have a valid LatLong property. This view is useful if you want to render Location objects from different find calls on one map. When this view is requested, MapPoint Web Service calculates the best possible map view to fit all locations on the map. The following code shows how to define and use the ViewByBoundingLocation object to render a map:

```
//Define an array of locations
//In this case 4 has been randomly chosen
Location[] myLocations = new Location[4];

//Obtain LatLong values for each Location object
. . .

//Define view by Location and assign locations
ViewByBoundingLocations viewByBoundingLocations
                = new ViewByBoundingLocations( );
viewByBoundingLocations.Locations = myLocations;

//Get a map
MapSpecification mapSpec = new MapSpecification( );
mapSpec.Views = new MapView[] {viewByBoundingLocations};
. . .
```

These four locations are rendered on the map shown in Figure 8-1.

View by height and width

In this case, a map view is defined by the height and width of the area that you want to cover on the ground. The height and width you express essentially equal the ground distance in either miles or kilometers. It is important to keep in mind that this height and width is different from the height and width of the map image that you want to render. If you want to render 50 km of height and 100 km of width on the ground, you can do so on a 200 × 200 pixel map image. Although the height and width specified for the map are different from the height and width of the map image, they are related to each other via map scale, which we will look at in detail later in this chapter.

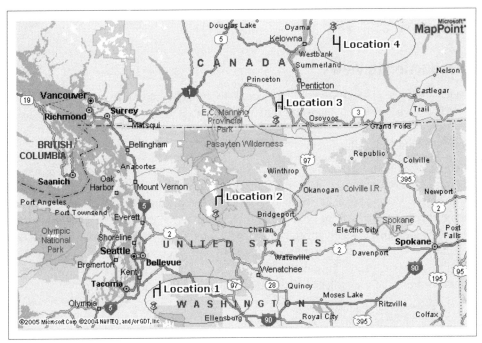

Figure 8-1. View by bounding locations map

When a map is rendered using ground height and width, it is rendered to contain at least the requested area, which means that MapPoint Web Service may render more area than requested depending on the aspect ratio. Programmatically, this view is represented by the ViewByHeightWidth class, which defines the map view using height and width specifications as integers. When this view is requested, MapPoint Web Service calculates the best possible map view to fit the requested area on the map. The following code shows how to define a ViewByHeightWidth object to render a map:

```
//Define a center point
LatLong centerPoint = new LatLong();
centerPoint.Latitude = centerLatitude;
centerPoint.Longitude = centerLongitude;


//Define view by height and width
ViewByHeightWidth viewByHW = new ViewByHeightWidth();
viewByHW.CenterPoint = centerPoint;

//Define height and width on the ground
//In this case area covering
//200 km and
//300 km
//on the ground
viewByHW.Height = 200;
viewByHW.Width = 300;
```

```
//Create map specification
MapSpecification mapSpec = new MapSpecification( );
mapSpec.Views = new ViewByHeightWidth[] {viewByHW};

//Get a map
. . .
```

The rendered map requested in the previous code is shown in Figure 8-2.

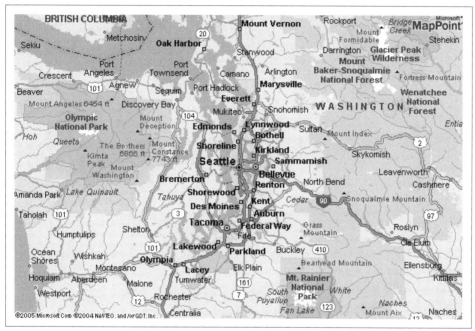

Figure 8-2. Map rendered with 200 × 300 KM in ground distance

The same map rendered with 20 × 30 km height and width, respectively, is shown in Figure 8-3.

Although the image (bitmap) size here is constant, a change in the map's height and width caused the scale to change, creating a "zoom in" effect.

View by scale

In order to understand view by scale, you need to understand the notion of scale first. *Scale* can be defined as (map image size) / (map size in real world); so, if you have a map of the world as a globe rendered on a 1 inch map image, the scale is 1: 520,000,000, since the world's diameter is 520,000,000 inches. This means that one inch on the image represents 520,000,000 actual inches in the world. Remember though, that the image size (such as 400 × 600 pixels and 2,000 × 2,000 pixels) has no impact on the scale; to control the scale of a rendered map, you need to use view

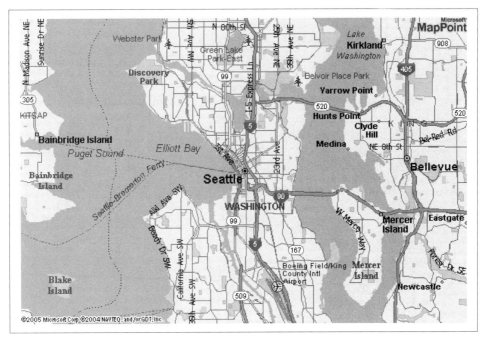

Figure 8-3. Map rendered with 20 × 30 KM in ground distance

by scale. This view is represented by the ViewByScale object. To use this object, set a center point as LatLong object and scale value. The scale ranges are dependent on the MapPoint data sources. The following code shows how to use the ViewByScale object:

```
//Define a center point
LatLong centerPoint = new LatLong( );
centerPoint.Latitude = centerLatitude;
centerPoint.Longitude = centerLongitude;

//Define view by scale
ViewByScale viewByScale = new ViewByScale( );
viewByScale.CenterPoint = centerPoint;

//Define scale value
viewByScale.MapScale = 20000;

//Create map specification
MapSpecification mapSpec = new MapSpecification( );
mapSpec.Views = new ViewByScale[] {viewByScale};

//Get a map
. . .
```

This view is extremely useful in controlling the zoom levels for rendered maps. Also, note that you can use this view for device-specific resolution map rendering; by default, MapPoint Web Service renders maps at 96 dpi; however, you can alter this value to match your device-specific resolution, as shown below:

```
//Define scale value
viewByScale.MapScale = 20000 * 96/120;
```

A resolution of 120 dpi is applied to the scale to match the device's dpi resolution.

View by bounding rectangle

This view defines the map area by a bounding rectangle. Unlike the view by bounding locations, there are only two LatLong objects involved in defining the rectangle: one for the northeast corner and one for the southwest corner. When a bounding rectangle is defined using a LatLongRectangle object, a map that covers the specified area is rendered. This view is useful if you want to render a specific area on the map (unlike the area dictated by the number of points, as in ViewByBoundingLocations). This view is programmatically represented by the ViewByBoundingRectangle object. The following code shows how to use this view:

```
//Define northeast point
LatLong northEastPoint = new LatLong();
. . .

//Define southwest point
LatLong southWestPoint = new LatLong();
. . .

//Define view by bounding rectangle
ViewByBoundingRectangle vbr = new ViewByBoundingRectangle();
vbr.BoundingRectangle = new LatLongRectangle();
vbr.BoundingRectangle.Northeast = northEastPoint;
vbr.BoundingRectangle.Southwest = southWestPoint;

//Create map specification
MapSpecification mapSpec = new MapSpecification();
mapSpec.Views = new ViewByBoundingRectangle[] {vbr};

//Get Map
. . .
```

This code generated the map shown in Figure 8-4.

The map has covered the corners defined by the northeast and southwest latitude, longitude combinations.

Now that you know what map views are, let's look at map styles before moving on to look at the Render APIs in detail.

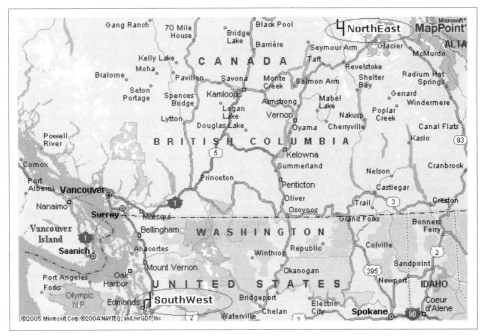

Figure 8-4. Map rendered for view by bounding rectangle

Understanding Map Styles

Map Style in MapPoint Web Service is a rendering-specific flag that indicates what kind of detail is rendered on the map. To that end, Map Style can be used to control which information is rendered on the maps.

For example, when you use Road map style, the maps are rendered with full road data; however, when you choose to use Political map style, maps display only political entities (such as countries, and regions). Map Style in MapPoint Web Service is programmatically represented using the MapStyle enumeration. There are currently 31 Map Styles supported in MapPoint Web Service; it is important to keep in mind that Map Styles are data source-dependent—not all map styles are supported by all data sources.

With this introduction to map views and map styles, let's next look at how Rendering APIs works.

Anatomy of Render APIs

MapPoint Web Service provides Render APIs for you to render maps using the RenderServiceSoap.GetMap method. The GetMap method takes a MapSpecification object as an argument that defines the map to be rendered and returns an array of

MapImage objects. The MapSpecification object defines the map to be rendered in terms of the view, data source, route (only for rendering a route), pushpins, or polygons (only to render polygons), along with optional map options that give you control over map features such as size and style. Table 8-2 shows the fields of the MapSpecification class, and Table 8-3 shows the MapOptions class fields.

Table 8-2. MapSpecification fields

Field	Description
DataSourceName	Name of the data source name as a string.
HighlightedEntityIDs	An array of the IDs of geographic entities that should appear as selected on the map. Valid array range is 0 through 50.
Options	The map rendering options (MapOptions object), such as image format, panning and zooming factors, identification of the requested map as an overview map, route highlight colors, font size, and map style.
Polygons	An array of Polygon objects to render.
Pushpins	An array of pushpins (Pushpin objects) to render on the map. Valid array range is 0 through 100.
Route	The route (Route object) to render on the map. Required if the Views property is null.
Views	An array of map views (MapView objects) to render. One map image is returned for each map view. Valid array range is 0 through 50. Required if the Route property is null.

Table 8-3. MapOption class fields

Field	Notes
ConstructionClosureHighlightColor	The highlight color (RouteHighlightColor enumeration) used for parts of a route that are closed due to construction. Default is red.
ConstructionDelayHighlightColor	The highlight color (RouteHighlightColor enumeration) to use for parts of a route where delays due to construction can be expected. Default is DefaultColor.
FontSize	The relative font size (MapFontSize enumeration) used for map labeling. Default is Medium.
Format	The format (ImageFormat object) of the map image to return.
IsOverviewMap	Identifies whether the requested map should be rendered as an overview map.
PanHorizontal	A positive or negative number reflecting the percentage of the map image to pan west (negative) or east (positive).
PanVertical	A positive or negative number reflecting the percentage of the map image to pan south (negative) or north (positive).
ReturnType	Identifies whether the RenderServiceSoap.GetMap method should return a map image or a standard or secure URL to a cached map image. MapReturnType enumeration.

Table 8-3. MapOption class fields (continued)

Field	Notes
RouteHighlightColor	The highlight color (RouteHighlightColor enumeration) to use for a route (other than construction areas). Default is Green.
Style	The map style (MapStyle enumeration) to use.
Zoom	Identifies the amount the map image is magnified, expressed as a fractional percentage.

The GetMap method returns an array of MapImage objects out of which the first MapImage contains the actual rendered map. The returned MapImage object contains either the map image serialized into a byte array or the URL to the map image stored on MapPoint Servers. The following code shows how to use MapSpecification object to get a map:

```
//Find a place to render
FindServiceSoap findService = new FindServiceSoap( );

//Assign credentials
. . .

//Find place
FindSpecification findSpec = new FindSpecification( );
findSpec.DataSourceName = "MapPoint.NA";
findSpec.InputPlace = "Seattle, WA";
FindResults foundResults = findService.Find(findSpec);

//Get the view
ViewByHeightWidth view
    = foundResults.Results[0].FoundLocation.BestMapView.ByHeightWidth;

//Create a RenderServiceSoap instance
RenderServiceSoap renderService  = new RenderServiceSoap( );

//Assign to credentials
. . .

//Define MapSpecification
MapSpecification mapSpec  = new MapSpecification( );

//Assign DataSource
mapSpec.DataSourceName = "MapPoint.NA";

//Assign view
mapSpec.Views = new MapView[] {view};

//Get Map
MapImage[] mapImages = renderService.GetMap(mapSpec);
```

```
//Get the map image stream
System.IO.Stream streamImage
        = new System.IO.MemoryStream(mapImages[0].MimeData.Bits);

//Load the image stream into a bitmap
Bitmap bitmapImage = new Bitmap(streamImage);
```

The MapImage instance returned by the GetMap method contains the map image as a byte array that can be used in your application, which works well for a Windows application. But what if you have a web application where you have an image tag and all you need is a URL to display the map?

Rendering for Windows Versus Rendering for the Web

Using the GetMap method, you can get either a map image as a byte array or a URL that contains the map image stored on MapPoint Web Service servers. Once you have the image URL, you can set it to an image tag for a web application. By default, the GetMap method returns the map image as a byte array, but you can use the MapOptions object to change this option to return the map URL by setting the ReturnType property:

```
//Create map specification
MapSpecification mapSpec  = new MapSpecification();

//Assign data source and views
..

//Define map options
mapSpec.Options = new MapOptions();

//Request map URL
mapSpec.Options.ReturnType = MapReturnType.ReturnUrl;

//Get map
MapImage[] mapImages =
            renderService.GetMap(mapSpec);

//Get the URL
string url = mapImages[0].Url;
```

From this code, MapPoint Web Service returns a URL to the map image when the MapOptions.ReturnType is set to either the MapReturnType.ReturnUrl or the MapReturnType.ReturnSecureUrl enumeration. This method is very efficient since the SOAP message response from MapPoint Web Service contains only a URL instead of the entire image.

However, keep in mind that a returned URL is valid for returning up to ten images within five minutes of the call to the GetMap method. After five minutes or ten images (whichever occurs first), accessing the URL returns a session time-out message.

Rendering Maps

Now that you know about views, map styles, and how to get a map image for both Windows and web applications, in this section of the chapter, let's look at how to render places, addresses, pushpins, and routes.

Rendering Places and Addresses

Rendering a place or address on a map starts with some type of Find call—either a Find call for a place or a FindAddress call. Once you successfully find a place or an address, use the found location's best map view to get the map using the RenderServiceSoap.GetMap method. For example, to render New York City on a map, start with the Find call and pass the found location's best map view to the GetMap method:

```
//Find New York, NY
FindServiceSoap findService  = new FindServiceSoap( );
//Assign credentials
. . .
//Define find specification
FindSpecification findSpec = new FindSpecification( );
//Assign data source
findSpec.DataSourceName = "MapPoint.NA";
//Assign input place
findSpec.InputPlace = "New York, NY";
//Find place
FindResults foundResults = findService.Find(findSpec);

//Get the best map view
ViewByHeightWidth view =
            foundResults.Results[0].FoundLocation.BestMapView.ByHeightWidth;

//Get Render Service Soap
RenderServiceSoap renderService  = new RenderServiceSoap( );
//Assign credentials
. . .
//Define map specification
MapSpecification mapSpec  = new MapSpecification( );
//Assign data source
mapSpec.DataSourceName = "MapPoint.NA";
//Assign the view
mapSpec.Views = new MapView[] {view}

//Get the map image
MapImage[] mapImages = renderService.GetMap(mapSpec);

//Get the bitmap image and assign it to a picture box
System.IO.Stream streamImage =
            new System.IO.MemoryStream(mapImages[0].MimeData.Bits);
Bitmap bitmapImage = new Bitmap(streamImage);
```

```
//Assign it to the picture box
pictureBox1.Image = bitmapImage;
```

When this code is executed, MapPoint Web Service renders the map shown in Figure 8-5.

Figure 8-5. Place map with default map options

This map was rendered using all default map options, such as style, zoom level, and map image size; with the default settings, the map image size was 240 pixels high and 296 pixels wide. What if you need a map 400 pixels high and 600 pixels wide? In order to render a map image with different dimensions, use the `MapOptions.Format` property of the `MapOptions` object. The `Format` property is of type `ImageFormat` object, and it holds the definition for the map image settings, such as the height, width, and Mime type of the image. To get a 400 × 600 map image, set the `MapOptions` as follows:

```
//Create MapSpecification object
MapSpecification mapSpec = new MapSpecification();

//Assign views and data source
. . .

//Create MapOptions
mapSpec.Options = new MapOptions();

//Set Map Image Format Settings
mapSpec.Options.Format = new ImageFormat();

//Set height
mapSpec.Options.Format.Height = 400;

//Set width
mapSpec.Options.Format.Width = 600;
```

```
//Get map
MapImage[] mapImages =
         renderService.GetMap(mapSpec);
```

Once you add the map image specifications for width and height, the map is rendered using the desired settings, as shown in Figure 8-6.

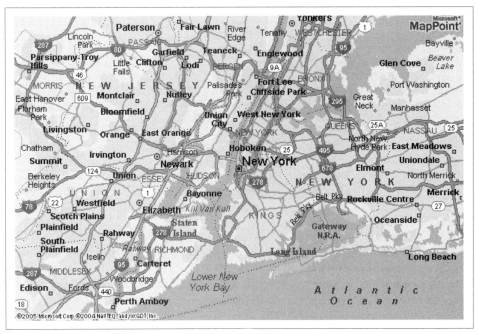

Figure 8-6. A 400 × 600 map rendered for New York, NY

The map is now the desired size, but there is still a problem—even though we know the map center is New York, there is no clear indication of which place you were looking for. To work around this issue, you can place a pushpin on New York City as a visual indication using the MapSpecifications.Pushpins property.

Rendering Pushpins

To render pushpins on a map, you need to define them and assign them to the corresponding MapSpecification.Pushpins property. This property takes an array of Pushpin objects that define the exact locations (as latitude/longitude coordinates) to be marked with pushpins. To add a pushpin to the map in Figure 8-6 to show that exactly where New York City is, add a Pushpin to the MapSpecification object:

```
//Create a pushpin
Pushpin pin = new Pushpin();
```

```
//Assign data source
pin.IconDataSource = "MapPoint.Icons";

//Assign icon name
pin.IconName = "1";

//Assign label
pin.Label = this.inputPlace.Text;

//Assign location
pin.LatLong = foundLocation.LatLong;

//Add pushpin to map specificiation
mapSpec.Pushpins = new Pushpin[] {pin};
```

Adding this code renders a map with a pushpin as shown in Figure 8-7.

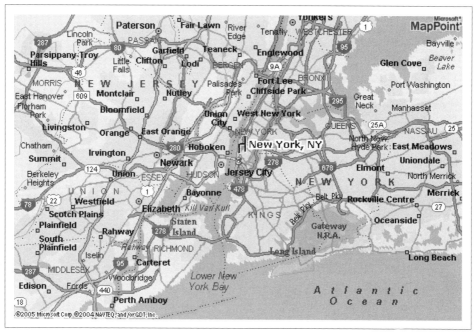

Figure 8-7. Map rendered with a pushpin

The MapSpecifications.Pushpins property is an array of pushpins, so of course you can draw more than one pushpin. However, the maximum limit to the number of pushpins that can be rendered on one map is 100. If you have more than 100 pushpins to be displayed on one map, the best solution is to implement pagination without cluttering the map with too many pushpins. If you look at how each pushpin is defined, it has a data source (standard data source is MapPoint.Icons, which has number of pushpins that you can use), a label, and a latitude/longitude.

For a full list of icons supported by MapPoint.Icons data source, go to *http://msdn.microsoft.com/library/default.asp?url=/library/en-us/ mappointsdk/HTML/mpn35devTablesIcons.asp.*

Of course, you can also upload your own icons to the MapPoint Web Service servers using the Customer Services site to use them with your render calls. Since you know how to render one pushpin, let's learn how to add more pushpins.

Rendering points of interest

One of the most frequently used scenarios for rendering maps and pushpins is to find a place and render points of interest around it. For example, first find New York City, and then render all coffee shops within five miles:

```
//Define a find nearby specification
FindNearbySpecification fnbSpec = new FindNearbySpecification();
//Assign data source
fnbSpec.DataSourceName = "MapPoint.FourthCoffeeSample";
//Assign original location
fnbSpec.LatLong = foundLocation.LatLong;
//Assign distance
fnbSpec.Distance = 5.0;

//Assign entity type
fnbSpec.Filter = new FindFilter();
fnbSpec.Filter.EntityTypeName = "FourthCoffeeShops";

//Find nearby coffeeshops
FindResults findResults = findService.FindNearby(fnbSpec);

//Add all locations to an array list
System.Collections.ArrayList pinList =
            new ArrayList();
foreach(FindResult findResult in findResults.Results)
{
    //Create a pushpin
    Pushpin pin = new Pushpin();
    pin.IconDataSource = "MapPoint.Icons";
    pin.IconName = "CoffeeShopIcon";
    pin.LatLong = findResult.FoundLocation.LatLong;
    pin.Label = findResult.FoundLocation.Entity.DisplayName;
    pinList.Add(pin);
}

//Add the original location pin
Pushpin originalLoc = new Pushpin();
originalLoc.IconDataSource = "MapPoint.Icons";
originalLoc.IconName = "33";
originalLoc.LatLong = foundLocation.LatLong;
originalLoc.Label = "New York, NY";
pinList.Add(originalLoc);
```

```
//Assign pins to the map specification
mapSpec.Pushpins = pinList.ToArray(typeof(Pushpin)) as Pushpin[];

//Get map
```

After finding coffee shops around the input place, I added them to an `ArrayList` so that I can assign all the coffee shop locations, along with the original location, to the `MapSpecification.Pushpins` property to render on a map. When this code is executed, a map is rendered as shown in Figure 8-8.

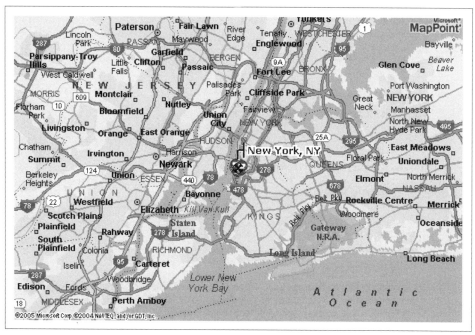

Figure 8-8. Rendering multiple pushpins on a map

The map is not usable because the original map view is optimized to display the input location (New York, NY) but not the points of interest around it. You need to recalculate the map view to be optimized for all of these locations before rendering it. There are two methods you can use to perform the recalculation of the map view with all the pushpins around:

- The `ViewByBoundingLocations` view to set `MapSpecification` views

- The `RenderServiceSoap.GetBestMapView` method to calculate the map view and then assign it to the `MapSpecification.Views` property

Either way, you will get a better-looking map. In the following code, I have added each coffee shop to another array list that holds all location objects to be used for `ViewByBoundingLocations` view, which will be defined later using those locations:

```csharp
//Add all locations to an array list
System.Collections.ArrayList locationList =
                new ArrayList();

//Add all pushpins to an array list
System.Collections.ArrayList pinList =
                new ArrayList();
foreach(FindResult findResult in findResults.Results)
{
    //Create a pushpin
    Pushpin pin = new Pushpin();
    pin.IconDataSource = "MapPoint.Icons";
    pin.IconName = "CoffeeShopIcon";
    pin.LatLong = findResult.FoundLocation.LatLong;
    //pin.Label = findResult.FoundLocation.Entity.DisplayName;
    pinList.Add(pin);

    //Add location
    locationList.Add(findResult.FoundLocation);
}

//Add the original location pin
Pushpin originalLoc = new Pushpin();
originalLoc.IconDataSource = "MapPoint.Icons";
originalLoc.IconName = "33";
originalLoc.LatLong = foundLocation.LatLong;
originalLoc.Label = "New York, NY";
pinList.Add(originalLoc);


//Define view
ViewByBoundingLocations vbl = new ViewByBoundingLocations();
//View by Locations
vbl.Locations = locationList.ToArray(typeof(Location)) as Location[];

//Assign pins to the map specification
mapSpec.Pushpins = pinList.ToArray(typeof(Pushpin)) as Pushpin[];

//Assign view
mapSpec.Views = new MapView[] {vbl};

//Get map
```

When this code is executed, MapPoint Web Service recalculates the map view to fit all locations within an optimized view for all the encompassing locations. The map rendered for the new view is shown in Figure 8-9.

The map clearly shows all the coffee shops without much clutter, but some coffee shops overlap each other. How can you avoid this issue?

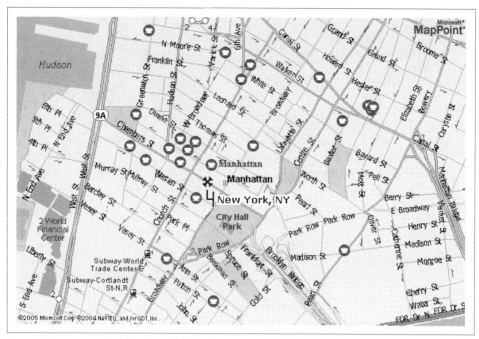

Figure 8-9. Map rendered with recalculated view

Avoiding icon collision

MapPoint Web Service allows you to render pushpins without icon collisions using the `MapOptions.PreventIconCollisions` property:

```
//Prevent Icon Collisions
mapSpec.Options.PreventIconCollisions = true;
```

When this flag is set to `true`, the map is rendered as shown in Figure 8-10 in "icons on stick" mode to prevent icon collisions.

As you can see, the map is now free of colliding icons and is much more readable.

Suppressing standard entity types

To improve the readability, you can also suppress standard entities from the map. For example, in the map shown in Figure 8-10, there are two subway stations rendered on the map along with the coffee shops. For improved readability, you can suppress that extraneous information using the `MapSpecification.HideEntityTypes` property. This property takes an array of standard entity type names that needs to be eliminated from rendering; the map in Figure 8-11 is rendered when you chose to eliminate the MetroStation entity type from rendering:

```
//Hide entity types
mapSpec.HideEntityTypes = new string[] {"MetroStation"};
```

The map no longer renders the subway stations.

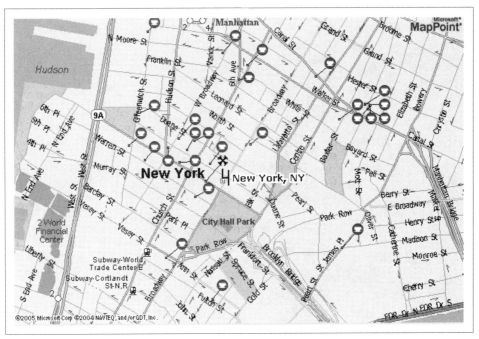

Figure 8-10. Rendering icons without collisions

 You can get a full list of standard entity types supported by each data source at *http://msdn.microsoft.com/library/default.asp?url=/library/en-us/mappointsdk/HTML/index.asp.*

Converting pushpins to pixel coordinates

Sometimes, you may need to know the pixel coordinates of the pushpins rendered on the map or the latitude and longitude coordinates of the pushpin pixel coordinates. Render Service offers two methods, ConvertToPoint and ConvertToLatLong, to calculate pixel position from a LatLong object and to obtain LatLong objects from pixel coordinates on a rendered map. The key to converting location to pixel and pixel to location on a map is the map view, which MapPoint Web Service uses to perform these calculations. If you have a requirement to build an application to obtain latitude and longitude when a user clicks on a map, it can be accomplished as follows:

```
//Define a pixel coordinate array
PixelCoord[] pixels = new PixelCoord[1];
pixels[0] = new PixelCoord( );
//Trap OnMouseDown event and X, Y coordinates
pixels[0].X = e.X;
pixels[0].Y = e.Y;
```

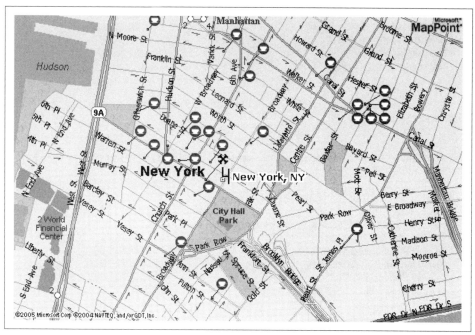

Figure 8-11. Route rendered on a map

```
//Get the latitude longitude from the point
LatLong[] latlongs =
    renderService.ConvertToLatLong(pixels, mapSpec.Views[0],
                                   400, 600);
```

The method `ConvertToLatLong` takes the pixel position, current map view, and the height and width of the map image (not the map distance covered on the ground) and returns the latitude and longitude coordinates for the corresponding pixel positions.

Rendering Routes

Although we have talked enough about rendering points, we have not yet discussed rendering routes on a map. As it turns out, the same `MapSpecification` object and the `GetMap` method can be used to render routes. The only difference is that while rendering routes, in addition to the map view, you also need to assign the route to be rendered on the map. The assigned `Route` object must have either the `Route.Specification` or the `Route.CalculatedRepresentation` present. Here is an example of rendering a route:

```
//Route between two locations
LatLong[] latLongs = new LatLong[2];
latLongs[0] = new LatLong();
latLongs[1] = new LatLong();
//Define start location
```

```
latLongs[0].Latitude = 40;
latLongs[0].Longitude = -120;
//Define stop location
latLongs[1].Latitude = 41;
latLongs[1].Longitude = -121;

//Create a route service
RouteServiceSoap routeService = new RouteServiceSoap();
//Add credentials
. . .
//Calculate route
Route route = routeService.CalculateSimpleRoute(latLongs, "MapPoint.NA",
                                    SegmentPreference.Quickest);

//Get a map view of the route
ViewByHeightWidth[] views = new ViewByHeightWidth[1];
views[0] = route.Itinerary.View.ByHeightWidth;

//Create Start Pushpin
Pushpin start = new Pushpin();
start.IconName = "1";
start.IconDataSource = "MapPoint.Icons";
start.Label = "Start";
start.LatLong = latLongs[0];

//Create Stop Pushpin
Pushpin stop = new Pushpin();
stop.IconName = "1";
stop.IconDataSource = "MapPoint.Icons";
stop.Label = "Stop";
stop.LatLong = latLongs[1];


//Define map specification
MapSpecification mapSpec = new MapSpecification();
mapSpec.DataSourceName = "MapPoint.NA";
//Assign view
mapSpec.Views = views;
//Assign route
mapSpec.Route = route;
//Assign start and stop locations
mapSpec.Pushpins = new Pushpin[] {start, stop};

//Assign map options
mapSpec.Options = new MapOptions();
mapSpec.Options.Format = new ImageFormat();
mapSpec.Options.Format.Height = 400;
mapSpec.Options.Format.Width = 600;

//Get map
. . .
```

When this code is executed, the map in Figure 8-12 is rendered.

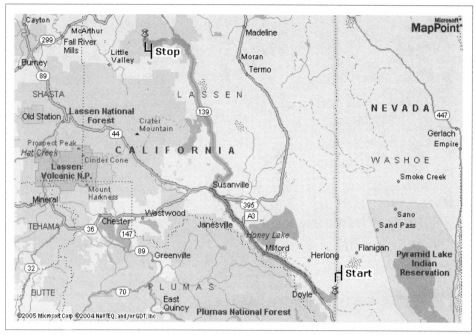

Figure 8-12. Standard route map

If you pass only the route and not the view, the entire route is rendered on the map. So, if you have a long route and want to render only a section of it, you can use the views; in case of a missing view specification, GetMap renders the entire route on the map. Also, keep in mind that any itinerary present in the Route object is ignored during the GetMap method.

You render routes using the standard GetMap method, but if you want to render LineDrive route maps, use the GetLineDriveMap method.

Rendering LineDrive Maps

Before we get into rendering LineDrive maps, let's look at what exactly they are. *LineDrive maps* are route maps that show the map of a route in an intuitive format, much as you might draw directions for a friend on a piece of paper. LineDrive provides the essential information about a route in an easy-to-use format that includes start and end points, names of streets and cross-streets, and mileage information. The core difference between a regular route map and a LineDrive map is that a LineDrive map gives more emphasis to starting/ending points and turns. For example, if you are driving from Redmond, WA to Portland, OR, a regular route map may look like Figure 8-13.

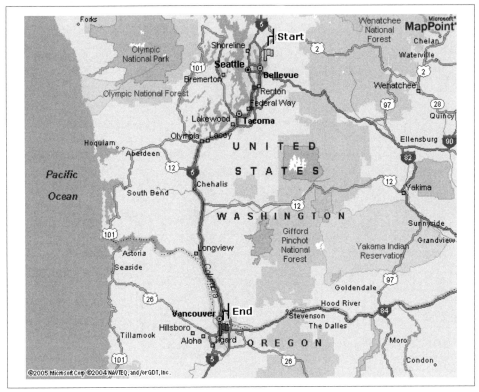

Figure 8-13. Regular route map

Rendering the same route on a LineDrive map gives you the map shown in Figure 8-14.

More emphasis is given to the turns and the starting and end points in the LineDrive map. It is important to note that a LineDrive route is not always identical to the route created using the standard map style. LineDrive maps also have some limitations in that they:

- Do not support Pan or Zoom
- Are not available for Australia (MapPoint.AP data source) or Brazil (MapPoint. BR data source)
- Are not drawn to scale

To render a LineDrive map, you still need a valid Route object (after all, a LineDrive map is just a variation in rendering a route). Call the GetLineDriveMap method using a valid LineDriveMapSpecification object. The LineDriveSpecification object specifies the size of the map, the route to be rendered, and the palette to be used for rendering the LineDrive map. You can pick a palette style using the PaletteType enumeration. The available options for the PaletteType enumeration are shown in Table 8-4.

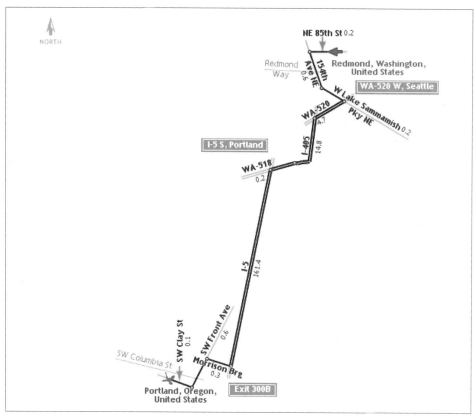

Figure 8-14. LineDrive Map for the same route as in Figure 8-13

Table 8-4. LineDrive palette options

Item	Description
Color	Returns a full color representation of the LineDrive map. This is the default value.
GrayScale	Returns a grayscale representation of the LineDrive map.
Monochrome	Returns a black and white representation of the LineDrive map.

The following code shows how to use the LineDriveSpecification object to render a LineDrive map displaying a route:

```
//Create an instance of RenderServiceSoap and
//Assign Credentials
RenderServiceSoap renderSoap =
                new RenderServiceSoap( );


//Create a LineDriveMapSpecification object
LineDriveMapSpecification lineDriveSpec =
                new LineDriveMapSpecification( );
```

```
//Assign the route to be rendered
//Assumes that the route is pre-calculated.
lineDriveSpec.Route = myroute;

//Set the LineDriveMapOptions such as Palette
LineDriveMapOptions lineDriveOptions =
                    new LineDriveMapOptions();
//Return Map Url
lineDriveOptions.ReturnType = MapReturnType.ReturnUrl;
//Set palette type as Color map
lineDriveOptions.PaletteType = PaletteType.Color;

//Assign options to the specification
lineDriveSpec.Options = lineDriveOptions;

//Get LineDrive maps
LineDriveMapImage[] lineDriveMaps
              = renderSoap.GetLineDriveMap(lineDriveSpec);

//Display the LineDrive Maps
. . .
```

The GetLineDriveMap returns the LineDriveMapImage array. Depending on the driving directions, the LineDrive map may be split into many map images, so you have to check for the image array length and display them accordingly. Also, to display the driving directions along with each LineDrive map image, match each LineDriveMapImage instance with the corresponding driving directions using the FirstDirectionID and LastDirectionID properties. The following code shows how to display LineDriveMapImage array along with the matching driving directions:

```
//Get LineDrive Maps
LineDriveMapImage[] lineDriveMapImages =
              renderSoap.GetLineDriveMap(lineDriveSpec);
//Now process them to display the map and the driving directions
foreach(LineDriveMapImage lineDriveImage in lineDriveMapImages)
{
    //Display the map image
    //Something like: Assign the url to your img tag
    . . .

    //Display the matching driving directions
    FormatDirectionsForLineDriveImage(lineDriveImage,
                                      lineDriveSpec.Route);
}
```

The helper function FormatDirectionsForLineDriveImage is shown in the following code:

```
//Returns the matching driving directions for a LineDriveImage
private string FormatDirectionsForLineDriveImage(
                    LineDriveMapImage lineDriveMapImage,
                    Route route)
{
```

```
        if(lineDriveMapImage == null || route == null)
            return string.Empty;

        System.Text.StringBuilder stringBuffer = new System.Text.StringBuilder( );

        //For each route segment
        foreach(Segment segment in route.Itinerary.Segments)
        {
            //For each direction entry
            foreach(Direction direction in segment.Directions)
            {
                //See if the id of the direction falls in the range for the current
                //LineDrive image
                if(direction.ID >= lineDriveMapImage.FirstDirectionID ||
                    direction.ID <= lineDriveMapImage.LastDirectionID)
                {
                    //If so display it
                    stringBuffer.Append(direction.Instruction);
                    //Append a line break for display formatting purposes
                    stringBuffer.Append("<BR>");
                }
            }
        }
        //Return the matching directions
        return stringBuffer.ToString( );
    }
```

Use the `LineDriveMapImage.FirstDirectionID` and `LineDriveMapImage.LastDirectionID` properties to match the driving directions. Now that you have seen rendering of both points and routes, let's look at rendering polygons.

Rendering Polygons

In Chapter 6, we looked at finding polygons depending on various spatial filters; in this section, we'll learn how to render the polygons using render service.

Rendering polygons in MapPoint Web Service is fairly straightforward; just like rendering roads and pushpins, you use the `RenderServiceSoap.GetMap` method to render polygons by specifying which polygons to render using the `MapSpecification` object. Before getting into the rendering details, let's look at how polygons are represented programmatically in MapPoint Web Service.

In MapPoint Web Service, polygons are programmatically represented by `Polygon` class instances. Each `Polygon` class exposes a set of fields listed in Table 8-5 that define the identity and style of the polygon.

Table 8-5. Polygon class fields

Field	Description
DataSourceName	Name of the data source that the current polygon belongs to
EntityID	An integer that uniquely identifies the polygon entity in a given data source

Table 8-5. Polygon class fields (continued)

Field	Description
BorderColor	An ElementColor object defining the color and level of transparency that is used when drawing the outside border of the polygon
FillColor	An ElementColor object defining the color and level of transparency that is used when shading the polygon
Label	The text to display when rendering the polygon

The BorderColor and FillColor use the ElementColor object to set the colors and transparency of the polygon. The ElementColor class defines the Red, Blue, and Green components of the color, along with the Alpha value, which defines transparency. Valid values range from 0 to 255. The fields exposed by the ElementColor class are shown in Table 8-6.

Table 8-6. ElementColor class fields

Field	Component value
A	Alpha
R	Red
G	Green
B	Blue

Let's look at the following code, which defines a polygon using the Polygon class:

```
//Define a polygon instance
Polygon polygon = new Polygon( );

//Assign data source name and id
polygon.DataSourceName = "your poly data source";
polygon.EntityID = 23354;

//Define border color
ElementColor borderColor = new ElementColor( );
borderColor.A=221;
borderColor.B=255;
borderColor.G=255;
borderColor.R=128;

//Define fill color
ElementColor fillColor = new ElementColor( );
fillColor.A=90;
fillColor.B=255;
fillColor.G=255;
fillColor.R=128;

//Assign border and fill colors
polygon.BorderColor=borderColor;
polygon.FillColor=fillColor;
```

Once you have a valid polygon, it is easy to render it using the GetMap method:

```
//Define a RenderServiceSoap instance
RenderServiceSoap renderSoap = new RenderServiceSoap();

//Assign credentials
. . .

//Define a MapSpecification object
MapSpecification mapSpec = new MapSpecification();

//Assign rendering data source
spec.DataSourceName = "MapPoint.NA";

//Assign views and map options
. . .

//Create a polygon
//Define a polygon instance
Polygon polygon = new Polygon();

//Assign data source name and id
polygon.DataSourceName = "your poly data source";
polygon.EntityID = 23354;

//Define border color
ElementColor borderColor = new ElementColor();
borderColor.A=221;
borderColor.B=255;
borderColor.G=255;
borderColor.R=128;

//Define fill color
ElementColor fillColor = new ElementColor();
fillColor.A=90;
fillColor.B=255;
fillColor.G=255;
fillColor.R=128;

//Assign border and fill colors
polygon.BorderColor=borderColor;
polygon.FillColor=fillColor;

//Assign to Polygons array
mapSpec.Polygons = new Polygon[1] {polygon};

//Render them on a map
MapImage[] mapImages = renderSoap.GetMap(mapSpec);
```

Creating Polygon instances and assigning them to the MapSpecification.Polygons field is all it takes to render polygons using the GetMap method. Now that you know how to render points, routes, and polygons, let's look at map interaction, such as panning and zooming, in the context of rendering.

Map Interaction

Once you have rendered your initial map, your users may want to interact with it by zooming in, zooming out, or panning around the map. In order to provide this functionality, you need to implement panning and zooming on your map using the same RenderServiceSoap.GetMap method with more specific map options.

Programming Map Zoom

MapOptions object offers the Zoom property, of type double, with which you can set the zoom level of any given map. The MapPoints.Zoom property identifies the factor by which the map image is magnified; when a map is rendered, the Zoom value is initially set to one. To zoom in by 50%, set the Zoom value to 0.5; to zoom in again another 50%, set the Zoom value to 0.25; each time you divide the zoom value by 2, you zoom in 50% more than the previous level. The same logic works for zoom out. To zoom out the map by 50%, simply multiply the Zoom value by 2. After setting the new Zoom value to the MapSpecification object, call the GetMap method again with the same specification to zoom in or out; you can also get the initial map with the view zoomed in or out by setting the appropriate value. The following code shows how to set the zoom value to get the initial map with the view zoomed in by 50%:

```
//Create render service
RenderServiceSoap renderService = new RenderServiceSoap( );

//Set credentials
. . .

//Create Map Specification
//Or assign to an existing map specification

//Zoom in by 50%
mapSpec.Options.Zoom = mapSpec.Options.Zoom/2;

//Get Map
MapImage[] maps = renderService.GetMap(mapSpec);
```

The Zoom value is set to the MapOptions.Zoom value and passed to the GetMap method; one thing to keep in mind regarding the Zoom value is that it must be a positive value, and it can't be zero.

Programming Map Pan

Similar to zoom, MapOptions object offers two properties, PanVertical and PanHorizontal, both of type double, which you can use to pan rendered maps. The MapPoints.PanVertical and MapPoints.PanHorizontal properties identify the factor by which the map image is panned. When a map is originally rendered, both the vertical and horizontal pan factors are set to zero. To pan the map north by 50% (half of the view), set the PanVertical value to 0.5, and to pan north by another 50%, increment the PanVertical value by 0.5 again; each time you increment the pan value by 0.5, you pan the map by another 50%. The same logic works for pan horizontal. However, there are a couple of things you need to keep in mind:

- Positive pan values indicate pans east or north
- Negative pan values indicate pans west or south
- To pan northeast, southwest, southeast, or northwest, you need to set both pan vertical and pan horizontal values.

The following code shows how to set the pan the initial map by 20% north:

```
//Create render service
RenderServiceSoap renderService = new RenderServiceSoap( );

//Set credentials
. . .

//Create Map Specification
//Or assign to an existing map specification
. . .

//Pan map North by 20%
mapSpec.Options.PanVertical =
            mapSpec.Options.PanVertical + 0.20

//Get Map
MapImage[] maps = renderService.GetMap(mapSpec);
```

Similarly, to pan the same map south instead of north, use the following pan factor:

```
//Pan map South by 20%
mapSpec.Options.PanVertical =
            mapSpec.Options.PanVertical - 0.20

//Get Map
MapImage[] maps = renderService.GetMap(mapSpec);
```

Along the same lines, to pan the map northwest, set both PanVertical and PanHorizontal as follows:

```
// +ve value for North
mapSpec.Options.PanVertical
        = mapSpec.Options.PanVertical + 0.20;

//-ve value for West
mapSpec.Options.PanHorizontal
        = mapSpec.Options.PanHorizontal - 0.20;

//Get Map
MapImage[] maps = renderService.GetMap(mapSpec);
```

While these pan settings work well at higher zoom levels, you will soon realize that the 20% pan factor pans the map more than you would like it to pan at lower zoom levels; to compensate, you just need to multiply the pan factor by the zoom factor:

```
//Compensate map pan with zoom factor
mapSpec.Options.PanVertical
        = mapSpec.Options.PanVertical + 0.20 * mapSpec.Options.Zoom;
//Compensate map pan with zoom factor
mapSpec.Options.PanHorizontal
        = mapSpec.Options.PanHorizontal - 0.20 * mapSpec.Options.Zoom;

//Get Map
. . .
```

Compensating the map pan with zoom value makes sure the panning is nonlinear at different zoom levels.

Asynchronous Programming

The asynchronous programming techniques that we have seen in Chapter 6 are applicable to Render Service as well. Depending on which application you are developing (for either Windows or the Web), you have two different options to use asynchronous programming for getting maps and enabling map interaction such as panning and zooming.

Asynchronous Programming for Windows Applications

When you use Visual Studio .NET to generate the MapPoint Web Service proxy class, it also generates the necessary methods for asynchronous programming. For example, if you look for the RenderServiceSoap.GetMap method, you also find the RenderServiceSoap.BeginGetMap and RenderServiceSoap.EndGetMap methods in the proxy class. The Begin and End method pairs together enable the asynchronous programming patterns for your Web Service client applications. Using these methods is easy; in a synchronous scenario, your Find call looks as follows:

```
//Call the GetMap Method
MapImage[] mapImages = renderSoap.GetMap(mapSpec);
//Now display the map
. . .
```

If this code is running on the UI thread, it gets blocked until the GetMap returns the map image array and results in an unresponsive application during that time. To avoid this situation, create a worker thread and use it to call GetMap methods so that your UI thread is free during this long network round-trip. In fact, that's exactly what the BeginGetMap and EndGetMap methods do behind the scenes. To implement the previous code using asynchronous methods, you would do something similar to the following code. First, define a "callback" method for your asynchronous method calls:

```
private void RenderServiceCallback(IAsyncResult ar)
{
    RenderServiceSoap renderSoap
      = ar.AsyncState as RenderServiceSoap;
    if(renderSoap == null)
      return;
    MapImage[] mapImages = renderSoap.EndGetMap(ar);
    //Display map
    . . .
}
```

Next, modify your GetMap call to be an asynchronous BeginGetMap call:

```
//Async call to GetMap
AsyncCallback callback = new AsyncCallback(RenderServiceCallback);
rendersoap.BeginGetMap(mapspec, callback, rendersoap);
```

The BeginGetMap call invokes the GetMap method on a different (worker) thread and passes a pointer to the RenderSeviceCallback method as a "callback" method; when the GetMap method returns the MapResult array, the callback delegate is invoked so that the RenderServiceCallback method gets executed on the UI thread again. In the RenderServiceCallback method, you need to obtain the MapImage array returned by the GetMap method by calling the EndGetMap method and displaying it. Keep in mind that the HTTP session is kept alive during this asynchronous operation behind the scenes—so this pattern is only asynchronous at your application thread level, not at the HTTP communication level.

Asynchronous Programming for Web Applications

As with AJAX, discussed in Chapter 6, you can use the combination of XML over HTTP and asynchronous JavaScript to create web applications that give the user a rich experience.

AJAX-Enabling Your Web Applications

Since the basics of AJAX implementation have already been covered in Chapter 6, in this section I will discuss the items specific to render. To AJAX-enable your rendering, you need to implement:

- An ASP.NET page (or an HTTP handler) that can take a place or an address and return map URL from MapPoint Web Service
- AJAX JavaScript and an image (img tag) on the web client that invokes the previously mentioned ASP.NET page and retrieves the map URL to display in the page

Also, when you are implementing the ASP.NET page that returns the map URL to the HTML page, you have to cache the corresponding MapSpecification at HTTP Session scope to enable map interaction, such as panning and zooming.

Where Are We?

In this chapter, you have seen how map rendering works in MapPoint Web Service. To render maps, use a valid MapSpecification object to call the RenderServiceSoap. GetMap method. Once a map is rendered, it allows you to interact by setting appropriate MapOptions to the MapSpecification object. RenderServiceSoap also offers methods to convert pixels on any given map to latitude and longitude coordinates and vice versa. Finally, using the Render Service, you can render not only maps, but points, routes, and polygon shapes.

PART III

MapPoint Location Server

CHAPTER 9

Programming Microsoft Location Server

While MapPoint 2004 and MapPoint Web Service both provide APIs to understand location information and process location data, Microsoft Location Server provides an ability to integrate real-time location into your application to provide location-based applications and services; to that end, Microsoft Location Server transcends into a real-time location platform that answers the basic question "Where am I?"

Location-based services are provided to a user based on his real-time location and can range from a simple service, such as listing nearby restaurants, to more complex features, such as analyzing real-time traffic conditions and finding the least congested route to a destination. For location-based services to work, a locatable device, such as a wireless mobile device or a pager, is usually necessary to identify the user's geographical location. In essence, location-based services are all about identifying the best and nearest possible service based on where the user currently is.

Developing location-based services conventionally is tedious and expensive because GPS hardware and software are required. However, with the Microsoft Location Server, you don't need a GPS device to find your real-time location; you can find your location (or your customer's location) using a mobile phone number.

In this chapter, I will discuss the inner workings of the Microsoft Location Server in detail; at the end I will go over the installation process of the Microsoft Location Server before tackling the programming aspects in the next chapter.

Microsoft Location Server Terminology

Before I get into the details of how Microsoft Location Server works, you'll need to familiarize yourself with the following terminology:

Mobile Operator

A company that provides communication services for mobile devices, such as cell phones and pagers. For example, in the United States, some companies that provide mobile communication services, such as Sprint, Verizon, and Nextel, fall into this category.

Provisioning

> *Provisioning* is the process of registering an enterprise user with Microsoft Location Server. A user who is registered with Microsoft Location Server is called a *provisioned user*. Each provisioned user must have an associated mobile device number (or phone number) that can be used by the mobile operator to identify the user's real-time location.

Provider

> A *provider* is a software plug-in for Microsoft Location Server developed to communicate with a specific network carrier, such as a cell phone company, either to obtain the location of a mobile device or to send a Short Message Service (SMS) message to a mobile device. Providers used for getting the location of a mobile device are called *location providers*, and providers used for sending SMS messages are called *notification providers*. Location and notification providers are unique to each mobile operator, and this is where the value of the Microsoft Location Server comes into the picture—it eliminates the carrier-specific complexity and provides an aggregated set of APIs for the developers to build applications.

Locatable Contact

> A *locatable contact* is a provisioned user who can be contacted by another provisioned user within an enterprise.

With this introduction to the key terminology used in Microsoft Location Server, let's see how it works to obtain real-time location from the cellular phone networks.

How Does Location Server Work?

Microsoft Location Server does not require GPS-like hardware to get real-time locations; instead, it locates a provisioned user's mobile device by communicating with a mobile operator. In a typical scenario, a user requests her position using a client that communicates with Microsoft Location Server; this client can be a mobile phone (such as a SmartPhone) or a portable computer (such as a laptop).

When Microsoft Location Server receives the request from the client, it identifies the mobile operator for the user and sends a location request to the mobile operator. The mobile operator responds by sending back the real-time location of the user, expressed as latitude and longitude coordinates. Microsoft Location Server then returns that location to the user's client, where it can be used for rendering a map or finding nearby points of interests, depending on the application. All communications that are specific to a mobile operator are hidden from end users and developers. Thus, Microsoft Location Server works as an aggregator for mobile operators by abstracting implementation details specific to the mobile operator to obtain a real-time location. Figure 9-1 summarizes this process.

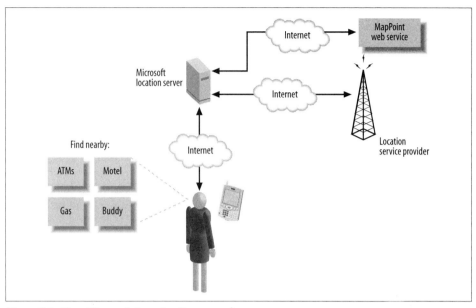

Figure 9-1. How Microsoft Location Server works

One important thing to keep in mind is that the accuracy of the locations returned by the Microsoft Location Server depends on the mobile operators and methods used to locate the devices on their networks. For example, some cell phone carriers use cell tower triangulation technique to determine the location of a phone; in this method the phone's location is determined by the cell towers around it. As you can imagine, this method does not always yield an accurate location. Some carriers use an assisted GPS technique, which results in a very accurate location of the phone. Table 9-1 provides an overview of technologies used by different network carriers and the approximate location accuracy of each technique used.

Table 9-1. Location Accuracy and the techniques used

Technique used	Approximate location accuracy
Cell Sector	Urban Areas (1–3 Kilometers)
	Suburban Areas (3–20 Kilometers)
Assisted GPS (AGPS)	10–50 meters
Time Difference of Arrival (TDOA)	100 meters
Angle of Arrival (AOA)	100 meters

Now that you know how Microsoft Location Server works in general, let's look at the internals to understand its architecture.

Microsoft Location Server Architecture

Microsoft Location Server consists of three core components:

- Microsoft Location Server Web Service
- Microsoft Location Server database
- Microsoft Location Server providers

In this section, I will go through each one in detail.

Microsoft Location Server Web Service

Microsoft Location Server Web Service is a programmable web service that developers can use to build real-time location client applications for a variety of platforms, including Microsoft Windows, the Web, and mobile devices. This web service exposes an API for finding the real-time locations of users and their contacts, finding points of interest, and managing contacts. Unlike MapPoint Web Service, which is hosted by Microsoft, Microsoft Location Server Web Service is hosted within your enterprise. In order to host this web service, you need Internet Information Server (IIS) 5.0 or higher, along with Secure Socket Layers (SSL).

It is important to note that Microsoft Location Server Web Service is always hosted with Secure Socket Layers (SSL) enabled to mitigate privacy-related issues while communicating the real-time location over the wire. Due to this precaution, to communicate with Microsoft Location Server Web Service, your client (Pocket PC, Pocket PC emulator, or development computer) must be able to establish a trusted connection via SSL. A client can establish a trusted connection when MapPoint Location Web Service is deployed with a root certificate issued by authorities such as Verisign, Cybertrust, Thawte, or Entrust. However, during development, if Microsoft Location Server Web Service is deployed using a certificate generated by your enterprise, you must install the certificate on the client manually.

 For information on adding certificates to a mobile device, see the Microsoft Knowledge Base article, *Sample to Add Root Certificates to Pocket PC 2002.*

Microsoft Location Server Database

The Microsoft Location Server database is a Microsoft SQL Server 2000 database used for storing information about provisioned users, contacts, and mobile operators, along with data related to points of interest (Find Nearby) categories. Microsoft Location Server exposes a set of management APIs for performing tasks such as provisioning users, managing contacts, and managing Find Nearby categories.

You'll need SQL Server 2000 with Service Pack 3 (SP3) or later to install the Microsoft Location Server database.

Microsoft Location Server Providers

Microsoft Location Server providers are software plug-ins required for communication with mobile operators. Usually, there is a location provider and a notification provider for each mobile operator. Because the implementation of location and notification providers is unique to each mobile operator, Microsoft Location Server does not currently expose APIs for developing location or notification providers.

The Microsoft Location Server includes a demonstration location provider for testing purposes. This demo provider simulates real-time location scenarios against a configurable file with phone numbers and associated latitude and longitude pairs.

Working with the Demo Location Provider

There are a few scenarios where you may need to use Demo Location Provider (a plug-in that actually talks to mobile phone carriers to get the location of a mobile phone) for programming with MapPoint Location Server:

- Your mobile phone carrier is not (yet) supported by MapPoint Location Server.
- You want to develop a demo application before asking the actual phone carriers for a location.
- You want to test/troubleshoot your MapPoint Location Server application without using the mobile operator's network.

In these cases, you can use the Demo Location Provider that ships with Microsoft Location Server. The Demo Location Provider works off of a text file to return a simulated location for a provisioned user. You can manually edit this text file and hardcode locations against the provisioned phone numbers for testing purposes.

The good news is that no extra code (that is specific to the demo provider) needs to be written to work with the Demo Location Provider. To locate a phone number using the Demo Location Provider, follow these steps:

1. Add a user (provision the phone number) either using the MMC or Server API.
2. Add Demo Location Provider as the location provider for that user.
3. Edit the *TestLocations.txt* file located in the *Program Files\Microsoft MapPoint Location Server\MLS\WebService\Bin* folder to add a simulated location for the user's mobile phone in the following format:

```
Mobile Phone Number, Status Code, Latitude, Longitude, Delay
```

So, an example simulated location for a mobile phone—for example, (425) 555-1212— would be:

```
14255551212,Success,47.6446802586242,-122.130220099595,1
```

Now you can locate this phone number using either the locator clients that ship with Microsoft Location Server or the APIs.

For more information about the demo provider, see the Microsoft Location Server Administrator's Guide, Version 1.0, which is included with Microsoft Location Server.

Figure 9-2 shows how all the core components work together to obtain the real-time location of a mobile device.

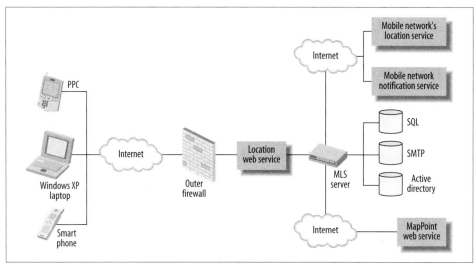

Figure 9-2. Location Server architecture

Now that you know the core components of the Location Server and how they work together, let's look at how to install the Location Server within your enterprise.

Installing the Location Server

In a production environment, Microsoft Location Server components should be distributed among multiple computers for security reasons; however, when you are developing and testing Microsoft Location Server applications, you may want to install all the components on a single computer. In this section, we'll see how to set up your Microsoft Location Server environment and install Microsoft Location Server on a single computer for development and testing.

 For the latest version of the Microsoft Location Server, go to *http://go. microsoft.com/fwlink/?linkid=25704*.

To use Microsoft Location Server, you also need a valid MapPoint Web Service account. For more information about MapPoint Web Service or to sign up for a

MapPoint Web Service evaluation account, visit the MapPoint Web Service web site at *http://www.microsoft.com/mappoint/products/webservice/default.mspx*.

Installation Overview

To install Microsoft Location Server, you need Microsoft Windows Server 2003, Standard Edition in a new Active Directory domain as your web server and Microsoft SQL Server 2000 as the Microsoft Location Server database.

 For a complete list of Microsoft Location Server prerequisites, see Chapter 2, *Installing Microsoft Location Server*, in the Microsoft Location Server Administrator's Guide.

The installation process consists of four primary tasks, each with a number of subtasks. The four primary tasks are:

1. Install and configure Windows Server 2003, Standard Edition.
2. Install and configure SQL Server 2000 Developer Edition and apply the latest service pack (SP3a).
3. Generate a Secure Sockets Layer (SSL) certificate and configure Internet Information Services (IIS) for SSL.
4. Install and configure Microsoft Location Server and verify your installation.

Microsoft Location Server requires you to preconfigure Windows Server 2003, SQL Server 2000, and Internet Information Server with SSL before installing the Location Server itself.

 For detailed information and step-by-step instructions for preconfiguration and installation, go to *http://msdn.microsoft.com/library/default. asp?url=/library/en-us/dnmaploc/html/MLSSetup.asp?frame=true*.

Once you successfully install Microsoft Location Server, there are two kinds of applications you can develop:

Real-time location applications
    Using the Location Web Service that you installed, you can build real-time location applications using mobile devices provisioned within your enterprise.

Location Server applications
    Using the Location Server APIs, you can build applications to manage users, contacts, and providers and to find nearby points of interest.

In the following sections, I will outline how to access both location web service APIs and server APIs once the Microsoft Location Server is installed.

Accessing the Location Service APIs

Microsoft Location Server Web Service allows you to develop real-time location-based services, such as finding your exact location or locating your contacts' exact locations. This web service also provides API functionality to manage contacts and privacy settings for any given provisioned user, making programming with Microsoft Location Server Web Service no different from programming with any web service.

Once you have successfully installed Microsoft Location Server, you can access the Location Server Web Service APIs using the following URL:

> *https://YourFullDomainName/mmlsservice/locationserver.wsdl*

The Location Server Web Service is hosted by your enterprise on your full domain name that is only accessible via any valid provisioned enterprise user credentials. To program with this web service, you can either use WSDL.EXE or Visual Studio .NET (2003 or later) to generate .NET proxy classes that can be added as references to your project.

 If you are planning to develop applications using mobile devices such as PocketPC or SmartPhone, your client should be able to trust the (SSL) certificate presented by the server hosting the Location Server Web service. Read the following knowledge base article to add a root certificate manually: *http://support.microsoft.com/default.aspx?scid= kb;en-us;322956.*

Accessing the Location Server APIs

Using the Microsoft Location Server server-side APIs, you can develop a variety of applications that can be run on any Microsoft Location Server; it is important to keep in mind that the applications developed using the Server APIs are purely Microsoft Location Server administrative applications and are not related to any real-time location scenarios. Administrative applications for Microsoft Location Server can be categorized into four major categories:

User management applications
> Adding (provisioning) new users, updating/removing existing users, and so on.

Contact management applications
> Adding new contacts, updating current contacts, and removing old contacts for the provisioned users.

Privacy management applications
> Managing your enterprise-level privacy settings programmatically, including setting notification modes for provisioned users and setting contact level locatable permissions.

Find Nearby Category management

This category of applications allows you to manage the find nearby categories that can be enabled for finding nearby points of interest. Usually enterprises are required to add, update, and delete the find nearby categories specific to their business needs and the Server API provides a way to programmatically manage them.

Keep in mind that all of the above-mentioned functionality is already available via the Microsoft Management Console (or MMC) for the Microsoft Location Server; however, there may be instances where you need to write scriptable applications as part of the Location Server administration, which is where the Server APIs will come in handy.

To build such applications, how do you access Location Server APIs? When you install the Microsoft Location Server successfully, you will see the following Location Server Management APIs installed as part of the server installation:

`MS.LocationServer.Types.dll`

This assembly contains all the Location Server data types, such as LocatableUser and LocatableContact.

`MS.LocationServer.Management.dll`

This assembly contains all of the classes that provide methods to manage the Location Server, including the ServerAPI class containing all of the management methods.

`MS.LocationServer.Core.dll`

This assembly contains classes required by the management API types. It should only be used to add as a reference to your project; you should never have to use the types from this assembly directly in your source code.

To develop Location Server applications, copy the aforementioned assemblies to your development machine and either add them to your local Global Assembly Cache or copy them to your local application Bin folder.

Additionally, to develop Location Server Applications, you also need sufficient privileges to access the Location Server Database. You also should have an SSL root certificate on your development computer to establish a more secure connection to the computer running SQL Server. Note that in the Microsoft Location Server environment, the database server is configured with Microsoft Windows authentication mode. Your enterprise domain alias should have proper access rights to connect to the Microsoft Location Server Database.

Finally, to successfully run a Location Server management application, the account running the application must be a member of the `MLSADMINISTRATORS` security group.

Microsoft Location Server Supported Providers

Before we cover the detailed programming aspects of the Microsoft Location Server, Table 9-2 shows a list of mobile network providers that are enabled to work with Microsoft Location Server in various countries.

Table 9-2. Currently supported providers

Country/Region	Mobile network providers
United States	Nextel, Sprint
Canada	Bell Mobility
Nordic and Baltic regions	Telia Sonera
Western Europe	Teydo

There are currently many other mobile network providers working with Microsoft to enable locating via Microsoft Location Server.

 You can visit *http://www.microsoft.com/mappoint/products/locationserver/ operators.mspx* for an up-to-date list of providers who work with Microsoft Location Server.

Where Are We?

In this chapter, we have looked at the architectural details of the Microsoft Location Server and how it works to obtain real-time location of a mobile device from the mobile carrier networks. The real-time location web service is hosted within an enterprise (not by Microsoft). Location Server also provides Server Management APIs for administrative application development, such as user management, contact management, and privacy management.

Next, let's look at programming with Location Service APIs and Location Server Management APIs in detail.

CHAPTER 10

Programming with Location Server APIs

Microsoft Location Server exposes APIs for building real-time location-based applications as well as server management and administration applications. You develop location-based applications using Microsoft Location Server Web Service, and you develop management and administration applications using the Microsoft Location Server management API. As you will see later in this chapter, most of the administrative tasks that can be performed with the Location Server Web Service can be accomplished by the Server Management API as well; however, it is important to keep in mind that the web service runs under the context of the currently logged-in user, whereas the management API runs under the context of the administrator.

In this chapter, let's take a detailed look at programming both Location Server Web Service and Location Server Management APIs.

Programming with Location Server Web Service

Microsoft Location Server Web Service provides APIs for functionalities such as finding real-time locations, finding nearby points of interest, finding contacts, and adding and removing contacts. Because this web service is hosted within your enterprise, you need your network domain credentials to access it. In the following sections of this chapter, we will examine the Microsoft Location Server Web Service APIs in detail.

Anatomy of Location Web Service APIs

As you learned in Chapter 9, Location Server Web Service is hosted within your enterprise and not hosted by Microsoft. So, in order to develop with the Location Server Web Service, you need to access the WSDL (Web Service Description Language) document for the Location Server Web Service. If your enterprise's Location Server is installed on a domain (*www.YourFullDomainName.com*), your Location Server Web Service WSDL can be accessed using the following URL:

https://www.YourFullDomainName.com/mmlsservice/locationserver.wsdl

Note that the Location Server Web Service is only accessible to valid provisioned domain user accounts; to access the above WSDL, you must be a domain user on your enterprise's network and provisioned in the Microsoft Location Server as a user.

The previous WSDL contains only one SOAP endpoint (LocationService.asmx) which translates into the LocationServiceSoap class when added to your current project as a web reference. The LocationServiceSoap class provides all the necessary functionalities, such as getting real-time location, adding, updating and removing contacts, and changing personal privacy settings. Table 10-1 shows the methods offered by the LocationServiceSoap class. In this table, the current user is the original submitter of the request.

Table 10-1. LocationServiceSoap class methods

Method	Description
GetPositions	Returns the user's or contact's positions synchronously as an instance of the PositionResults class.
GetPositionsAsync	Returns the user's or contact's positions asynchronously. This method is an asynchronous version of the GetPositions method. However, you must call the GetPositionsAsyncResults method to complete the process of getting positions.
GetPositionsAsyncResults	Completes the asynchronous request invoked by the GetPositionsAsync method. This method returns the positions that correspond to the domain and alias pairs as an instance of the PositionResults class. This method must be called with a valid token obtained by calling the GetPositionsAsync method.
GetNearbyCategories	Gets Find Nearby categories based on the current user's culture.
GetVisibility	Gets the status for the current user's Visible property.
SetVisibility	Sets the status for the current user's Visible property.
GetNewContactNotification	Gets the value of the NotifyOnNewContact property for the current locatable user.
SetNewContactNotification	Sets the value of the "Notify on Contact" option for the current user.
GetDefaultCulture	Returns the default culture for the current user in string format; for example: "en-US" for English, United States.
SetDefaultCulture	Sets the default culture for the current user.
GetUserInfo	Returns the current user's information as an instance of the LocatableUser class.
AddContact	Adds a contact to the current user's list of contacts.
UpdateContact	Updates the specified contact in the current user's contact list.
DeleteContact	Deletes the specified contact entry from the current user's list of contacts.
FindProvisionedUser	Allows partial input of the LocatableUser object properties or a user's email address to search the provisioned users on the location server and returns contact information as an array of LocatableContact class instances.
GetContacts	Returns a list of contacts for the current user as an array of LocatableContact objects.

The categorizations of various methods provided by the `LocationServiceSoap` class are shown in Figure 10-1.

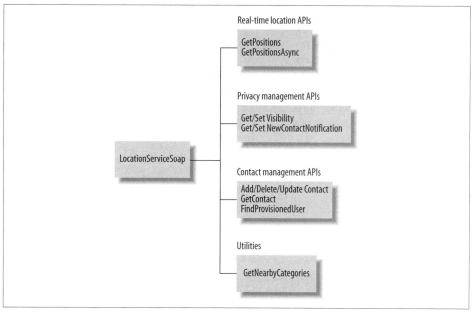

Figure 10-1. LocationServiceSoap method categorization

The methods available on the `LocationServiceSoap` type fall into three main categories:

Real-Time Location APIs
> Provide core functionality to get real-time location based on mobile phone numbers; the methods in this category are `GetPositions` and `GetPositionsAsync`.

Privacy Management APIs
> Provide core functionality to manage self privacy, including the `GetVisibility`, `SetVisibility`, `GetNewContactNotification`, and `SetNewContactNotification` methods.

Contact Management APIs
> Provide core functionality to add new contacts and delete or update existing contacts. The methods in this category include `GetContacts`, `AddContact`, and `DeleteContact`.

All these methods that run from `LocationServiceSoap` run the context of a provisioned user; in other words, `LocationServiceSoap` methods cannot be used to manipulate the privacy settings or contact management for users other than the logged-in user. Since Location Server depends on the Active Directory-based domain accounts to provision users within an enterprise, the authentication to the Location Server Web Service is performed using the enterprise domain account credentials:

```
//Create an instance of the LocationServiceSoap proxy class
LocationServiceSoap locationService = new LocationServiceSoap();
//Create an instance of the NetworkCredential class
//and add the credentials required to access the Web service
NetworkCredential credentials =
        new NetworkCredential("user", "password", "domain");
locationService.Credentials = credentials;
```

Next, let's look at various tasks that can be performed using the Location Server Web Service.

Finding a Real-Time Location

MapPoint Location Server Web Service exposes the GetPositions method, which you can use to request a real-time location of yourself or your contacts (such as your colleagues within the same enterprise).

If you are requesting your own location, pass your domain alias as an argument to the GetPositions method; however, you must be a valid provisioned user to successfully request your location.

If you are requesting the location of your contacts, you need to pass the following criteria:

- You must be a valid provisioned user.
- Your contacts must be valid provisioned users.
- Your contacts have granted you permission to locate them.
- Your contacts have their status set to visible (not in stealth mode).

Once you meet the above criteria, you can pass the domain aliases of the contact users whose location you want to find as an argument to this method. If you fail to meet any of the above criteria, your request to locate your contact results in a failure. The third and fourth bullets act as layers of defense to protect your contacts' privacy.

When a location request succeeds, GetPositions returns an instance of the PositionResults class, which contains the positions for the domain aliases passed to the method. The PositionResults class instance contains a property that exposes an array of Position class instances that contain the position information expressed as latitude and longitude coordinates. The order of the Position array elements corresponds to the order of the domain aliases passed to this method. The following code snippet shows how to invoke the GetPositions method:

```
//Create an instance of the LocationServiceSoap proxy class
LocationServiceSoap locationService = new LocationServiceSoap();

//Create an instance of the NetworkCredential class
//and add the credentials required to access the Web service
```

```
NetworkCredential credentials =
        new NetworkCredential("user", "password", "domain");
locationService.Credentials = credentials;
try
 {
   //Get the positions from the GetPositions method
   PositionResults positionResults =
     locationService.GetPositions(new string[] {@"domain\contact"});
   //Process the positions
   foreach(Position position in positionResults.Positions)
   {
     //Get each contact's lat/long
     LatLong ll = position.LatLong;

   }
   }
catch(System.Web.Services.Protocols.SoapException MyException)
 {
   //Process exceptions here
 }
```

Once a location is obtained as latitude/longitude coordinates, you can display it on a map using the MapPoint Web Service Rendering Service.

Microsoft Location Server Web Service also exposes the GetPositionsAsync method and a corresponding GetPositionsAsyncResults method for invoking asynchronous location requests. The difference between these methods and the proxy-generated asynchronous methods (BeginGetPositions and EndGetPositions) generated by Visual Studio .NET is that the Visual Studio .NET-generated methods run the invocation process on a background thread to free up the UI thread, which keeps the HTTP connection open until the response from Microsoft Location Server Web Service is complete. The GetPositionsAsync method closes the HTTP connection as soon as the request is complete, making the request and response truly asynchronous. The GetPositionsAsync method may be required with mobile operators that cannot locate a mobile device when an HTTP connection is open. If you are working with a mobile operator that does not have this issue and you are developing your client application using the asynchronous model, use the asynchronous methods generated by Visual Studio .NET.

Adding and Removing Contacts

MapPoint Location Web Service offers two methods, AddContact and DeleteContact, which can be used to add and remove contacts for provisioned users. You can use the FindProvisionedUser method to look up the provisioned users within your enterprise so that you can to add them to your contact list. Note that although you can add a contact to your contacts list, you can locate that contact only if he grants you permission to do so. This explicit opt-in model is an important privacy feature of Microsoft Location Server.

The following code snippet shows how to add a contact to your contact list. First, find a provisioned user using his phone number:

```
//Create a LocationService Proxy.
LocationServiceSoap locationService = new LocationServiceSoap();

//Define and add credentials to the proxy
. . .

//Create a ProvisionedUser instance and
//assign the search value.
ProvisionedUser provisionedUser = new ProvisionedUser();
provisionedUser.DomainAlias = @"DOMAIN\user";

//Create a locatable device instance and assign the value.
LocatablePhoneNumber phone = new LocatablePhoneNumber();
phone.CountryCode = "001";
phone.LocalCode = "111";
phone.ShortNumber = "1111111";

//Find out if this user is provisioned
try
 {
   LocatableContact[] users = locationService.FindProvisionedUser(
                              provisionedUser, phone,  -1);

   foreach(LocatableContact user in users)
   {
    //Process found provisioned users
    . . .
   }
 }
catch(SoapException exception)
 {
   //Your exception process goes here
 }
```

As you can see, `FindProvisionedUser` takes either a partially-defined `ProvisionedUser` instance or a `LocatablePhoneNumber` instance to look up the provisioned users to match from the Active Directory within an enterprise. It is important to note that at least one of these two arguments is required. When both are present, both arguments are used for the lookup. The rules detailed in the following sections must be followed for the partially defined `ProvisionedUser` instance used for the lookup.

If lookup is based on domain alias

Partial domain alias searching is permitted. For example, if there is a user "John Doe" in domain "XYZ" with an user alias "jdoe," the following searches return valid results:

- "jdoe" returns an exact match for "XYZ\jdoe".
- "XYZ\jdoe" returns an exact match for "XYZ\jdoe".
- "XYZ/jdoe" returns an exact match for "XYZ\jdoe".

The following searches fail to return the provisioned user:

- "Doe" will fail. (This case assumes that the alias "Doe" does not belong to another valid user.)
- Searching for "jdo" will fail. (This case assumes that the alias "jdo" does not belong to another valid user.)

If lookup is based on display name

Partial display name searching is allowed. This search is performed using a "starts-with" condition. For example, if the display name is "Mr. Jon Doe," searching for "John" will yield "Mr. Jon Doe" as one of the results.

The minimum number of characters that needs to be supplied for a display name partial search is two.

If lookup is based on first name and last name

Partial searching is allowed for first and last name searches. The only rule is that the sum of the characters from both first name and last name together must be greater than or equal to two. The following searches return results for "John Doe:"

- Searching for "John" as the first name and "Doe" as the last name will return "John Doe" as one of the matches.
- Searching for "J" as the first name and "Doe" as the last name will return "John Doe" as one of the matches.
- Searching for "John" as the first name and "D" as the last name will return "John Doe" as one of the matches.
- Searching for "Jon" as the first name and "" (empty) as the last name will return "John Doe" as one of the matches (or may fail due to too many matches).
- Finally, searching for "J" as the first name and "D" as the last name may fail due to too many matches.

If lookup is based on phone number

The locatablePhonenumber parameter is optional and can be null; however, when provided, an exact match is returned if its match is in the database. When a phone number is provided, the short number (last seven digits of the phone number) must be provided to be considered for the search.

If lookup is based on email address

Email address searches allow a "starts-with" partial search. If you provide a complete email address including a @ sign, however, an exact match is returned if its match is in the database.

The third argument for the FindProvisionedUser method indicates the number of provisioned users to return that match the input query; value -1 indicates the Location Server Web Service to return all found provisioned users. When the requested number of provisioned users does not match the matched provisioned user count, an exception is thrown.

Once a provisioned user is found using a query such as the one shown previously, you can add her as your contact:

```
//Create an instance of the LocationServiceSoap proxy class
LocationServiceSoap MyLocationService = new LocationServiceSoap( );
//Create an instance of the NetworkCredential class
//and add the credentials required to access the Web service
NetworkCredential MyCredentials =
        new NetworkCredential("user", "password", "domain");
MyLocationService.Credentials = MyCredentials;
 try
 {
 //Add a new contact for the current user
 LocatableContact MyLocatableContact =
     MyLocationService.AddContact(@"domain\contactuser",
                                 true, true);
 }
catch(SoapException MyException)
 {
 //Process exceptions here
 . . .
 }
```

As you can see, the AddContact method takes three arguments:

contact user domain alias
> Indicates the domain alias of the contact that is being added

isActive flag
> Indicates whether the contact relationship is active; you may add someone as a contact but block her from locating you by setting this flag to false. If you set this value to true, it means that the contact can locate you.

notifyOnLocate flag
> Indicates via an SMS message or email that you are being located by your contact when this flag is set to true. This flag works as a record of all locate attempts made by your contacts.

Note that if you try to add a contact that you already have in your contact list, this method throws an exception. Along similar lines, the methods DeleteContact and UpdateContact take the contact domain alias to either remove the contact relationship or modify the existing contact relationship respectively.

Programming Privacy Settings

As a Location Server user, you may be worried about your privacy—specifically, you don't want to be tracked all the time even if you give permission to your contacts to track you. For situations like this, Location Server gives you the flexibility to control the privacy settings so that you can enable who can track you; it even gives you a way to go into stealth mode by becoming completely invisible to your contacts.

Managing contact privacy settings

Using the LocationServiceSoap.UpdateContact method, you can enable or disable the ability for your contacts to locate you. Similar to the AddContact method, this method takes three arguments that indicate the contact user, locatable permissions flag (isActive), and notification on the locate flag. To disable a contact from locating you, set the isActive flag to false:

```
//Create a LocationServiceSoap proxy instance
LocationServiceSoap locationService = new LocationServiceSoap( );
//Create and add the credentials required to access the Web service
NetworkCredential credentials =
            new NetworkCredential("user", "password", "DOMAIN");
locationService.Credentials = credentials;

try
{
 //Update the contact - turn off their ability to locate you
 LocatableContact locatableContact =
            MyLocationService.UpdateContact(@"DOMAIN\contactuser",
                                            false, false);
}
catch(SoapException MyException)
{
 //Your exception processing goes here
 . . .
}
```

To enable the same contact to be able to locate you, you just need to call the same method with the isActive flag set to true:

```
//Update the contact - turn on their ability to locate you
 LocatableContact locatableContact =
            MyLocationService.UpdateContact(@"DOMAIN\contactuser",
                                            true, true);
```

Going into stealth mode—becoming invisible to all contacts

Using the LocationServiceSoap.SetVisibility method, you can become completely invisible to all of your contacts, meaning that even if your contacts have permission to locate you, they will be not be able to if you set your visibility to false. The following code snippet shows how to turn off your visibility completely using the SetVisibility method:

```
//Create a LocationServiceSoap proxy instance
LocationServiceSoap locationService = new LocationServiceSoap();
//Create and add the credentials required to access the Web service
NetworkCredential credentials =
        new NetworkCredential("user", "password", "DOMAIN");
locationService.Credentials = credentials;

try
{
 //Set the visibility for the current user - Go Stealth mode
 locationService.SetVisibility(false);
}
catch(SoapException MyException)
{
 //Your exception processing goes here
 . . .
}
```

Similarly, you can set your visibility to true so that your contacts can locate you:

```
//Set the visibility for the current user - Become visible
 locationService.SetVisibility(true);
```

If your visibility is set to false and your contacts try to locate you, they get an error indicating that you are not locatable; however, it does not indicate that you chose to be invisible to your contacts.

Finding Nearby Points of Interest

To find nearby points of interest, MapPoint Location Web Service exposes the LocationServiceSoap.GetNearbyCategories method, which returns find nearby categories. Find nearby categories are groups of points of interest of the same type; for example, banks, ATMs, pizza shops, and pubs could belong to these categories. You can use this list of categories to search for points of interest that are close to your location. The following code shows how to retrieve find nearby categories.

```
//Create an instance of the LocationServiceSoap proxy class
LocationServiceSoap locationService = new LocationServiceSoap();
//Create an instance of the NetworkCredential class
//and add the credentials required to access the Web service
NetworkCredential credentials =
        new NetworkCredential("user", "password", "domain");
locationService.Credentials = MyCredentials;
```

```
//Get the Find Nearby categories
try
{
  FindNearbyCategory[] findNearbyCategories =
              locationService.GetNearbyCategories();

  foreach(FindNearbyCategory findNearbyCategory in
                                  findNearbyCategories)
  {
    //Process find nearby category
    . . .
  }
}
catch(SoapException exception)
{
  //Process exceptions here
  . . .
}
```

Once you retrieve the find nearby categories using this method, you can call the `FindServiceSoap.FindNearby` method to retrieve the actual points of interest. So, why do you need this layer of abstraction from the huge yellow page categories and listings available in MapPoint Web Service? Enterprise customization! As an enterprise, you may have business requirements to make specific find nearby categories available to your employees. In this case, a system administrator can define specific find nearby categories that are useful for provisioned users that can later be exposed to your enterprise users via the Location Server client, enabling them to find the specific groups of points of interest around their current location.

Programming with the Location Server Management API

You use the Microsoft Location Server management API to develop server-side applications for Microsoft Location Server. *Server-side applications* include applications for provisioning users within an enterprise, automating the addition and removal of contact lists for provisioned users, removing provisioned users, and so on. Note that the management API does not expose a real-time location API. To program with the management API, you need to add the following assemblies as references to your project:

Microsoft.MapPoint.LocationServer.Types.dll
  Contains Microsoft Location Server data types.

Microsoft.MapPoint.LocationServer.Management.dll
  Contains classes that provide methods for managing Microsoft Location Server. In this assembly, the type ServerAPI exposes methods to manage Microsoft Location Server.

Microsoft.MapPoint.LocationServer.Core.dll

Contains classes required by the management API types. This assembly should be used only to add as a reference to your project; do not use types from this assembly directly in your source code.

In the following sections, we'll look at the Microsoft Location Server management API in detail.

Anatomy of Location Server Management APIs

Microsoft Location Server provides the Server Management APIs to build applications to automate administrative tasks such as adding users, managing contacts for users, and managing find nearby categories. All of the Server Management APIs are provided via the `ServerAPI` class in the `Microsoft.MapPoint.LocationServer.Types.dll` assembly; this class provides a set of methods that enables you to develop applications in four major categories:

User management
Enables you to develop applications to add new users and update existing users in the Microsoft Location Server.

Contact management
Enables you to develop applications to add, update, and remove the contacts for the provisioned users.

Privacy management
Enables you to develop applications to modify provisioned user privacy settings.

Find nearby category management
Enables you to develop applications to add, update and remove find nearby categories.

Table 10-2 shows the methods exposed by the ServerAPI class.

Table 10-2. ServerAPI class methods

Method	Description
Initialize	Initializes a connection to the MapPoint Location Server database. Call this method on a `ServerAPI` instance.
GetContacts	Returns a list of contacts as an array of `LocatableContact` objects for the user represented by the domain and alias.
AddContact	Adds a new contact for a given user.
UpdateContact	Updates a specified contact in a given user's contacts list.
DeleteContact	Deletes the specified contact from the contacts list of a given user.
FindProvisionedUser	Allows partial input of `LocatableUser` object properties or an email address of a user to search provisioned MapPoint Location Server users and returns contact information as an array of `LocatableContact` instances.

Table 10-2. ServerAPI class methods (continued)

Method	Description
GetDefaultCulture	Retrieves the default culture for a given user, in string format (e.g., "en-US" for English, United States).
SetDefaultCulture	Sets the default culture for a given user.
AddUser	Adds a new user to MapPoint Location Server. Adding a user is also called provisioning a user.
UpdateUser	Updates an existing user (a user that has already been provisioned) in MapPoint Location Server.
DeleteUser	Deletes an existing (provisioned) user from the MapPoint Location Server.
GetAllUsers	Returns all provisioned users as an array of strings in MapPoint Location Server.
GetLocatableUser	Searches for a provisioned user by domain and alias.
GetNewContactNotification	Gets the NotifyOnNewContact property of the LocatableUser object for the user identified by the domain and alias.
SetNewContactNotification	Sets the NotifyOnNewContact property of the LocatableUser object for the user identified by the domain and alias.
GetVisibility	Gets the Visible property of the LocatableUser object that represents the user identified by the domain and alias.
SetVisibility	Determines whether the user is visible to other users or contacts.
GetNearbyCategories	Gets the Find Nearby categories as an array of FindNearbyCategory objects based on the culture name.
AddNearbyCategory	Adds a Find Nearby category to MapPoint Location Server.
UpdateNearbyCategory	Updates an existing nearby category in the MapPoint Location Server.
DeleteNearbyCategory	Deletes an existing Find Nearby category from the MapPoint Location Server.

Figure 10-2 shows the methods and their categorization.

The server management APIs provide everything that the Location Server Web Service provides except for the real-time location APIs. In this section, let's look at each of the categories in detail.

> If you are using the ServerAPI class to develop applications for Microsoft Location Server, make sure to invoke the Initialize method before calling any other methods of the ServerAPI class. This method call is required to establish a connection to the Microsoft Location Server database.

Programming User Management

Before getting into the details of user management, let's take a brief look at how the users are organized within Microsoft Location Server. All enterprise users provisioned within the Microsoft Location Server are represented using the ProvisionedUser class. The ProvisionedUser class acts as a base class for locatable

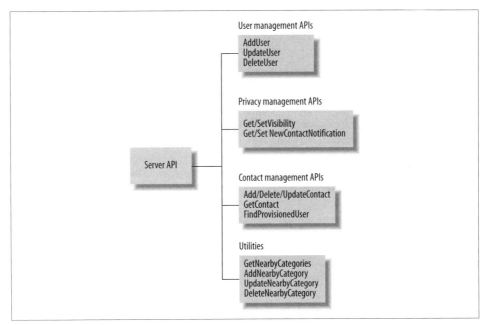

Figure 10-2. Server management API categorization

users and contacts. A *locatable user* is essentially a provisioned user with a valid locatable phone number; along the same lines, a *locatable contact* is a provisioned user with a valid contact relationship. Figure 10-3 shows this relationship pictorially.

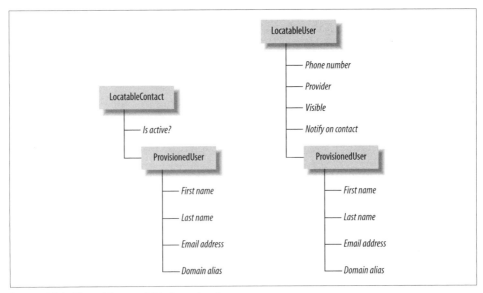

Figure 10-3. User object model in Location Server

In essence, the previous discussion can be summarized as:

```
Locatable User = Provisioned User + Locatable Phone Number
Locatable Contact = Provisioned User + Contact Relationship
```

With this introduction, let's look at user management API in the Location Server APIs.

Adding users

The ServerAPI class in the Microsoft.MapPoint.LocationServer.Management.dll assembly exposes the method AddUser, which is used to provision users for Microsoft Location Server. This method takes a LocatableUserinstance as an input parameter. A LocatableUser instance is an object representation of a domain user with a unique locatable endpoint (a phone number). The following code shows how to provision a user:

```
//Create a new instance of the ServerAPI class.
ServerAPI serverAPI = new ServerAPI();
try
{
 //Create a new instance of the LocatableUser class.
 LocatableUser newUser = new LocatableUser();
 //Set the domain and alias.
 newUser.DomainAlias = @"domain\user";
 //Set the culture name.
 newUser.CultureName = "en-US";
 //Set the locatable endpoint (the user's mobile device number).
 newUser.LocatableEndpoint =
        new LocatablePhoneNumber("001", "111", "1111111");
 //Set the location provider name
 newUser.LocationProviderName = "Your Location Provider Name";
 //Set the notification provider name
 newUser.NotificationProviderName =
             "Your Notification Provider Name";
 //Set the notification endpoint
 newUser.NotificationEndpoint = "user email address";
 //Initialize the database connection for ServerAPI operations.
 serverAPI.Initialize("SQL Server Name", "LocationServerDB");
 //Add the new domain user to Microsoft Location Server.
 serverAPI.AddUser(newUser);
}
catch(Exception exception)
{
 //Process exceptions
 . . .
}
```

In this code, a user with the domain alias "domain\user" has been added to the Microsoft Location Server. Note that the LocatableEndPoint (phone number), LocationProviderName, NotificationEndPoint (email address or SMS number), and NotificationProviderName are optional parameters; however, domain alias and default culture name are mandatory to add a new user. Also note that any newly added provisioned user will be visible by default.

Managing provisioned users

Similar to the AddUser method, the ServerAPI class also provides methods for managing users who are already provisioned. You can use the DeleteUser method to delete a provisioned user from Microsoft Location Server, and the UpdateUser method to update the properties of a provisioned user. The following code shows how to update a provisioned user's locatable phone number:

```
//Create a new instance of the ServerAPI class
ServerAPI serverAPI = new ServerAPI();
try
{
  //Create a LocatableUser instance
  LocatableUser user = new LocatableUser();
  //Set the domain alias
  user.DomainAlias = @"DOMAIN\user";
  //Update the culture name
  user.CultureName = "de-DE";
  //Update the Locatable end point - This is the user's new mobile device number
  user.LocatableEndpoint = new LocatablePhoneNumber("001", "425", "2222222");

  //Initialize the database connection for ServerAPI operations
  serverAPI.Initialize("SQL Server Name", "MSLocationServer");
  //Now Update the domain user profile
  serverAPI.UpdateUser(user);
}
catch(Exception MyException)
{
  //Process your exceptions
  . . .
}
```

In this code, both the default culture and phone number are updated using the ServerAPI.UpdateUser method. Note that you cannot update the user's domain alias using the UpdateUser method.

Programming Privacy Management

If you recall from our earlier discussions, Location Server Web Service can only update privacy settings for the logged-in user; however, the ServerAPI class can be used in administrative mode to update the privacy settings of any provisioned users in the Microsoft Location Server, including enabling and disabling contact relationships and visibility for any given provisioned user. You can use the ServerAPI.GetVisibility and ServerAPI.SetVisibility methods to set the user level visibility settings.

The following code snippet shows how to set visibility for a provisioned user within Microsoft Location Server:

```
//Create a new instance of the ServerAPI class
ServerAPI serverAPI = new ServerAPI( );
try
{
  //Initialize the database connection for ServerAPI operations
  serverAPI.Initialize("SQL Server Name", "MSLocationServer");

  //Now Set the Visibility flag for the domain alias DOMAIN\user
  //false means that the user is not visible and others can not
  //locate this user even if he/she is on their contact list
  serverAPI.SetVisibility(@"DOMAIN\user", false);

}
catch(Exception exception)
{
  //Process your exceptions
  . . .
}
```

The only difference between the SetVisibility of the ServerAPI and the LocationServiceSoap is that you need to pass the domain alias that you want to modify the privacy settings for; this makes sense since you are running ServerAPI in administrator mode; Location Server Web Service, however, implicitly assumes the logged-in user's settings.

Programming Contact Management

Using the ServerAPI class, you can add, remove, and update contacts for provisioned users. The capability to manage contacts is extremely useful if you are setting up a standard contact list for all provisioned users within your enterprise. The ServerAPI class exposes the methods AddContact, UpdateContact, and DeleteContact for adding, updating, and deleting contacts, respectively. As mentioned earlier, the primary difference between the Microsoft Location Server Web Service methods and the ServerAPI class methods is that the web service method calls run in the current user's context and the ServerAPI methods calls run under the administrator's context. Therefore, when you call the AddContact method using the Microsoft Location Server Web Service, you are adding a contact to your own contact list, whereas when you call the AddContact method of the ServerAPI class, you are adding a contact for the provisioned user whom you specify as an argument to this method.

The following code snippet shows how to call the AddContact method to add a contact for a provisioned user.

```
//Create a new instance of the ServerAPI class.
ServerAPI serverAPI = new ServerAPI( );
```

```
//Call the Initialize method.
 serverAPI.Initialize("sql server name", "LocationServerDB");

//Original user to whom the contact is being added
string userAlias = @"domain\user";
//Contact domain alias
string contactAlias = @"domain\newcontact";
try
{
 LocatableContact locatableContact =
             serverAPI.AddContact(userAlias, contactAlias, true, true);
 . . .
}
catch(Exception exception)
{
 //Process exceptions
 . . .
}
```

In this code, a new contact, "domain\newcontact" has been added to the provisioned user "domain\user" using the ServerAPI.AddContact method; the two boolean flags passed to this method indicate whether the contact relationship is active and whether the user wants to be notified when the contact tries to locate him, respectively.

Along the same lines, you can also update an existing contact relationship using the ServerAPI.UpdateContact method:

```
//Original user to whom the contact is being added
string userAlias = @"domain\user";
//Contact domain alias
string contactAlias = @"domain\newcontact";
try
{
 LocatableContact locatableContact =
             serverAPI.UpdateContact(userAlias, contactAlias, false, true);
 . . .
}
catch(Exception exception)
{
 //Process exceptions
 . . .
}
```

This call updates the contact relationship to be a "non-active" relationship (due to the flag isActive being set to false), and as a result, the provisioned user newcontact cannot locate the provisioned user user.

Programming Find Nearby Category Management

Using the ServerAPI class you can add, update, and delete find nearby categories that are appropriate for your enterprise. The ServerAPI class exposes the methods

AddNearbyCategory, UpdateNearbyCategory, and DeleteNearbyCategory for adding, updating, and removing find nearby categories.

Find nearby categories are logical groupings of points of interest; they directly map to the entity model presented in the MapPoint Web Service. If you plan to define a find nearby category by the name "dining places," you need to specify the exact entity type name and the associated data source name that corresponds to the find nearby category in MapPoint Web Service. In this case, if you plan to use NavTeq's provided yellow page listing categories to define the "dining places" category, you need to specify the entity type name as "SIC3578" and the data source name as "NavTech.NA."

So, to add a find nearby category, you need to complete the following steps:

1. Find nearby category name.
2. Find nearby category culture and distance unit.
3. Find nearby category localized names (to display them in different cultures).
4. Find the entity type that defines the find nearby category.
5. Apply this to a MapPoint Web Service data source name that contains the entity type specified in item 4.

Use the method AddNearbyCategory to add a nearby category; this method takes a valid instance of the FindNearbyCategory class as an argument to add the nearby category; a valid FindNearbyCategory object defines the aforementioned five properties for the ServerAPI to be able to add a nearby category successfully.

The following code shows adding a find nearby category called Dining Places and maps the entity type SIC3578 from the data source NavTech.NA:

```
//Create a new instance of the ServerAPI class
ServerAPI serverAPI = new ServerAPI();

//Initialize the database connection for ServerAPI operations
serverAPI.Initialize("SQL Server Name", "LocationServerDB");

//Step 1 & 2

//Create a new instance of the FindNearbyCategory class
FindNearbyCategory category = new FindNearbyCategory();
//Set the default culture.
category.DefaultCulture = "en-US";
//Set the distance units.
category.DistanceUnit = DistanceUnit.Mile;
//Set the key name.
category.KeyName = "DiningPlaces";

//Step 3

//Set the localized names.
//In this case we have two localized names
//Set the name for English (US)
```

```
FindNearbyCategoryName[] findNearbyCategoryNames
                    = new FindNearbyCategoryName[2];

findNearbyCategoryNames[0] = new FindNearbyCategoryName( );
findNearbyCategoryNames[0].Culture = "en-US";
findNearbyCategoryNames[0].DisplayName
                    = "Dining Places";
findNearbyCategoryNames[0].DisplayDescription
                    = "Dining Places related to my enterprise.";
//Set the name for German (Germany) Culture.
findNearbyCategoryNames[1] = new FindNearbyCategoryName( );
findNearbyCategoryNames[1].Culture = "de-DE";
findNearbyCategoryNames[1].DisplayName
                    = "Speisenden Pl?tze";
findNearbyCategoryNames[1].DisplayDescription
                    = "Speisenden Pl?tze";

//Assign the localized names to the instance
//of the FindNearbyCategory class
category.Names = findNearbyCategoryNames;


//Step 4 & 5

//Create a new instance of the FindNearbySpecification class
FindNearbySpecification findNearbyCategorySpecification =
                              new FindNearbySpecification( );
//Define the data source
findNearbyCategorySpecification.DataSourceName = "NavTech.NA";

//Define the entity type
findNearbyCategorySpecification.Filter = new FindFilter( );
findNearbyCategorySpecification.Filter.EntityTypeName = "SIC3578";

//Assign the FindNearbySpecification to the category
category.FindNearbySpecification = findNearbyCategorySpecification;

//Finally . . .
//Add the find nearby category
serverAPI.AddNearbyCategory(category);
. . .
```

Note that the find nearby category key name (DiningPlaces, in this example) is a required field and should not exceed 128 characters in length. Also, the default culture must be always defined, along with an associated localized name. For example, if you define the default culture as "fr-FR" with no associated localized French name for your find nearby category, the AddNearbyCategory throws an exception.

Along similar lines, you can also update a find nearby category using the ServerAPI. UpdateNearbyCategory method. To update the entity type and data source mapping to a find nearby category that you have already defined, use the UpdateNearbyCategory method. The following code snippet shows updating the entity type and data source mapping for the dining places nearby category that we created previously:

```
//Create an instance of the ServerAPI and initialize
. . .

//Create a FindNearbySpecification
FindNearbySpecification findNearbyCategorySpecification
              = new FindNearbySpecification();
//Update this value from NavTech.NA to Acxiom.US.SIC_G.58
findNearbyCategorySpecification.DataSourceName = "Acxiom.US.SIC_G.58";

findNearbyCategorySpecification.Filter = new FindFilter();

//Update this value from SIC3578 to SIC5813
MyFindNearbyCategorySpecification.Filter.EntityTypeName = "SIC5813";

//Assign the FindNearbySpecification to the category
category.FindNearbySpecification = MyFindNearbyCategorySpecification;

//Now update the category
serverAPI.UpdateNearbyCategory(category);
```

The find nearby category data source and entity type mapping have been changed from NavTech.NA and SIC3578 to Acxion.US.SIC_G.58 and SIC5813, respectively.

Finally, you can use the ServerAPI.DeleteNearbyCategory method to delete the existing nearby category definitions in the Microsoft Location Server. The DeleteNearbyCategory method takes the nearby category key name as an argument to delete the existing nearby category method. To delete the nearby category, dining places, call the DeleteNearbyCategory method:

```
//Delete the category using the keyname value
serverAPI.DeleteNearbyCategory("DiningPlaces");
```

The key name of the nearby category is the primary key within an instance of the Microsoft Location Server.

Comparing Location Server API to Location Web Service API

So far in this chapter, you have seen both Microsoft Location Server Web Service APIs and the Location Server Management APIs and learned how to program with them. Since most of the API functionality is common across these two sets of APIs, I thought it would be a good idea to wrap up the discussion with a comparison table by pointing out key differences as shown in Table 10-3.

Table 10-3. API comparison chart

API feature	Available with Location Web Service	Available with Location Web Server
Get Real-time Location	Yes	No
Add Contacts	Yes	Yes

Table 10-3. API comparison chart (continued)

API feature	Available with Location Web Service	Available with Location Web Server
Update Contacts	Yes	Yes
Delete Contacts	Yes	Yes
Set Visibility	Yes	Yes
Add Nearby Categories	No	Yes
Update Nearby Categories	No	Yes
Delete Nearby Categories	No	Yes
Get Nearby Categories	Yes	Yes
Provision Users	No	Yes
Update Provisioned Users	No	Yes
Delete Provisioned Users	No	Yes
Find Provisioned Users	Yes	Yes

It is important to keep in mind that the applications built with the Server APIs always run in the context of the Microsoft Location Server Administrator, while the applications built with the Location Server Web Server always run in the context of a provisioned user.

Where Are We?

In this chapter, you have seen how to develop:

- Real-time location applications using Location Server Web Service
- User, Contact, and Privacy Management applications using Location Server Web Service and the Server APIs
- Find nearby category management applications using the Location Server APIs

In the case of real-time location applications, the Location Server Web Service is hosted within your enterprise, providing a SOAP XML-enabled web service to obtain the real-time location of a provisioned mobile phone number from the mobile operator networks. For building server applications, you will need to access the server API assemblies directly so that you can build and use them on a Microsoft Location Server instance installed in your enterprise.

Finally, keep in mind that Microsoft Location Server works with different network providers to provide the real-time location using mobile phone numbers; the list of providers may change from time to time, and it is recommended that you check the Microsoft Location Server product home page (*http://www.microsoft.com/mappoint/ products/locationserver/default.mspx*) for up-to-date information about the supported network providers.

MSN Virtual Earth

Programming with Virtual Earth

Virtual Earth (*http://virtualearth.msn.com*) is the latest web product from the Microsoft MapPoint team. Even though there are currently no official APIs available, the openness of Virtual Earth allows some friendly "hackability." Virtual Earth is implemented using a mix of both server-side and client-side technologies, including ASP.NET and AJAX (Asynchronous JavaScript and XML).

In this section, I want to show you some of the interesting hacks that you can build around Virtual Earth.

Let's get started!

 This section is based on beta product and undocumented APIs; the APIs and the architecture may change significantly in future versions of Virtual Earth.

Anatomy of Virtual Earth

When you visit the Virtual Earth site at *http://www.virtualearth.msn.com*, you will see a site that looks similar to Figure 11-1. You will also notice a couple of interesting facts:

- Map interaction is enabled using the mouse and keyboard.
- Map interaction does not require a page-refresh.
- Search, pan, and zoom are preformed asynchronously for a better user experience.

All this is made possible by using JavaScript on the client browser to communicate with the Virtual Earth servers asynchronously. One of the neat things about JavaScript is that you can look at the implementation, since the code exists on the client side. If you look at the source of the Virtual Earth site, you will notice the following JavaScript files:

MapControl.js
    Defines the Map Control object and all related properties and methods.

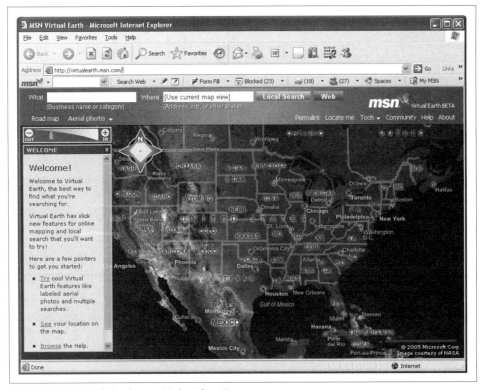

Figure 11-1. Virtual Earth map (Color Plate 8)

VE.js

Contains the code to display the map, zoom, and pan controls. This is the core script that runs the Virtual Earth site.

Configurations.js

Contains the configuration values, such as the search service, locate service, and the map image server endpoints.

If you want to use Virtual Earth map on your site, the JavaScript you need is the *MapControl.js*, which can be obtained from the Virtual Earth site at: *http:// virtualearth.msn.com/js/MapControl.js*. Even though the Map Control is completely written in JavaScript, you can create an instance just like any other object using its constructor:

```
var map = new VE_MapControl(32.69, -117.13, 12, 'r', "absolute", 400, 10, 400, 300);
```

Don't worry about the details of the parameters yet; we will take a detailed look at these in the next section. The VE_MapControl class takes nine parameters to create a map control instance that you can use to call the methods and subscribe to its events.

Tables 11-1 and 11-2 provide a list of the important methods and events exposed by the Map Control.

Table 11-1. Map Control methods

Method	Description	Example

SetCenterAndZoom	Centers the map on the specified latitude and longitude and zooms the map to the specified zoom level.	`map.SetCenterAndZoom(`
		`   47.6,  // lat`
		`   -122.33, //lon`
		`   12);   // zoom`

SetCenter	Centers the map on the specified latitude and longitude coordinates.	`map.SetCenter(`
		`   47.6,      // lat`
		`   -122.33); // lon`

SetZoom	Sets the map zoom level to the specified zoom value. Valid values range from 1 to 19.	`map.SetZoom(7);  //zoom`
ZoomIn	Zooms in the map to one level below than the current level.	`map.ZoomIn( );`
ZoomOut	Zooms out the map to one level above the current level.	`map.ZoomOut( );`

SetMapStyle	Sets the current map style to the specified style. The map style argument should be one of the following:
	
	r
	   Displays Road maps
	
	a
	   Displays Aerial maps
	
	h
	   Displays Hybrid maps (Aerial with labels)
		`//Set Road Map style`
		`map.SetMapStyle("r");`
		
		`//Set Aerial Map style`
		`map.SetMapStyle("a");`
		
		`//Set Hybrid Map style`
		`map.SetMapStyle("h");`

GetCenterLatitude	Gets the map center latitude coordinate.	`var latitude = map.` `GetCenterLatitude( );`
GetCenterLongitude	Gets the map center longitude coordinate.	`var longitude = map.` `GetCenterLongitude( );`
GetZoomLevel	Gets the map's current zoom level.	`var currentZoom = map.` `GetZoomLevel( );`
Resize	Resizes the map to the specified height and width.	`map. Resize(500, //width` `200 //height);`

PanMap	Pans the map to the specified pixel positions. The arguments are expressed as the difference between the x and y screen coordinates.	`//Pan 10 pixes on X and 20`
		`// pixels on Y`
		`map.PanMap(10, 20);`

PanToLatLong(latitude, longitude);	Pans the map to the specified latitude and longitude coordinates.	`map.PanToLatLong(47, -` `122);`

Table 11-1. Map Control methods (continued)

Method	Description	Example
| AddPushpin | Adds a pushpin at the specified latitude and longitude coordinate. | ```
map.AddPushpin(
'myPushpin', // Pin ID
47.6,         // latitude
-122.33,      // longitude
24,           // width
24,           // height
'bluepin',    // CSS class
'My Pushpin', //
innerHtml
25 //Z-Index);
``` |
| RemovePushpin | Removes the specified pushpin from the map. | ```
map.RemovePushpin(
    'myPushpin'); //Pin ID
``` |
| ClearPushpins | Removes all the pushpins from the map. | `map.ClearPushpins();` |
| SetViewPort | Sets the view of the map based on two latitude and longitude sets, one for the northwest corner and the other for the southeast corner. | ```
map.SetViewport(
47.648,   // latitude 1
-122.145, // longitude 1
47.6317,  // latitude 2
-122.1117); // longitude
2
``` |

Table 11-2. Map Control events

Event Name	Description	Example
| onMouseClick | Fires an event when the mouse is clicked on the map. The event argument exposes the latitude and longitude where the mouse click occurred. | ```
//Wire-up the event
map.onMouseClick=function(e)
{
    alert(e.latitude+',
        '+e.longitude);
};

// Disable the event
map.onMouseClick=null;
``` |
| onMapChange | Fires an event when the map has changed (such as when it has been zoomed, dragged, or panned). | ```
//Wire-up the event
map.onMapChange=function(e){
alert('map changed');
}
//Disable the event
map.onMapChange=null;
``` |

Using this JavaScript control, you can build applications to show anything that you can layer on top of maps—a bunch of photographs that you want to show by location (where they were taken), or a group of friends blogging from different cities who you want to show on a map. The information integration scenarios that we discussed in MapPoint 2004 and MapPoint Web Service can be also be done with Virtual Earth. The integration of information on maps as a layer is also known as *Mash-up*.
```

Programming with MapControl.js

In this section, we'll be displaying the map and changing map styles, as well as trying out Pan, Zoom, Mouse Clicks and more. Finally, we'll add Pushpins, layering RSS/XML feeds. All of this can be accomplished using only HTML and JavaScript.

Map Control Basics

Displaying a map using Map Control is very easy in Virtual Earth. All you need is a plain HTML page with some script tags. To start, let's create a new blank HTML page and add the *mapcontrol.js* as a reference from *http://virtualearth.msn.com*:

```
<!DOCTYPE HTML PUBLIC "-//W3C//DTD HTML 4.0 Transitional//EN">
<html>
    <head>
        <title>Virtual Earth Hacks</title>
        <script src="http://virtualearth.msn.com/js/mapcontrol.js"></script>
    </head>

    <body>
    </body>
</html>
```

Next, to create an instance of the map control with proper parameters, use the following constructor:

```
var map = VE_MapControl(CenterLatitude,
                        CenterLongitude,
                        DefaultZoom,
                        MapStyle,
                        ControlLayout,
                        PositionLeft,
                        PsotionTop,
                        MapWidth,
                        MapHeight);
```

Each of these parameters has a job to perform:

CenterLatitude
> The initial center point latitude for the map.

CenterLongitude
> The initial center point longitude for the map.

DefaultZoom
> The initial zoom value with which the map control is loaded. Valid values are from 1-19 (1 is zoomed out all the way, and 19 is zoomed down to the street level).

MapStyle

The style to use when displaying the map. There are currently 3 style options: aerial, road, and hybrid. In order to indicate a style you need to pass the following values as a parameter to the constructor:

a

Displays an aerial satellite image of the map display.

r

Displays a road map-style map.

h

Displays a combination of aerial photos with street labels.

ControlLayout

The way in which the control should be positioned on the page. The two options are *relative* and *absolute*. Use relative if you are using the map in a table or a div that you want it to wrap if someone resizes the html page. Use absolute if you don't want your map to reposition itself on the page.

PostionLeft

The position to the left of the control on the page. Use it only if you want an absolute layout. If you want a relative layout, pass an empty string (' ').

PostionTop

The position on the top of the control on the page. Use it only if you want an absolute layout. If you want a relative layout, pass an empty string (' ').

MapWidth

The width of the control in pixels.

MapHeight

The height of the control in pixels.

The following JavaScript statement shows how to create a new instance of the map control with a specific set of initial values:

```
var map = null;
map = new VE_MapControl(44, //Latitude
                        -99, //Longitude
                        3, //Zoom Level
                        'r', //Road MapStyle
                        "absolute", //Layout
                        10, //Left
                        10, //Top
                        700, //Width
                        500); //Height
```

To display a map, you need to render this control by adding to the body of the HTML page. This can be done in two ways. Either add to the body using a script:

```
document.body.appendChild(map.element);
```

or add the map to a div element inside another element (for example, a table cell named mapholder) on the page:

```
document.getElementById("mapholder").appendChild(map.element);
```

That's it; when this script is placed in the body:

```
<!DOCTYPE HTML PUBLIC "-//W3C//DTD HTML 4.0 Transitional//EN">
<html>
    <head>
        <title>Virtual Earth Hacks</title>
        <script src="http://virtualearth.msn.com/js/mapcontrol.js"></script>
    </head>
    <body>
        <script type="text/JavaScript">
            var map = null;
            map = new VE_MapControl(44, -99, 3, 'r', "absolute", 10, 10, 700, 500);
            document.body.appendChild(map.element);
        </script>
    </body>
</html>
```

A nice-looking map will be rendered on the page as shown in Figure 11-2.

 If you are running Windows XP SP2 or Internet Explorer 7.0, you may get security warnings before running the page. You have to manually allow the script to run on your computer to show the map.

Alternatively, you can also display the map in a table cell:

```
<!DOCTYPE HTML PUBLIC "-//W3C//DTD HTML 4.0 Transitional//EN">
<html>
    <head>
        <title>Virtual Earth Hacks</title>
        <script src="http://virtualearth.msn.com/js/mapcontrol.js"></script>
    </head>
    <body>
        <table border=1px>
            <tr>
                <td colspan=2 align=center>
                    <b>Map shown in a table</b>
                </td>
            </tr>
            <tr>
                <td width=40%>
                    This is my content part
                </td>
                <td width=50%>
                    This is the map part
                    <div id=mapholder></div>
                </td>
            </tr>
        </table>
        <script type="text/JavaScript">
```

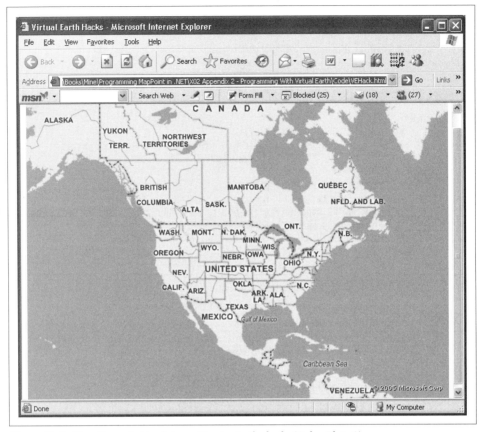

Figure 11-2. Map Control: Absolute positioning in the body (Color Plate 9)

```
      var map = null;
      map = new VE_MapControl(44, -99, 3, 'r', "relative", '', '', 500, 300);
      document.getElementById("mapholder").appendChild(map.element);
    </script>
  </body>
</html>
```

The resulting map is shown in Figure 11-3.

If you see the Internet Explorer Image Tool Bar menu on the map when the mouse hovers over the map, you can disable it by adding the following meta tag to the header of your HTML page:

```
<META HTTP-EQUIV="imagetoolbar" CONTENT="no">
```

Finally, you can also move the map initialization code into a function that can be called by the HTML body element's onLoad event:

```
<!DOCTYPE HTML PUBLIC "-//W3C//DTD HTML 4.0 Transitional//EN">
<html>
    <head>
```

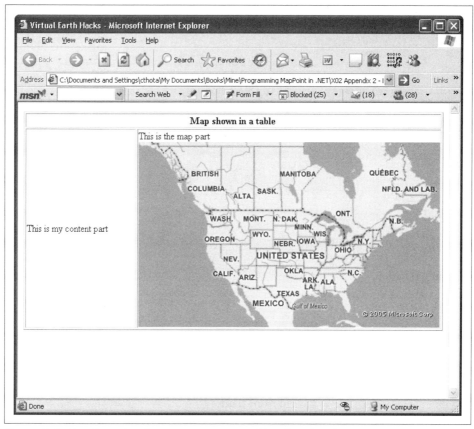

Figure 11-3. Map Control: Relative positioning in a table cell (Color Plate 10)

```
<title>Virtual Earth Hacks</title>
<script src="http://virtualearth.msn.com/js/mapcontrol.js"></script>
<script type="text/JavaScript">
    var map = null;
    function LoadMap()
    {
        map = new VE_MapControl(44, -99, 3, 'r', "relative",
                                '', '', 500, 300);
        document.getElementById("mapholder").appendChild(map.element);
    }
</script>
</head>
<body onload="LoadMap();">
    <table border=1px ID="Table1">
        <tr>
            <td colspan=2 align=center>
                <b>Map shown in a table</b>
            </td>
        </tr>
        <tr>
```

```
              <td width=40%>
                  This is my content part
              </td>
              <td width=50%>
                  This is the map part
                  <div id=mapholder></div>
              </td>
          </tr>
      </table>
  </body>
</html>
```

 The default map generated by these scripts has pan and zoom functionalities tied to your mouse clicks and keyboard strokes.

Now that you have the map, let's see how you can change the map style.

Changing the map style

Once you create a map control, you can change the map style simply by calling the
SetMapStyle method:

```
//Show Hybrid mapstyle
map.SetMapStyle('h');
```

You can send r to see the road style maps and a to see aerial maps with no labels. By
adding a button to the previous HTML page and using the SetMapStyle method, you
can change the map style to hybrid from road:

```
<!DOCTYPE HTML PUBLIC "-//W3C//DTD HTML 4.0 Transitional//EN">
<html>
    <head>
        <title>Virtual Earth Hacks</title>
        <script src="http://virtualearth.msn.com/js/mapcontrol.js"></script>
        <script type="text/JavaScript">
            var map = null;
            function LoadMap()
            {
                map = new VE_MapControl(44, -99, 3, 'r',
                                        "relative", '', '',
                                        500, 300);
                document.getElementById("mapholder").appendChild(map.element);
            }
        </script>
    </head>
    <body onload="LoadMap();">
        <table border=1px ID="Table1">
            <tr>
                <td colspan=2 align=center>
                    <b>Map shown in a table</b>
                </td>
            </tr>
```

```
        <tr>
            <td width=40%>
                <input type=button onclick="map.SetMapStyle('h');"
                value="Show Hybrid!" ID="Button1" NAME="Button1"></input>
            </td>
            <td width=50%>
                This is the map part
                <div id=mapholder></div>
            </td>
        </tr>
    </table>
</body>
</html>
```

The resulting page and map displayed when the button is clicked is shown in Figure 11-4.

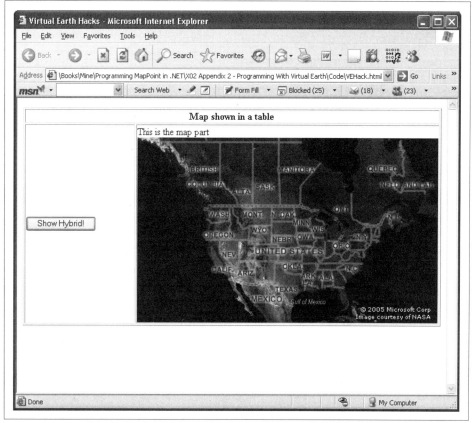

Figure 11-4. Switch map style using the SetMapStyle method (Color Plate 11)

Now that you know how to change the map style, let's look at how to trap the map events.

Trapping the Virtual Earth Map Control events

Map Control exposes a set of events, including onMouseClick and onMapChange. To wire up one of those events, create a function that gets executed with the event arguments:

```
map.onMouseClick=function(e){DisplayLatLong(e.latitude, e.longitude);};
```

where the DisplayLatLong function is defined as:

```
function DisplayLatLong(latitude, longitude)
{
    alert("You clicked on: " + latitude + ", " + longitude);
}
```

The event argument e contains the location contextual information, such as the latitude and longitude of the event, so that you can use that information to perform custom actions. The document HTML reads as follows:

```
<!DOCTYPE HTML PUBLIC "-//W3C//DTD HTML 4.0 Transitional//EN">
<html>
    <head>
        <title>Virtual Earth Hacks</title>
        <script src="http://virtualearth.msn.com/js/mapcontrol.js"></script>
        <script type="text/JavaScript">
            var map = null;
            function LoadMap( )
            {
                map = new VE_MapControl(44, -99, 3, 'r',
                                        "relative", '', '', 500, 300);
                document.getElementById("mapholder").appendChild(map.element);
                map.onMouseClick=function(e){
                                DisplayLatLong(e.latitude, e.longitude);};
            }

            function DisplayLatLong(latitude, longitude)
            {
                alert("You clicked on: " + latitude + ", " + longitude);
            }
        </script>
    </head>
    <body onload="LoadMap( );">
        <table border=1px ID="Table1">
            <tr>
                <td colspan=2 align=center>
                    <b>Map shown in a table</b>
                </td>
            </tr>
            <tr>
                <td width=40%>
                    <input type=button onclick="map.SetMapStyle('h');" value="Show
Hybrid!" ID="Button1" NAME="Button1"></input>
                </td>
                <td width=50%>
                    This is the map part
```

```
                    <div id=mapholder></div>
                </td>
            </tr>
        </table>
    </body>
</html>
```

When you click on the map, a message is displayed as shown in Figure 11-5; the numbers depend on the latitude and longitude coordinates that you have clicked on.

Figure 11-5. onMouseClick event handler message

Along the same lines, you can also wire up events like onMapChange, onMouseUp, and onMouseDown.

Map Interaction Using Map Control

Now that you know how to display a basic map, change map styles, and trap map events, you can build some map interaction around the map. The basic interactions that you would want to see on a map are panning and zooming. Map Control exposes the PanMap, ZoomIn, and ZoomOut methods to control panning and zooming.

Panning the map

You can use the PanMap method to pan around the map. This method takes pixel position difference as arguments for both x and y coordinates. For example, if you want to pan the map to your left by 100 pixels, call the PanMap method:

```
//Pan left
map.PanMap(-100, 0);
```

Along the same lines, calling this method with 100 and 0 parameters pans the map to the right by 100 pixels:

```
//Pan right
map.PanMap(100, 0);
```

Similarly, you can pan the map up and down by passing the y coordinates while keeping the x coordinate assigned to 0:

```
//Pan Up
map.PanMap(0, -100);
```

```
//Pan Down
map.PanMap(0, 100);
```

You can also pan the map to corners such as southeast and northwest by passing both x and y coordinates:

```
//Pan South East
//(or Bottom-Right)
map.PanMap(100, 100);
```

Finally, to pan the map to specific latitude and longitude coordinates, call the PanToLatLong method:

```
map.PanToLatLong(
    47.6045, // latitude
    -122.3305); // longitude
```

Zooming the map

To perform any zoom operations, you can use the ZoomIn and ZoomOut methods. These methods don't take any parameters, and they increment or decrement the zoom level by one depending on whether you are zooming in or zooming out.

To zoom in to one level below the current level, simply call the ZoomIn method:

```
//Zoom In
map.ZoomIn();
```

Similarly, to zoom out to one level above the current level, simply call the ZoomOut method:

```
//Zoom Out
map.ZoomOut();
```

Finally, to set a specific zoom level, call the SetZoom method:

```
map.SetZoom(7); // zoom level
```

Displaying Your Data on Maps

One of the values of using maps is that you can use them to visualize the data geographically; you can display a variety of items, such as news, photos, blogs, etc. on a map once the location is known. Since all these items are basically point information, you can easily display them with Virtual Earth MapControl using the AddPushpin method.

Adding a pushpin

The AddPushpin method adds an icon on the map at the specified latitude and longitude coordinate. A simple use of the AddPushpin method is shown in the following example:

```
map.AddPushpin(
    'myPushpin', // pin id
    47.6,        // latitude
```

```
-122.33,      // longitude
24,           // width
24,           // height
'bluepin',    // CSS class
'X',          // pincontent
25);          // z index
```

This method takes the latitude and longitude among the other elements to add a pushpin at the specified location; one of the most interesting parameters of all the above is the pincontent parameter. This parameter contains the content that will be displayed as the pushpin. When this code is executed, a pin is added to the map as shown in Figure 11-6.

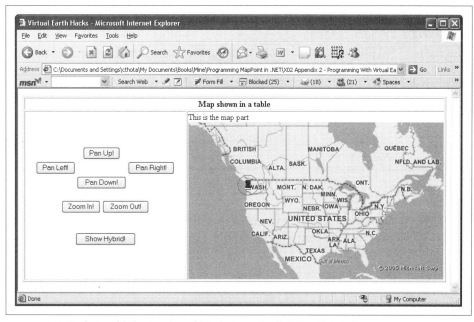

Figure 11-6. Pushpin added using the AddPushpin method (Color Plate 12)

Since each pushpin is a div element in Virtual Earth, and since each div can have rich inner HTML, you can pass any valid HTML code as part of this pin content parameter; in the following example, see how an image thumbnail can be passed as the pushpin content:

```
map.AddPushpin('myPushpin', // pin id
        47.6,         // latitude
        -122.33,      // longitude
        24,           // width
        24,           // height
        '',            // CSS class
        "<img src='http://cache.corbis.com/CorbisImage/thumb/14/19/74/14197458/
    IH212078.jpg'>",
                      // pincontent
        25);          // z index
```

This code adds a pushpin with the Space Needle thumbnail picture over Seattle, as shown in Figure 11-7.

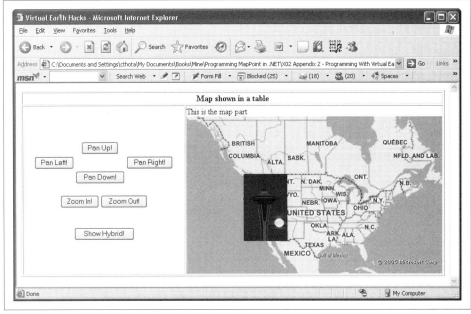

Figure 11-7. The Space Needle shown as an icon over Seattle (Color Plate 13)

As you can imagine, you can easily extend this inner HTML code to show pop-ups when a user's mouse is hovered over the icon.

 When adding a pushpin, always set the Z-Index above 24; otherwise, your pushpin will not be visible.

Removing pushpins

Once you add a pushpin, you can remove it with its ID using the `RemovePushpin` method:

```
map.RemovePushpin('myPushpin');
```

Similarly, you can remove all pushpins on the map using the `ClearPushpins` method:

```
map.ClearPushpins();
```

As you can see, adding and removing a pushpin is easy in Virtual Earth; next, we'll add several pushpins from a data source, such as an XML file.

Adding pushpins from RSS feed

Let's say you have a bunch of points specified as an RSS feed (an XML file):

```
<?xml version="1.0"?>
<rss version="2.0" xmlns:geo="http://www.w3.org/2003/01/geo/wgs84_pos#">
<channel>
    <title>Chandu's Fav Places</title>
    <link>http://www.csthota.com</link>
    <description>Chandu's Fav Places</description>
    <item>
        <title>Coffee Shop</title>
        <description>Starbucks Coffee. Umm, Caramel Machiato!</description>
        <geo:lat>37.757329</geo:lat>
        <geo:long>-122.399081</geo:long>
    </item>
    <item>
        <title>Video Store</title>
        <description>Hollywood Video - Love it!</description>
        <geo:lat>37.758051</geo:lat>
        <geo:long>-122.400984</geo:long>
    </item>
    <item>
        <title>Home</title>
        <description>Home, Sweet Home!</description>
        <geo:lat>37.758035</geo:lat>
        <geo:long>-122.397129</geo:long>
    </item>
    <item>
        <title>Sages Italiano</title>
        <description>Italian food in my hood!</description>
        <geo:lat>37.755929</geo:lat>
        <geo:long>-122.397881</geo:long>
    </item>
</channel>
</rss>
```

This XML file can be loaded and displayed on the Virtual Earth map using the following JavaScript function:

```
function LoadXml(xmlfile)
{
    if(!documentSource)
        return;

    var doc = null;
    doc=new ActiveXObject("msxml2.DOMDocument.3.0");
    doc.async=false;
    doc.resolveExternals=false;
    doc.validateOnParse=false;
    // Load the XML file into the DOM instance.
    doc.load(xmlfile);
    if(!doc)
    {
```

```
        return;
    }
    //Loop now
    var nodeList = doc.selectNodes("//./item");
    for(i=0;i<nodeList.length;i++)
    {
        if(nodeList.item(i))
        {
            var item = nodeList.item(i);
            var title=item.selectSingleNode("title").text;
            var description=item.selectSingleNode("description").text;
            var latitude=item.selectSingleNode("geo:lat").text;
            var longitude=item.selectSingleNode("geo:long").text;
            //Add pushpin
            map.AddPushpin(i, latitude, longitude, 24, 24, 'mypin', title, 25);
        }


    }
}
```

When this function is called in the HTML page, the pushpins are added on the map as shown in Figure 11-8.

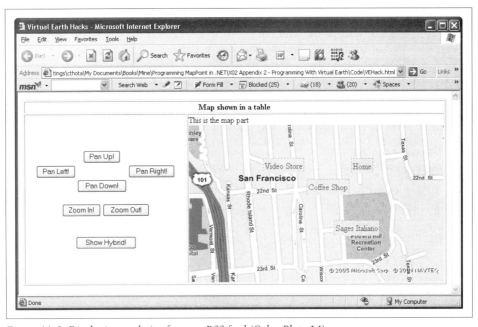

Figure 11-8. Displaying pushpins from an RSS feed (Color Plate 14)

Adding pushpins on the map can be done directly on the client side (browser) using JavaScript from an XML feed. You can also extend this code to center the map on the pushpins that are being added using the map.SetViewPort method.

Where Are We?

There are currently no official APIs provided by Virtual Earth, and the APIs discussed here are the undocumented APIs that can be used for noncommercial purposes only. If you are an enterprise in need of a mapping application, consider either MapPoint 2006 or MapPoint Web Service. Having said that, the MapPoint team is working hard to enable Virtual Earth experience in the MapPoint Web Service, and it is expected to be available early next year to the developer community.

So, there you have it: we have arrived at the tail end of programming an array of products and technologies with MapPoint using C# and .NET, ranging from Map-Point 2006 to MapPoint Web Service to Location Server to Virtual Earth, and including a wide variety of technologies to suit different needs and requirements. I would like to leave you with one final note: the world of web services is a fast-changing one—so, I will keep you posted with any new features or existing feature updates via articles and blog posts. If you have any questions in the meantime, please don't hesitate to contact me at *Chandu.Thota@microsoft.com*.

Managing Your Data on MapPoint's Customer Services Site

Enabling MapPoint Web Service to use your custom data with find service methods such as `FindNearby` and `FindById` is possible by uploading your data to MapPoint servers. There are two ways to upload/download your data to/from the MapPoint Customer Services site: you can use either the MapPoint Customer Services site itself or the Customer Data Web Service.

In both cases, you can upload new data or update existing data. However, to delete uploaded data, you have to use the MapPoint Customer Services Site Web UI. It is also important to note that neither one of these two options support incremental updates. If you upload a data source, modify it using the CSS, and then re-upload the same data source, your changes will be lost, so it is essential to back up your data before uploading each time to the MapPoint Servers.

Now, let's take a look at these two options in detail.

Using the MapPoint Customer Services Site

You can upload custom points of interest data using the MapPoint Web Service Customer Services site (*https://mappoint-css.partners.extranet.microsoft.com/cscV3/*) web interface. The user interface for this functionality is available on the home page of the site under the data sources section shown in Figure A-1.

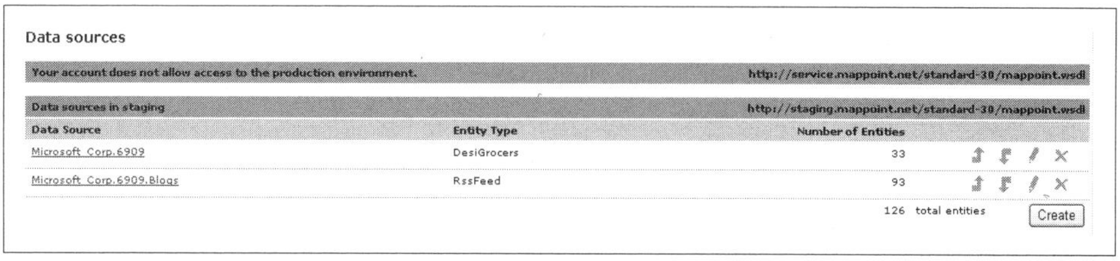

Figure A-1. Data management UI from the customer services site

Location data files that you upload to MapPoint Web Service must be in either Access XML file format or flat file format and must meet specific requirements. To find out more about the specific requirements, refer to the Formatting MapPoint Web Service Data Source Files topic on MSDN *http://msdn.microsoft.com/library/default.asp?url=/library/en-us/mappointsdk/HTML/mpn35FormattingDataSources.asp?frame=true*.

You can perform a maximum of 50 location data uploads within a 24-hour period. This restriction includes uploading new data as well as updating existing data. To upload your data using the UI, follow these steps:

1. On the home page, scroll down to the data sources section for the environment that you want, and click Create.

2. In the "Data source name" field, type a name for the new data source. The name you type is appended to the customer's name and the account ID assigned to you by MapPoint Web Service, which is displayed to the left of the text box.

3. In the "Entity type" field, assign an entity type for the data source. The entities in a data source require an entity type, and all entities within the data source must be of the same type. The *entity type* is the category you want associated with your data, such as Stores, Distributors, or ATMs. The entity type can be anything you want as long as it is a valid XML name (which contains no spaces or reserved characters).

4. Type the filename and path of the data file, or click Browse to locate the file on your computer.

5. From the Geocoding level (matched method) drop-down list, choose a geocoding level. The geocoder works through the geocoding hierarchy in the order shown in the drop-down list (Street, PostCode, City, Subdivision, CountryRegion) seeking a match for each entity either below or at the level you select. If the latitude and longitude columns in the data source file are empty for any of the entities, they will be geocoded as part of the upload process. Sometimes the geocoder returns multiple results for an address. Select the "Reject ambiguous matches" checkbox to leave the latitude and longitude fields blank for any entity for which multiple matches are returned. Otherwise, the latitude and longitude coordinates for the first match are used.

6. Click Create.

The MapPoint Customer Services site home page includes a section for recently uploaded data jobs. Refresh the page to see the status of your upload job. You can click on the "View details" link to see additional information about the job or to see whether the job has successfully completed, along with the number of entities that are successfully uploaded and the number of entities that failed to load.

Now that you know how to upload data using the Customer Services Site UI, let's look at how you can programmatically upload the data using the Customer Data Web Service.

Using Customer Data Web Service

The Customer Data Service enables you to upload and download your point of interest data to the MapPoint servers programmatically. Even though Microsoft hosts it as part of MapPoint Web Service, Customer Data Service is only used in customer data management, whereas MapPoint Web Service offers a core mapping platform for location based application development.

 You can access the Customer Data Service WSDL at: *https://mappoint-css.partners.extranet.microsoft.com/CustomerData-30/CustomerDataService.wsdl.*

To access Customer Data Service Web Service, you need to use your MapPoint Web Service Customer Services Site credentials.

A Look at Customer Data Service APIs

As I said earlier, Customer Data Service supports both upload and download of your entity data programmatically. If you are developing with Customer Data Service, the main class that you need to use is the CustomerDataService class. Depending on the task (upload or download) you need to invoke the StartUpload or StartDownload methods on the CustomerDataService class. Table A-1 shows the methods exposed on the CustomerDataService class.

Table A-1. CustomerDataService methods

Method	Description
StartUpload	Starts a location data upload job. This method returns a unique job ID that should be used in subsequent calls.
UploadData	Uploads the point-of-interest data. You can use this method to upload data in multiple chunks. This method returns the number of bytes that were uploaded in the current call.
GetJobState	Returns the state of the data upload job represented by the jobID parameter.
FinishUpload	Marks the data upload job represented by the job ID as complete and submits the uploaded data for geocoding.
StartDownload	Starts a location data download job. This method returns a unique job ID that should be used in subsequent calls.
GetDownloadFileURL	Returns a URL that can be used to access the data file for a given job.

So, how does the data upload/download work with Customer Data Service? Let's look in detail in the following two sections.

Uploading data using Customer Data Service

The upload process using Customer Data Service has the following three steps:

Create a new upload job. During this step, you create a new upload job using the `CustomerDataService.StartUpload` method. This method takes a specification object of type `UploadSpecification`, which specifies several job-specific parameters such as environment (production versus staging), geocoding match level (street, city, Zip Code, subdivision, or country/region), whether to ignore ambiguous records after geocoding, etc. Table A-2 shows the fields exposed on the `UploadSpecification` class.

Table A-2. UploadSpecification class fields

Field	Notes
DataSourceName	Represents the name of the data source that the point-of-interest data is being uploaded to.
EntityTypeName	Represents the name of the entity type of the data that is being uploaded.
Environment	Indicates which MapPoint Web Service environment should be used for the data upload. This field is of type `LocationDataEnvironment` enumeration. The default value is `Staging`.
MaximumGeocodingLevel	Indicates the maximum geocoding level (`GeocodingLevel` enumeration) to be used to geocode the point-of-interest data. The default geocoding level is street name and number.
RejectAmbiguousGeocodes	Indicates whether ambiguous addresses should be skipped or whether they should be assigned the latitude and longitude of the first address that matches the record.
GeometryType	Specifies whether the data is point data or polygon data (`GeometryType` enumeration).

Tables A-3, A-4, and A-5 provide possible values for various enumerations used with the `UploadSpecification` object.

Table A-3. LocationDataEnvironment enumeration

Item	Notes
Service	Indicates that the data upload is performed in the production environment
Staging	Indicates that the data upload is performed in the staging environment

Table A-4. GeoCodingLevel enumeration

Item	Notes
City	Indicates that the city level of geocoding is allowed. If this geocoding level is selected, all ambiguous addresses at street and postal code levels are geocoded against their city names.
CountryRegion	Indicates that the country/region level of geocoding is allowed. If this geocoding level is selected, all ambiguous addresses at street, postal code, and city levels are geocoded against their country names.

Table A-4. GeoCodingLevel enumeration (continued)

Item	Notes
PostalCode	Indicates that the postal code level of geocoding is allowed. If this geocoding level is selected, all ambiguous addresses at the street level are geocoded against their postal codes.
Street	Indicates that the point of interest data will be geocoded at the street name and number level. When an ambiguous address is found with this geocoding level, that record will not be marked as ambiguous and will not be geocoded at other levels, such as postal code or city.
Subdivision	Indicates that the subdivision/state level of geocoding is allowed. If this geocoding level is selected, all ambiguous addresses at street, postal code, and city levels are geocoded against their state/subdivision.

Table A-5. GeometryType enumeration

Item	Value
Point	Indicates that the data being uploaded is the point data
Polygon	Indicates that the data being uploaded is polygon data

Next, look at the following code to see how to start a data upload job:

```
//Create an instance of the customer data service proxy.
CustomerDataService cds = new CustomerDataService();
//Assign your credentials.
. . .

//Set PreAuthenticate to true
cds.PreAuthenticate = true;

//Define an upload specification object
//and assign all required fields.
UploadSpecification uploadspec = new UploadSpecification();
uploadspec.DataSourceName = myDataSourceName;
uploadspec.EntityTypeName = myEntityTypeName;
uploadspec.Environment = LocationDataEnvironment.Staging;
uploadspec.MaximumGeocodingLevel = GeocodingLevel.City;
uploadspec.RejectAmbiguousGeocodes = false;
uploadspec.GeometryType = GeometryType.Point;

//Start an upload job and obtain the job ID.
string jobID = cds.StartUpload(uploadspec);
```

A successful call to this method returns a unique job ID used in subsequent steps.

Upload your data. Using the job ID that you obtained in the first step, upload your custom point of interest data to the MapPoint servers with the CustomerDataService. UploadData method; this method takes a valid job ID, point of interest data as a memory buffer, and the bytes uploaded in previous upload calls for this job. The last parameter is useful if you are uploading small chunks of data instead of uploading all of the data at once. You have to upload your data in chunks if your data file is bigger than 1 MB. This method returns the number of bytes uploaded once you have successfully uploaded the data.

Assuming that your location data is contained in a simple text file, the following code shows how to use this method:

```
//String buffer to hold the poi data
string poidata = string.Empty;
//Get the contents from the poi file
System.IO.StreamReader sr = new StreamReader(@"C:\poi.txt");
poidata = sr.ReadToEnd( );
sr.Close( );
//Convert the string content into an array of bytes.
byte[] buffer = System.Text.Encoding.UTF8.GetBytes(poidata);
//Now upload the POI data.
long uploadedbytes = cds.UploadData(jobID, buffer, 0);
```

If you are uploading data in one call, set bytesPreviouslyUploaded to zero; if you are uploading the data in multiple chunks, this parameter value must match the cumulative sum of all individual uploads for the current job. For example, if you have 10 KB of data that you want to upload, the value of the bytesPreviouslyUploaded is zero if you upload all 10 KB in one CustomerDataService.UploadData method call. However, if you decide to upload the same 10 KB of data in five chunks of 2 KB each, then the values of the bytesPreviouslyUploaded parameter should be 0, 2,000, 4,000, 6,000, and 8,000 in corresponding consecutive CustomerDataService.UploadData method calls.

Here is an example of a text file with custom location data:

```
EntityID    Latitude    Longitude    nat_importance    Region    Name    street_
number     street_name    AddressLine    PrimaryCity    Subdivision    PostalCode
CountryRegion    Phone
6    42.720266    -87.870073    N    CHI    Knights Court    1149    Oakes Rd    1149
Oakes Rd    Racine    WI    53406    United States    262-8866667
7    42.719011    -87.859109    N    CHI    Fairfield Inn-Racine    6421
Washington Ave    6421 Washington Ave    Racine    WI    53406    United States
262-8865000
8    42.720513    -87.866756    N    CHI    Comfort Inn-Racine    1154    Prairie Dr
1154 Prairie Dr    Racine    WI    53406    United States    262-8866055
9    42.719168    -87.864424    N    CHI    Frank Gentile Oldsmobile    6801
Washington Ave    6801 Washington Ave
```

Submit your data for processing. Upon completing the second step, submit your points of interest data for processing by calling the CustomerDataService.FinishUpload method. If you do not call this method, your data will not be processed; in other words, your data will not be loaded into your data source. This method takes the job ID and the total number of byes uploaded as input parameters.

The following code shows the `CustomerDataService.FinishUpload` method call:

```
//Finish the data upload
cds.FinishUpload(jobID, 10000);
```

After the `CustomerDataService.FinishUpload` method is invoked, the services on Map-Point Web Servers upload your data to your data sources, but how do you know when an upload job is done? You can use the `CustomerDataService.GetJobState` method for that purpose.

Polling for an upload job status

You can use the `CustomerDataService.GetJobState` method to get the status of your data upload job. This method takes a valid job ID and returns the `JobState` enumeration to indicate the job status. The following code shows how to use the `CustomerDataService.GetJobState` method:

```
//Get job state by calling the GetJobState method.
JobState jobStatus = cds.GetJobState(jobID);
//Check the state
switch(jobStatus)
{
    case JobState.Pending:
    //Still Pending
    break;
    case JobState.Loading:
    //Still Loading
    break;
    default:
    //None of the above two
    break;
}
```

Now that you know how to upload data programmatically, let's look at how you can use Customer Data Service to download your data.

Downloading data using Customer Data Service

Using the Customer Data Service, you can also download your point of interest data; like the data upload process, the download process also has three basic steps.

Create a new download job. In this step, you create a new download job using the `CustomerDataService.StartDownload` method. You also have to specify several job-specific parameters, such as environment (production or staging), entity type, data source name, and so on, using the `DownloadSpecification` object. Table A-6 shows the fields defined in the `DownloadSpecification` object.

Table A-6. DownloadSpecification class fields

Field	Description
DataSourceName	Represents the name of the data source containing the point of interest data to be downloaded.
EntityTypeName	Represents the name of the entity type of the data that is being downloaded.
Environment	Indicates from which environment the data should be downloaded (of type LocationDataEnvironment enumeration). The default value is Staging.
Format	Indicates the file format (FileFormat enumeration) for the downloaded data. The default value is AccessXml2003.
Compressed	Indicates whether the data should be compressed. The default value is false.

A successful call to StartDownload method returns a unique job ID that you use in subsequent steps. This step also initiates the actual download process, in which the Customer Data Service downloads your point of interest data to a secure location that you can access through a URL. The following code demonstrates how to initiate a download process:

```
//Create the Customer Data Service proxy
CustomerDataService cds = new CustomerDataService();

//Set the PreAuthenticate property to true
DownloadService.PreAuthenticate = true;

//Assign your Customer Services Site credentials
. . .

//Define the DownloadSpecification object
DownloadSpecification specification = new DownloadSpecification();

//Assign download settings for my data source
specification.DataSourceName = "MyCompany.6909.ATM";
specification.EntityTypeName = "ATM";
//Set staging environment - this is default
specification.Environment = LocationDataEnvironment.Staging;
//Assign the desired file format
specification.Format = FileFormat.CommaDelimitedTextUTF8;
//Compress the file for faster downloads
specification.Compressed = true;

//Start the download job
string jobID = cds.StartDownload(specification);
```

The download specification takes the desired file format and supports compressed file formats as well (for example, a Zip file). Table A-7 shows the supported file formats for the data download.

Table A-7. Supported file formats

File Format	Description
AccessXml2003	Microsoft Access 2003 XML format. This is the default format used by the download methods.
AccessXml2002	Microsoft Access 2002 XML format.
TabDelimitedTextLatin1	Tab-delimited text format with Latin 1 [ISO 8859-1] encoding.
TabDelimitedTextUTF8	Tab-delimited text format with UTF-8 [ISO 10646-1:2000 Annex D] encoding.
PipeDelimitedTextLatin1	Pipe-delimited text format with Latin 1 [ISO 8859-1] encoding.
PipeDelimitedTextUTF8	Pipe-delimited text format with UTF-8 [ISO 10646-1:2000 Annex D] encoding.
CommaDelimitedTextLatin1	Comma-delimited text format with Latin 1 [ISO 8859-1] encoding.
CommaDelimitedTextUTF8	Comma-delimited text format with UTF-8 [ISO 10646-1:2000 Annex D] encoding.

AccessXml2003 is the default format for the downloaded file. Finally, when the Compressed flag is set to true on the download specification, the data is downloaded in compressed format as a Zip file.

Poll for the status of the job. Calling the StartDownload method initiates the actual download process, so you have to keep checking the job status using the GetJobState method until the download process is complete.

The following code shows how to poll for the job status to find out whether the download is complete or not:

```
//Get the job state
JobState jobState = DownloadService.GetJobState(jobID);

//Call IsWaitingState to check the
//status of the job
while(IsWaitingState(jobState))
{
    //Wait for 60 seconds before polling
    //again.
    Thread.Sleep(60 * 1000);
    //Get the job state again
    jobState = DownloadService.GetJobState(jobID);
}

// Determine whether the job is still being processed
bool IsWaitingState(JobState state)
{
    switch (state)
    {
        //If the job is in progress
        //or pending
        //IsWaitingState returns a value of true
```

```
        case JobState.Pending:
        case JobState.InProcess:
            return true;
        default:
            return false;
    }
}
```

I have added a small method, IsWaitingState, which checks the value of the JobState enumeration to determine whether the job is pending or in progress. Once the job state is returned as CompletedSuccess, it indicates that the download process is complete, and you can save the downloaded data to your local hard disk.

Download the data file and save it to your hard drive. When the download job is completed successfully, your point of interest data are downloaded to a secure location. You have to use the CustomerDataService.GetDownloadFileURL method to obtain the location of the file so that you can download it to your local hard drive.

The following code shows how to obtain the downloaded file URL and save it to your local disk:

```
//Get the URL to the download file
string fileUrl = DownloadService.GetDownloadFileURL(jobID);
//Define a valid local file path
string localFile = @"C:\Downloads\data.csv";
//Create a new WebClient instance.
System.Net.WebClient client = new System.Net.WebClient();
//Assign your Customer Services Site credentials
. . .
//Download the data to a local file
client.DownloadFile(fileUrl, localFile);
```

Also, it is important to remember that if you set the Compressed flag to true in the DownloadSpecifications, the data is downloaded as a Zip file.

Working with Polygons

In some cases, you may need more than just one point to represent your entities. For example, if you have a call center territory and you need to model it spatially, you cannot do that using a point, since it contains a set of points that make up the territory shape. If you need to define more than a single point location in a data source, you can create a polygon data source.

In MapPoint Web Service, like point data sources, polygon data sources include spatial and non-spatial entities. A *polygon data source* allows you to define one or more regions on a map. You can then use these regions to find spatial relations to other polygons (such as rectangles), point data sources, addresses, and specific geographic locations. For example, you may define the delivery area for a store as a polygon. You can then look up a customer's address and determine whether it is within the delivery area. Polygons can be as simple as a single ring of connected points, or may be complex, with an external ring containing numerous internal rings that define areas not included in the polygon.

What Is a Polygon?

Polygons are defined by an ordered series of latitude/longitude points (vertices) with an implied connection between consecutive vertices and between the last and first vertex. A polygon data source can contain one or more polygons, and a single polygon data source can contain up to 500 vertices. Each polygon consists of a single external ring and may include multiple internal rings. When you create a polygon, you must first define the external ring. Figure B-1 shows the external ring of a polygon with 6 vertices and the implied edges drawn between each.

In addition to the external ring, a polygon can contain one or more internal rings. Like the external ring, internal rings are defined by an ordered list of vertices, and no two implied edges may intersect. Therefore, each internal ring must be entirely contained within the external ring. In addition, you cannot create an internal ring within an existing internal ring. Figure B-2 shows a polygon with one external ring with two internal rings.

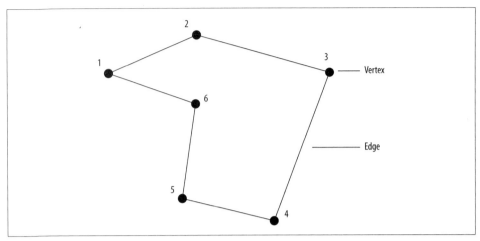

Figure B-1. Simple polygon with edges and vertices

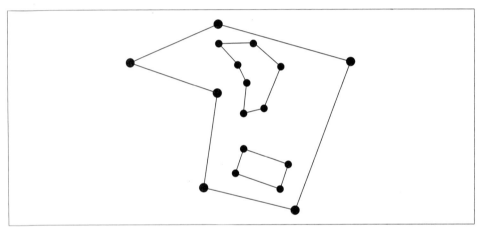

Figure B-2. Complex polygon with inner and outer rings

Polygon Relationships

In MapPoint Web Service, like point data sources, a polygon data source requires a unique identity (known as "Entity ID value"). However, unlike point data sources, it is not mandatory to provide the values for the latitude and longitude coordinates; when the latitude and longitude coordinates are not assigned, the values will be automatically set to the latitude and longitude of the center point of the bounding rectangle for the polygon. Any valid polygon that is defined in the MapPoint Web Service data sources can be used for a variety of spatial relationship checks, depending on the business's needs. For example, you can determine whether a latitude and longitude coordinate lies within a polygon. You can also determine whether a polygon is contained within another polygon (currently limited to a rectangle), or whether the rectangle and polygon are connected in any way. Figure B-3 shows the possible relationships between a rectangle and polygon.

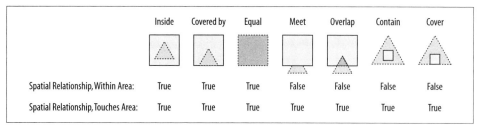

	Inside	Covered by	Equal	Meet	Overlap	Contain	Cover
Spatial Relationship, Within Area:	True	True	True	False	False	False	False
Spatial Relationship, Touches Area:	True	True	True	True	True	True	True

Figure B-3. Polygon spatial relationships

With this introduction, now let's look at how you can prepare polygon data.

Rules for Preparing Polygon Data

You can manually create an XML file that contains the polygon data; however, the resulting XML file must contain the following requirements:

- An embedded XSD schema with two namespaces:
  - xsd, which references *http://www.w3.org/2001/XMLSchema*
  - od, which references *urn:schemas-microsoft-com:officedata*
- A dataroot element, that contains:
  - One or more `CustomerPolygonEntity` elements
  - A generated attribute, which is set to a date-time value (for example, `generated="2004-05-21T17:11:40"`)

The `CustomerPolygonEntity` element must contain the following elements:

EntityID
    Unique ID within the given data source.

Latitude
    If you do not provide this value, MapPoint Web Service calculates the latitude value and adds it during the upload process.

Longitude
    If you do not provide this value, MapPoint Web Service calculates the Longitude value and adds it during the upload process.

EntityGeometry
    References poly namespace **http://s.mappoint.net/polygon-40/**.

The `EntityGeometry` element must contain a `Polygon` element. The `Polygon` element contains:

- One `ExteriorRing` element
- Zero or more `InteriorRing` elements

- The value for an `ExteriorRing` or `InteriorRing` element is a list of latitude and longitude coordinate pairs separated by semicolons with no semicolon at the end of the list and with no spaces between any characters—for example, latitude1,longitude1;latitude2,longitude2

The following rules apply to the polygons in the `ExteriorRing` or `InteriorRing` element:

- Each vertex is defined by a pair of latitude and longitude coordinate values.

- No two latitude and longitude pairs can be the same within a polygon.

- You do not need to close the polygon by specifying the final vertex of a polygon, as this will be a duplicate of the first vertex.

- Internal polygons cannot overlap or intersect external polygons.

- Each ring you define must contain at least three vertices.

Polygon Data Schema Document

The schema for the Polygon XML data document is as follows:

```
<?xml version="1.0" encoding="UTF-8"?>
<root xmlns:xsd="http://www.w3.org/2001/XMLSchema" xmlns:od="urn:schemas-microsoft-
com:officedata">
 <xsd:schema>
  <xsd:element name="dataroot">
    <xsd:complexType>
      <xsd:sequence>
        <xsd:element ref="CustomerPolygonEntity" minOccurs="0" maxOccurs="unbounded"/
>
      </xsd:sequence>
      <xsd:attribute name="generated" type="xsd:dateTime"/>
    </xsd:complexType>
  </xsd:element>
  <xsd:element name="CustomerPolygonEntity">
    <xsd:complexType>
      <xsd:sequence>
        <xsd:element name="EntityID" minOccurs="0" od:jetType="integer"
od:sqlSType="smallint" type="xsd:short"/>
        <xsd:element name="Latitude" minOccurs="0" od:jetType="double"
od:sqlSType="float" type="xsd:double"/>
        <xsd:element name="Longitude" minOccurs="0" od:jetType="double"
od:sqlSType="float" type="xsd:double"/>
        <xsd:any namespace="##other" />
      </xsd:sequence>
    </xsd:complexType>
  </xsd:element>
 </xsd:schema>
```

Polygon Data Sample Document

The following XML document shows a sample polygon that is defined with one exterior ring and one interior ring:

```
<dataroot xmlns:xsi="http://www.w3.org/2001/XMLSchema-instance" generated="2004-05-
21T17:11:40">
  <CustomerPolygonEntity>
    <EntityID>1</EntityID>
    <Latitude>42.00</Latitude>
    <Longitude>-100.00</Longitude>
    <poly:EntityGeometry xmlns:poly="http://s.mappoint.net/polygon-40/">
      <Polygon>
        <ExteriorRing>40,-98;40,-102;44,-102;44,-98</ExteriorRing>
        <InteriorRing>41,-101;43,-100;41,-101</InteriorRing>
      </Polygon>
    </poly:EntityGeometry>
  </CustomerPolygonEntity>
</dataroot>
</root>
```

APPENDIX C

Implementing Spatial Search Using SQL Server

The MapPoint Web Service provides a comprehensive set of find nearby (proximity search) APIs and custom data storage hosted in a secure environment on Microsoft servers. This setting works seamlessly for most business needs. However, while the MapPoint Web Service proximity search solution is effective for most scenarios, in some circumstances, implementing proximity searches independent of MapPoint Web Service may be necessary. There are three scenarios that might lead you to want to store and query your points of interest data locally within your enterprise network:

Sensitive or confidential information
> If your data is sensitive, such as information about crimes, for example, you may not want to upload the data to MapPoint Web Service.

Frequent changes
> If your data changes frequently, such as sales information that is updated in real-time, it may not be practical to upload your data to MapPoint Web Service continually.

Large datasets
> If you have a database containing millions of locations, you must store and manage it in a local Microsoft SQL Server database. MapPoint Web Service allows you to upload up to approximately 100,000 points of interest.

This section describes how to implement simple proximity searches locally within your enterprise using a SQL Server.

 This appendix assumes that you have a basic understanding of SQL Server, Stored Procedures, and ADO.NET.

Understanding Proximity Search

Proximity search works by applying the law of cosines, which calculates the distance between two points on the globe. Because the law of cosines takes into account the curvature of the earth, it is considered better than other methods, such as the Pythagorean Theorem. An abridged version of the law of cosines is as follows:

```
a = sin(latitude_1) * sin(latitude_2)

b = cos(latitude_1) * cos(latitude_2) *
      cos(longitude_2 - longitude_1)

c = arcos( a + b )

d = R*c
```

In this law, the following facts are true:

- `latitude_1`, `longitude_1`, `latitude_2`, and `longitude_2` are the points between which we want to measure the distance (latitude and longitude are expressed in radians)

- `R` is the Earth's radius (3,963.0 in miles or 6,378.5 in kilometers)

- `d` is the distance between the two points

This formula takes two latitude and longitude pairs, one for a location stored in your SQL data store, such as the address of an ATM, and one for a location provided by your end user, such as the user's current location around which she wants to find ATMs. During a proximity search, the distance is calculated between the user's current address and each business location within the specified search radius, and the results are then ordered by distance.

In the following sections, I will go through a step-by-step approach to building your own spatial proximity search using SQL Server.

Step 1: Create a Table to Store Your Business Location Data

Let's say you have business locations for which you want to enable proximity searching; in order to do that, you need to have your business listings and their corresponding location information expressed in latitude and longitude coordinates as radians. Once you have that data, you need to create a SQL table (say, `BusinessEntity`) to store your business listings:

```
CREATE TABLE [BusinessEntity] (
    [ID] [int] IDENTITY (1, 1) NOT NULL ,
    [Name] [nvarchar] NOT NULL ,
    [Latitude] [float] NOT NULL ,
    [Longitude] [float] NOT NULL ,
```

```
    [XAxis] [float] NOT NULL ,
    [YAxis] [float] NOT NULL ,
    [ZAxis] [float] NOT NULL ,
) ON [PRIMARY]
GO
```

 For the sake of simplicity, I'm only showing one property (Name) on the business entity; in reality, you can have as many properties as you want.

Once you created the table successfully, load your data into it using either SQL Data Transformation Services (DTS) or SQL Server Integration Services (SSIS).

 The name of the table that you choose in this step is used in the other steps, so if you choose a table name other than BusinessEntity, change the following stored procedures accordingly to match your own name.

Step 2: Calculate Axis Values for the BusinessEntities Table

Now that you have your business listings available in the SQL table, run the following SQL query (either using the SQL Server Enterprise Manager or SQL Query Analyzer) to calculate the values for the columns XAxis, YAxis and ZAxis:

```
UPDATE [BusinessEntity] SET XAxis = (cos(((4*((4*atn(1/5))-
    (atn(1/239))))/180)*[ BusinessEntity].Latitude)*cos(((4*((4*atn(1/5))-
    (atn(1/239))))/180)*[ BusinessEntity].Longitude));

UPDATE [BusinessEntity] SET YAxis = (cos(((4*((4*atn(1/5))-
    (atn(1/239))))/180)*[ BusinessEntity].Latitude)*sin(((4*((4*atn(1/5))-
    (atn(1/239))))/180)*[ BusinessEntity].Longitude));

UPDATE [BusinessEntity] SET ZAxis = (sin(((4*((4*atn(1/5))-
    (atn(1/239))))/180)*[ BusinessEntity].Latitude));
```

This query creates the values for the XAxis, YAxis, and ZAxis columns in the table. Now your data is ready to be searched for spatial proximity queries.

Step 3: Create the FindNearby Stored Procedure

Create a SQL stored procedure called FindNearby:

```
CREATE PROCEDURE FindNearby
    @CenterLat float,
    @CenterLon float,
    @SearchDistance float,
    @Units int
```

```
AS
declare @CntXAxis float
declare @CntYAxis float
declare @CntZAxis float
declare @EarthRadius float

-- Miles = 0
if(@Units = 0)
set @EarthRadius = 3963.0
else
set @EarthRadius = 6378.5

set @CntXAxis = cos(radians(@CenterLat)) * cos(radians(@CenterLon))
set @CntYAxis = cos(radians(@CenterLat)) * sin(radians(@CenterLon))
set @CntZAxis = sin(radians(@CenterLat))

select BusinessEntity.ID,
       BusinessEntity.Name,
       ProxDistance = @EarthRadius * acos( XAxis*@CntXAxis +
                      YAxis*@CntYAxis + ZAxis*@CntZAxis)

from   [BusinessEntity]

where  @EarthRadius * acos( XAxis*@CntXAxis + YAxis*@CntYAxis +
       ZAxis*@CntZAxis) <= @SearchDistance

order by ProxDistance ASC
```

Now you can execute FindNearby queries using your own SQL implementation.

Step 4: Using Your Find Nearby Stored Procedure Using C#

Now that you have the SQL Server implementation of the FindNearby ready, you can use it from your applications using the following C# code:

```
public void FindNearbyBusinessEntities(double latitude,
                                       double longitude,
                                       double distance)
{
    //Assume miles distance units for now
    //Change to 1 if you want Kilometers
    int units = 0;

    //Create SQL command
    //import System.Data.Sql namespace if you haven't already
    SqlCommand cmd = new SqlCommand("FindNearby");

    //Assign input values to the sql command
```

```
cmd.CommandType = CommandType.StoredProcedure;
cmd.Parameters.Add("@CenterLat", latitude);
cmd.Parameters.Add("@CenterLon", longitude);
cmd.Parameters.Add("@SearchDistance", distance);
cmd.Parameters.Add("@Units", units);

//Define a connection
SqlConnection sqlConn = null;
try
{
    //Open the connection
    sqlConn = new SqlConnection("your sql connection string");
    // If the connection is closed, open it
    if(sqlConn.State == ConnectionState.Closed)
        sqlConn.Open( );

    if(sqlConn.State == ConnectionState.Open)
    {
        cmd.Connection = sqlConn;
        SqlDataReader dreader =  cmd.ExecuteReader( );
        if(dreader != null)
        {
            while(dreader.Read( ))
            {
                //Get id of the business entity
                int id=0;
                if(!dreader.IsDBNull(0))
                    id = (int)dreader[0];

                //Get name of the business entity
                string name = string.Empty;
                if(!dreader.IsDBNull(1))
                    name = (string)dreader[1];

                //Do something userful with your entity such as
                //creating a puhspin object to render on map or
                //something
                . . .

            }
        }
    }

}
catch(Exception ex)
{
    //Handle your exception processing here
}
finally
{
    if(sqlConn != null)
```

```
        {
            if(sqlConn.State == ConnectionState.Open)
            {
                //Close sql connection
                sqlConn.Close();
            }
        }
    }
}
```

Now you have your own FindNearby capability that can be used in conjunction with other MapPoint Web Service features, such as rendering nearby business entities.

Index

We'd like to hear your suggestions for improving our indexes. Send email to *index@oreilly.com*.

About the Author

Chandu Thota is Microsoft's point man on MapPoint. You can see his picture at *http://msdn.microsoft.com/mappoint*. His weblog at *http://blogs.msdn.com/cthota* is a key resource for MapPoint developers.

Colophon

Our look is the result of reader comments, our own experimentation, and feedback from distribution channels. Distinctive covers complement our distinctive approach to technical topics, breathing personality and life into potentially dry subjects.

The animal on the cover of *Programming MapPoint in .NET* is a great frigate bird (*fregata minor*), also known as a man-of-war bird. Once thought of as a bad omen by Europeans settling in the Western Hemisphere, frigate birds are indeed unpopular with other tropical birds, whose prey they steal with their long, hooked beaks.

However, frigate birds are not bullies simply for the pleasure of harassing other birds. Although their diet consists solely of fish, their disproportionately small feet and lack of waterproofing oil on their feathers make catching fish difficult. Although their relatively large wingspan and light body weight enable them to swoop low to the ocean surface to snatch fish, their main food supply comes from chasing other birds and attacking them until they relinquish their fish, either by dropping fresh kills from their beaks or by regurgitating their recently eaten meals, both of which frigate birds will greedily gobble up.

Despite their inability to swim, frigate birds are tropical sea birds that come to land only to breed. About the size of a large chicken, they weigh only four pounds and have a wingspan of up to six feet, so they can fly for extremely long distances, sometimes staying on ocean updrafts for days. During the breeding season, males attract potential mates by puffing up their bare, bright red throat skin to the size of a human head, sometimes larger than the birds themselves.

While both parents tend the nest, males breed every year—twice as frequently as females, since eggs take nearly two months to hatch, and chicks are dependent on their mothers for food for a year and a half after hatching. Although frigate birds are not ready to breed until they are nine years old, they still have plenty of opportunities, since they have an average life span of 30 years.

Reba Libby was the production editor and the copyeditor for *Programming MapPoint in .NET*. Jeffrey Liggett proofread the book. Claire Cloutier and Adam Witwer provided quality control. Lucie Haskins wrote the index.

Karen Montgomery designed the cover of this book, based on a series design by Edie Freedman. The cover image is from *Cassell's Natural History*. Karen Montgomery produced the cover layout with Adobe InDesign CS using Adobe's ITC Garamond font.

David Futato designed the interior layout. This book was converted by Keith Fahlgren to FrameMaker 5.5.6 with a format conversion tool created by Erik Ray, Jason McIntosh, Neil Walls, and Mike Sierra that uses Perl and XML technologies. The text font is Linotype Birka; the heading font is Adobe Myriad Condensed; and the code font is LucasFont's TheSans Mono Condensed. The illustrations that appear in the book were produced by Robert Romano, Jessamyn Read, and Lesley Borash using Macromedia FreeHand MX and Adobe Photoshop CS. The tip and warning icons were drawn by Christopher Bing. This colophon was written by Reba Libby.

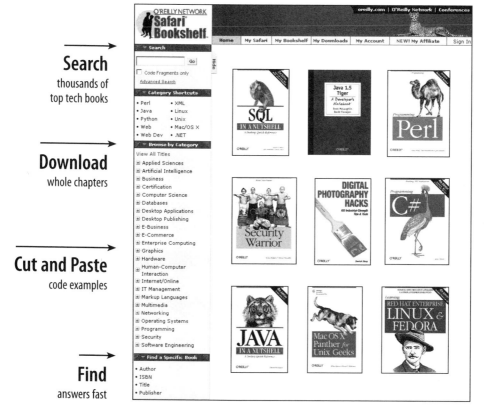

Related Titles from O'Reilly

.NET

ADO.NET Cookbook

ASP.NET Cookbook

ASP.NET 2.0 Cookbook

ASP.NET 2.0: A Developer's Notebook

C# Cookbook, *2nd Edition*

C# in a Nutshell, *2nd Edition*

C# Language Pocket Guide

Learning C#

.NET and XML

.NET Gotchas

Programming .NET Components, *2nd Edition*

Programming .NET Security

Programming .NET Web Services

Programming ASP.NET, *3rd Edition*

Programming C#, *4th Edition*

Programming MapPoint in .NET

Programming Visual Basic 2005

Programming Windows Presentation Foundation

Visual Basic 2005: A Developer's Notebook

Visual Basic 2005 in a Nutshell, *3rd Edition*

Visual Basic 2005 Jumpstart

Visual C# 2005: A Developer's Notebook

Visual Studio Hacks

Our books are available at most retail and online bookstores.

To order direct: 1-800-998-9938 • *order@oreilly.com* • *www.oreilly.com*

Online editions of most O'Reilly titles are available by subscription at *safari.oreilly.com*

The O'Reilly Advantage

Stay Current and Save Money